Keynote

ADVANCED
Workbook

NGL.Cengage.com/Keynote

PASSWORD   keynoteStdt#

Paula Mulanovic
Mike Harrison
Sandy Millin

NATIONAL
GEOGRAPHIC
LEARNING

Australia · Brazil · Mexico · Singapore · United Kingdom · United States

NATIONAL
GEOGRAPHIC
L E A R N I N G

Keynote Advanced
Workbook
Paula Mulanovic with Mike Harrison and
Sandy Millin

Publisher: Gavin McLean

Publishing Consultant: Karen Spiller

Project Manager: Karen White

Development Editors: Stephanie Parker,
    Ruth Goodman

Editorial Manager: Scott Newport

Head of Strategic Marketing ELT:
    Charlotte Ellis

Senior Content Project Manager:
    Nick Ventullo

Manufacturing Manager: Eyvett Davis

Cover design: Brenda Carmichael

Text design: MPS North America LLC

Compositor: MPS North America LLC

National Geographic Liaison: Leila Hishmeh

Audio: Tom Dick and Debbie Productions
    Ltd

Cover Photo Caption: Beatrice Coron
speaking at TED2011: The Rediscovery
of Wonder, February 28 – March 4, 2011,
Long Beach, CA. Photo: © James Duncan
Davidson/TED.

For product information and technology assistance, contact us at
Cengage Learning Customer & Sales Support, cengage.com/contact
For permission to use material from this text or product,
submit all requests online at **cengage.com/permissions**
Further permissions questions can be emailed to
permissionrequest@cengage.com

ISBN: 978-1-305-57834-0

National Geographic Learning
Cheriton House, North Way, Andover, Hampshire, SP10 5BE, United Kingdom

National Geographic Learning, a Cengage Learning Company, has a mission
to bring the world to the classroom and the classroom to life. With our English
language programs, students learn about their world by experiencing it. Through
our partnerships with National Geographic and TED Talks, they develop the
language and skills they need to be successful global citizens and leaders.

Locate your local office at **international.cengage.com/region**

Visit National Geographic Learning online at **NGL.Cengage.com/ELT**
Visit our corporate website at **www.cengage.com**

CREDITS

The publishers would like to thank TED Staff for their insightful feedback and expert guidance, allowing us to achieve
our dual aims of maintaining the integrity of these inspirational TED Talks, while maximizing their potential for teaching English.

Although every effort has been made to contact copyright holders before publication, this has not always been possible. If contacted, the publisher will
undertake to rectify any errors or omissions at the earliest opportunity.

The publishers would like to thank the following for permission to use copyright material:

Cover: © James Duncan Davidson/TED

Photos: 4 © James Duncan Davidson/TED; 7 © Mick House/Alamy Stock Photo; 8 © Vlue/Shutterstock.com; 14 (l, r) © James Duncan Davidson/TED;
17 © Andrey Arkusha/Shutterstock.com; 18 © Roberto Westbrook/Getty Images; 20 © Gary Burchell/Getty Images; 22 © Oleksiy Mark/Shutterstock.com;
24 © James Duncan Davidson/TED; 26 © Rawpixel Ltd/Getty Images; 28 © Keith Morris/Writer Pictures/Associated Press/AP Images; 30 © Morsa Images
/Getty Images; 32 © Denis Kennedy/Alamy Stock Photo; 34 © Ryan Lash/TED; 36 © joingate/Getty Images; 38 (tl) © David Paul Morris/Bloomberg/Getty
Images; 38 (tr) © Vodafone Limited; 38 (bl) © Studioshots/Alamy Stock Photo; 38 (br) © Associated Press/Tony Dejak/AP Images; 40 © Paul Bradbury
/Getty Images; 44 © TED Conferences, LLC; 46 © Jetta Productions/Getty Images; 48 © enotmaks/Getty Images; 50 © monkeybusinessimages/Getty
Images; 52 © Chris Ryan/Getty Images; 54 © James Duncan Davidson/TED; 56 © Maslowski Marcin/Shutterstock.com; 58 © AR Pictures/Shutterstock.com;
60 © PeopleImages.com/Ocean/Corbis; 62 © Russell Mountford/Getty Images; 64 © James Duncan Davidson/TED; 66 © Oliver Rossi/Getty Images;
68 © Susanna's Catering; 70 © Yavuz Arslan/ullstein bild/Getty Images; 72 (t) © Hero Images/Getty Images; 72 (m) © Marc Romanelli/Getty Images; 72 (b)
© Inti St Clair/Getty Images; 74 © James Duncan Davidson/TED; 76 © Hero Images/Getty Images; 78 © Kamal Kishore/Reuters; 80 © Hero Images/Getty
Images; 81 © Orla/Getty Images; 84 © Dafydd Jones/TED; 86 © Vincent Jary/Getty Images; 88 © Yagi Studio/Getty Images; 90 © Alex Brylov/Shutterstock
.com; 92 © Siri Berting/Getty Images; 94 © James Duncan Davidson/TED; 96 © 19th era/Alamy Stock Photo; 97 © Bob Thomas/Popperfoto/Getty Images;
98 © Muslianshah Masrie/Shutterstock.com; 100 © Peeter Viisimaa/Getty Images; 104 © Ryan Lash/TED; 106 © Aleph Studio/Shutterstock.com; 107 ©
rootstocks/Getty Images; 110 © Josie Elias/Getty Images; 112 (t) © Robert Daly/Getty Images; 112 (m) © equinoxvect/Shutterstock.com; 112 (b) © Hill Street
Studios/Getty Images; 114 (l, r) © James Duncan Davidson/TED; 116 © National Anthropological Archives, Division of Work & Industry, National Museum
of American History, Smithsonian Institution; 117 © Everett Collection Historical/Alamy Stock Photo; 118 (left col: tl) © Fuse/Getty Images; 118 (left col: tr)
© Ariwasabi/Shutterstock.com; 118 (left col: ml, right col: mr) © Monkey Business Images/Shutterstock.com; 118 (left col: mr) © Pavel L Photo and Video
/Shutterstock.com; 118 (left col: b) © Amos Morgan/Getty Images; 118 (right col: t) © Drop of Light/Shutterstock.com; 118 (right col: ml) © Tracy Whiteside
/Shutterstock.com; 118 (right col: bl) © Robert Kneschke/Shuterstock.com; 118 (right col: br) © jstudio/Shutterstock.com; 120 © Katie Fletcher/Getty Images.

Illustrations: MPS North America LLC

Printed in Greece by Bakis SA
Print Number: 05 Print Year: 2021

Contents

1 Necessities

1.1 Less stuff, more happiness

TEDTALKS

GRAHAM HILL is a modern entrepreneur: by 2007, when he was still only in his mid-30s, he'd already set up and sold two companies for a staggering ten million dollars each! Having originally studied architecture and design, Hill now runs two businesses alongside other projects dedicated to sustainability and ways we can live more simply. He describes himself as a webber, a designer and an environmentalist. As well as his TED Talk on living with less, he also spoke at TED about consuming less meat. At the time he'd been a weekday vegetarian for a year and he went on to write a book about it. The values in both talks are consistent: consume less – whether meat or stuff – enjoy it more, and it will ultimately be better for you and the planet.

In articles and on social media, Graham Hill describes his earlier years when he owned large properties and even employed a personal shopper. Travelling the world extensively taught him what he didn't need. He began to simplify and declutter his life, and over the next 15 years reduced his belongings to a fraction of what he'd once had. He says 'Intuitively, we know that the best stuff in life isn't stuff at all, and that relationships, experiences and meaningful work are the staples of a happy life'.

Hill claims 'editing' is the skill of the century. Is he persuasive enough to inspire us to edit our homes and lives too?

Graham Hill

CAREER PATHWAYS

1 Read the text. Answer the questions.

1 How many companies has Hill started and sold?
2 What jobs has he had?
3 How has he changed as a consumer over the years?
4 What ability does Hill think we need most these days?

TED PLAYLIST

2 Other TED speakers are interested in topics similar to the ones in Graham Hill's TED Talk. Read the descriptions of four TED Talks at the top of page 5. In your opinion, which is the best title for this playlist, a, b or c?

a Transforming recycling into art
b Raising awareness about sustainability
c The cost of modern living

3 Complete the six-word summary (1–4) that corresponds to each talk in the TED playlist. Use these words.

matter	outfit	rubbish	statistics

1 Waste is a _____ of taste.
2 Who's taking all the _____ out?
3 Making meaning out of huge _____ .
4 A new recycled _____ every day.

4 Match the verbs (1–5) with their collocates (a–e). Check your answers in the playlist descriptions.

1 to throw   a waste
2 to refresh   b the impact on
3 to clean up   c something away
4 to increase   d your creative drive
5 to reduce   e understanding

5 Which talk would you most like to see? Why? Watch the talk at TED.com.

▶ **Dan Phillips: Creative houses from reclaimed stuff**

Dan Phillips finds beauty and value in things that other people throw away as rubbish. He recycles all kinds of surprising things, incorporating them into brilliantly designed, low-tech housing built entirely of reused components. The buildings will refresh your creative drive and make you re-think what's beautiful.

▶ **Robin Nagle: What I discovered in New York City trash**

New York City inhabitants produce an astounding 11,000 tons of rubbish every single day. Who cleans up all that waste? Robin Nagle started a research project with the city's Department of Sanitation to find out. She walked the routes, operated mechanical brooms and even drove a dustbin lorry herself. In her talk, she explains why street cleaners are fundamental to any city, and what their (dangerous) work could teach us about our global environmental priorities.

▶ **Chris Jordan: Turning powerful stats into art**

The art that Chris Jordan creates is designed to increase our understanding of some of the staggering statistics associated with mainstream Western cultures. What do 40 million paper cups look like? How can we illustrate the 400,000 smokers who die every year? Jordan hopes that when people engage with these statistics in a visual, artistic way, they'll feel them more deeply and ask themselves the most important question: How do we change?

▶ **Jessi Arrington: Wearing nothing new**

Jessi Arrington is a colour-loving and original designer, who, in this short and snappy talk, shares her pleasure in buying her clothes from – and donating them to – second-hand shops. Her talk is a meditation on conscious consumption and our strong attachment to our belongings. Arrington suggests that second-hand shopping can be a fun adventure, as well as reducing the impact her wardrobe has on the environment and on her bank account.

AUTHENTIC LISTENING SKILLS Relaxed pronunciation

6 🎧 1 1 You are going to hear a podcast in which a member of the *Keynote* team talks about Dan Phillips's TED Talk, *Creative houses from reclaimed stuff*. Listen and underline examples of two-word combinations where *to*, *have* or *of* is reduced or changed.

1 Dan Phillips is not the usual polished TED presenter – he's kind of like a cowboy.
2 Listening to his lilting American accent and easy jokes, we feel as if we should have been sitting round the campfire with him.
3 We want to see more of the quirky yet functional wooden homes he builds.
4 We have to look again and listen to Dan's explanation to fully discover why they are so extraordinary.

LISTENING

7 🎧 1 2 Listen to the full podcast. Are these statements true (T) or false (F)?

1 Dan Phillips isn't a cowboy and he makes jokes. ☐
2 He isn't that interested in what materials he uses. ☐
3 Ninety per cent of his building materials are recycled. ☐
4 Karen tends to replace broken items with new ones. ☐
5 Phillips chooses to use things that are not perfect. ☐

8 🎧 1 2 Listen again. Answer the questions.

1 Why was Phillips pleased about the staircase he got?
2 Why and how did Phillips make 'bumpy tiles'?

3 In your own words, how is waste a matter of taste?
4 What, according to Karen, do you need to have in order to be good at recycling?
5 What does Karen say this talk might inspire us to do?

VOCABULARY IN CONTEXT

9 Read the extracts from the podcast. Choose the correct meaning of the words in bold.

1 ... the **quirky** yet functional wooden homes he builds.
  a stylish ☐
  b clever ☐
  c strange ☐
2 It's about being as **resourceful** as our parents ...
  a modest ☐
  b organized ☐
  c good at finding simple solutions ☐
3 I've got **an allotment**, ...
  a a small vegetable garden ☐
  b a field in the country ☐
  c a big garden ☐
4 … finding beauty in the irregular, [...] and the **flawed**.
  a unfashionable ☐
  b ugly ☐
  c damaged ☐
5 When we think **outside the box** in this way …
  a in tried and tested ways ☐
  b in new ways ☐
  c in the same way as someone else ☐

1.2 Luxury or necessity?

GRAMMAR The perfect aspect

1 Answer the quiz questions and compare your answers with the information about people's coffee-drinking habits in the article.

1 How many cups of coffee do you drink a day?
   a 0–2
   b 3–4
   c 5 or more

2 When do you drink your coffee?
   a in the morning
   b throughout the day
   c after meals

3 Why do you drink coffee, usually?
   a to feel alert
   b to focus
   c to relax

4 How do you rate the coffee experience in your life?
   a essential
   b optional
   c luxury

2 Read the text. Complete the sentences with the correct form of the verb in brackets. Use the present perfect, past perfect or future perfect.

3 Read the interview with a barista. Choose the correct options to complete the questions (a–e).

Q: (a) So, how long *did you work / have you been working* here?
A: Oh I dunno … I guess I ¹_____ (work) here on and off since 2005.

Q: (b) Have you *been working / worked* anywhere else?
A: My grandparents have a café and I ²_____ (work) there for fun before I worked anywhere for money.

Q: (c) It's delicious coffee. How have you *perfected / been perfecting* the art?
A: I ³_____ (have) to practise making a perfect latte, but I think it's in my blood.
I ⁴_____ (watch) coffee-making rituals before I even went to school and I ⁵_____ (spend) hours sitting in cafés since I can remember.

Q: What's the secret to making a really great coffee?
A: Well, you have to ⁶_____ (buy), roasted and ground good beans first. Then it's the combination of temperature and pressure.

Q: Anything else?
A: You have to ⁷_____ (heat) the perfect cup too! And then drink it in great company.

Q: (d) How many coffees *have you made / did you make*, do you think?
A: Fewer than my grandpa ⁸_____ (make) and not as many as I ⁹_____ (make) by the time I retire.

Q: (e) So, have you *found / been finding* your vocation?
A: Well, I absolutely love what I do. In a few years, I ¹⁰_____ (inherit) the café and can keep the family business going. But until then I can work in other places and study a little too.

Q: What are you studying?
A: I ¹¹_____ (start) a business course to help me run the business.

Coffee yesterday, today and tomorrow

If you ¹_____ (have / never) a cup of coffee made by an expert barista, it's time you did. It's one of life's affordable luxuries.

Europeans enjoy 725 million cups of coffee every day and Americans 400 million.
It ²_____ (integrate) into our culture to such an extent that takeaway coffee ³_____ (almost / attain) fashion accessory status. Americans drink an average of 1.6 cups of coffee a day whereas tea-drinking countries like Britain and Japan drink about half that, mostly at breakfast time. (Men reportedly drink coffee to focus and get the job done whereas women ⁴_____ (tend) to drink it to relax.)

In the 21ˢᵗ century our taste in coffee ⁵_____ (become) more sophisticated, but coffee drinking itself ⁶_____ (already / gain) high levels of popularity in the previous century. The first instant coffee was drunk in 1938 and, by 1946, coffee drinking ⁷_____ (reach) a peak in the US with 174 litres being consumed yearly per person. Interestingly, by 2005, consumption dropped to only 90 litres and for the past few years now we ⁸_____ (drink) a range of soft and energy drinks as well as coffee. By 2020, who knows? Perhaps we ⁹_____ (even / find) a replacement for coffee.

4 🎧1 3 Complete the barista's answers (1–11) in Exercise 3 with the correct form of the verb in brackets. Use the present perfect, past perfect or future perfect. Then listen and check your answers.

GRAMMAR EXTRA! *been or gone*

5 Complete the sentences with *been* or *gone*.

1 I've _____ working in a café for the summer and am starting university in October.

2 Customers have _____ leaving more tips recently! We must be doing a good job, don't you think?

3 She's _____ on holiday for three weeks so we've taken on a replacement.

4 She's _____ asking about the overtime she's owed; can you check the time sheets please?

5 Have you ever _____ to a coffee-tasting event?

6 We arranged to meet at 5 p.m., but when I arrived at the café at ten past, he'd already _____ !

6 Complete the sentences. Use these words and phrases.

| long gone | been there, done that | been and gone |
| has-been | gone to seed | |

1 I hadn't seen him for ten years at least and I was shocked at how he'd changed. He'd really _____ .

2 Do you remember when we were kids we used to spend all day playing outside? The days of being able to do that are _____ now, aren't they?

3 She doesn't seem very enthusiastic about anything I suggest – it's always '_____' !

4 She was a really great actress in her day, but I'm afraid she's a bit of a _____ now.

5 By the time we got round to booking tickets for the performance, it had already _____ .

DICTATION

7 🎧1 4 Listen to someone talking about coffee houses. Complete the paragraph.

The Grand Café in Oxford was started in 1650 _____
_____ .

However, the Queen's Lane Coffee House, _____
_____ ,

is the longest established coffee house in England. Twenty-five years after the first place opened, _____
_____ .

Over the years, they _____
_____ . If you
_____ in a

historic café _____
_____ .

Even before your first sip _____
_____ .

7

1.3 I'm wide awake

READING

1 Match each extract (1–6) with its source (a–f).

   1 'Sometimes I wake up grumpy, other times I just let him sleep.'

   2 '... it's difficult to motivate yourself to make the changes; difficult, that is, until you've had another sleepless night. I decided to start with the easiest things.'

   3 'Blissful nights in comfort and style: *Sky*, a modern four-poster made of solid acacia wood comes in two sizes …'

   4 'Tracey shows us her own bed in all its embarrassing glory.'

   5 'A rom-com, perfect for Sunday afternoon viewing, or for a night when you can't drop off.'

   6 'Finally she did open her eyes. At first she just saw strange lights until a figure appeared in the centre of her field of vision.'

   a A blog account of following some self-help advice.

   b A T-shirt slogan.

   c Part of the description of an artwork, *My bed* by Tracey Emin, by the Saatchi Gallery.

   d *The Girl who Kicked the Hornets' Nest*, novel by Stieg Larsson.

   e Description of the film, *Sleepless in Seattle,* in review.

   f Furniture catalogue description.

Title: A

B

Have you ever suffered from insomnia? Believe me it's awful. I'd been suffering for about six months when I finally decided, with the help of my doctor, to do something about it. I didn't want to take any medication so I read everything I could find about the problem and tried to solve it myself. After all, reading was one of the things I had time for when I wasn't sleeping. The first thing I discovered was that I was doing almost everything absolutely wrong. With so many bad habits, it's difficult to motivate yourself to make the changes; difficult, that is, until you've had another sleepless night. I decided to start with the easiest things.

C

Easier said than done not to take devices into the bedroom; I like being connected, checking posts or watching something before sleep. I left them in the living room and tried reading books again. It reminded me a little of my childhood when my parents read to me before sleep. With a couple of exceptions I kept it up.

D

I tried taking a bath before bed and playing some gentle music while I did so. It was certainly calming but I actually prefer a shower in the morning so I didn't keep it up. But, while looking for different music, I did start listening to the radio more and discovered some new Internet channels.

E

This advice meant I actually had to give myself a fixed time to retire to bed which I didn't like at all! I felt like a teenager again. So, I turned it around and started eating earlier than I had been doing. Actually, it proved not to be too difficult to eat between seven and eight o'clock most days and, if I was eating out, it wasn't a problem because I was going to bed later anyway.

F

I realized I hadn't thought of this before. It was quite full and messy and not exactly restful. I threw away the piles of papers and magazines that were on the floor by my bed, put all the clothes in the wardrobe and bought some new bedding. I discovered that I liked being in it and started to look forward to going to bed.

G

I'm not a fan of the gym. I tried it two years ago but didn't go enough to justify the cost. So, I started getting off the bus a stop early and walking a bit – when the weather was good, that is. And I started taking the stairs at work, all four flights, every day!

H

This proved to be the most difficult tip! I'd made some changes and was impatient to see some results. When I still couldn't get to sleep I felt disappointed. But every couple of nights it worked and that kept me motivated. It's just like they say: change doesn't happen overnight.

2 Read the blog post on page 8. Match the headings (1–8) with A–H in the text.

1 Getting exercise during the day helps you sleep at night
2 Create a relaxing bedtime routine
3 Don't take your laptop, tablet or smartphone to bed with you
4 Don't expect instant results – change takes time
5 Make sure your bedroom is a comfortable environment for sleeping
6 Getting a good night's sleep
7 Enough sleeplessness!
8 Avoid eating and drinking three hours before bedtime

VOCABULARY The prefixes *over* and *under*

3 Match the words with *over* or *under* with the definitions that mean the <u>opposite</u> (a–f).

1 to overwork ☐
2 to undervalue ☐
3 to overspend ☐
4 to oversleep ☐
5 to overdo ☐
6 to underestimate ☐

a to get up before the alarm
b to stay within budget
c to perform a task in a moderate way
d to be realistic about what something involves
e to consider something to be worth more than it is
f to do your job in a proportionate way

4 Complete the sentences with *over* or *under*.

1 Unfortunately the new collection was slightly _____ priced at the launch and not many items were actually sold.
2 His lack of concentration during the exam was the result of stress and _____ sleeping.
3 They pitched their idea for a new business to a board of investors who were interested in the idea but felt that the financial details were _____ developed.
4 The buses are becoming so _____ crowded that I've started cycling to work instead.
5 The café was horribly _____ staffed and after fifteen minutes they still hadn't been served.

WORDBUILDING Negative prefixes

5 Complete the negative words (1–8). Use these prefixes. Then match the meanings (a–h) with the words (1–8).

de	dis	in	im
il	mis	non	un

1 _____satisfied
2 _____comfortable
3 _____polite
4 _____-existent
5 _____efficient
6 _____understood
7 _____legible
8 _____centralized

a rude ☐
b time wasting and chaotic ☐
c difficult to read ☐
d controlled regionally ☐
e unhappy about service or quality ☐
f not present or available ☐
g not comprehended correctly ☐
h not pleasant to sit, lie on or use ☐

6 Complete the hotel review. Use the negative words from Exercise 5.

The European hotel chain Moss has recently carried out an extensive survey after customer reviews had been unexpectedly poor. The survey revealed that since the hotel organization was ¹_____ there's been more local variation across the group. Some of the feedback in two locations has shown a number of guests have been ²_____ . Comments about the hotels have ranged from the beds being ³_____ and staff being ⁴_____ and unhelpful to the management being ⁵_____ and requests for help being ⁶_____ . The restaurants haven't fared any better, with guests remarking that the handwritten menu is ⁷_____ and being frustrated to find that the advertised restaurant terrace is ⁸_____ . The hotel chain is now under review.

WORD FOCUS *sleep*

7 Match the *sleep* phrasal verbs with the definitions.

sleep in	sleep off	sleep on
sleep over	sleep through	

1 to make a decision or solve a problem overnight _____
2 to neutralize the unpleasant effects of too much food, drink, a physical complaint, etc. _____
3 to have an uninterrupted night's sleep despite noise _____
4 to stay at someone's house, often with several other people _____
5 to sleep past the alarm clock _____

8 Complete the sentences with the correct form of the verbs from Exercise 7.

1 He's a very deep sleeper; he could _____ an earthquake!
2 I'm sorry I still can't decide what to do; so far _____ the problem hasn't helped.
3 My daughter's friends often _____ at our house and vice versa – sometimes it saves finding a babysitter.
4 If it hadn't been for the postman ringing the doorbell, I would have _____ and missed my flight.
5 I prefer not to take medication when I get a headache. I tend to go to bed and try and _____ (it).

1.4 Keep it to the bare minimum

HEDGING

1 🎧 **1 5** Listen and make a note of three arguments that support the idea that a 'gap year' is a good idea for Ian.

1 _____
2 _____
3 _____

2 🎧 **1 5** Match the two parts of the sentences. Then listen again and check your answers.

1 I wonder if ☐
2 I'm guessing ☐
3 It seems to me that ☐
4 Personally, I feel that ☐
5 All I know is ☐

a I really want to study, but not immediately.
b it might not be a bad idea to find out more about it.
c we could have a chat about my plans?
d you'd be thinking of something abroad?
e you young people have too many choices and actually should just work like we had to do.

3 Put the words in the correct order to make hedging phrases.
a about / know / I / don't / but / you,
b might / possibly / you
c a / bad / be / idea / it / not / might / to
d me / seems / it / to
e right / you're / maybe
f reasonable / assume / that / it's / to
g expert, / no / but / I'm

4 🎧 **1 6** Complete the conversation with the hedging phrases from Exercise 3. Then listen and check your answers.

Bob: You know, Ian does have a point. I think ¹_____ there *are* some advantages of having a gap year.

Connie: Well, ²_____ have a trip ourselves. We've never been to New Zealand.

Bob: Now hold your horses! Let's not get carried away! ³_____ we're a little old for things like that.

Connie: I thought you'd say that. Things have changed, you know. ⁴_____ I don't think gap years are only for young people now! We'd be silver gappers, I think they call them.

Bob: Yes, ⁵_____ . Aren't they called grey gappers though? Let's look it up ... yes, grey not silver.

Connie: ⁶_____ I could do with a break from work and broadening my horizons a bit.

Bob: You know, ⁷_____ have something there! Gap years *should* be for people who've been working ten or fifteen years and need a break, not only for kids full of energy.

PRONUNCIATION Vowel sounds at word boundaries

5 🎧 **1 7** Look at the words in bold. Listen to what happens when one word ends in a vowel sound and the next begins with one. Is it a /w/, /j/ or /r/ sound? Write W, Y or R.

1 It'd help you decide exactly what to study and **be a** chance to broaden your horizons. _____

2 But **the experience** does help find out what to do ...
_____

3 Well, actually there's an information evening at school. Lots of people **are interested** ... _____

4 I think it's reasonable **to assume** that there *are* some advantages of having a gap year. _____

5 It seems to me **we're a** little old for things like that. _____

6 I'm **no expert**, but I don't think gap years are only for young people! _____

WRITING SKILL Hedging expressions

6 Read the report by a recent gap year student from Ian's school. Put the words in italics in the correct order to make hedging expressions.

a So, the type of work *be / necessarily / shouldn't* connected to what your line of study so far suggests.

b When choosing what and where to do it, *considering / worth / it's* that doing something, which really stretches you and takes you out of your comfort zone, will be most valuable.

c However, after having just completed one myself, I *conclude / probably / can* that this is true, but that arguably the individual doing it reaps more benefit than either of them.

d Certainly a gap year involving voluntary work will, *likelihood / all / in*, combine work that benefits both the local community and the planet.

e I'd like to add that if you are working with a team of people from different cultures and backgrounds, *be / be / could / it / said / to* an enjoyable and enriching experience, whatever the topic.

f The aim of this short report is to relate what I have learned on my gap year and to inform others thinking of taking one. *a / be / held / seems / that / there / to / view / widely* a gap year is an experience worth having and that what you do during this time will have social implications.

g In conclusion, *appear / would / it* that it's not necessarily what you do, but why you do it and who you do it with that matters. It certainly taught me to live with less by living out of a rucksack for six months.

h Firstly, *that / thought / often / it's* the work experience won't always be easy or appealing, but that it will be rewarding.

7 Number the sentences in Exercise 6 in the correct order to complete the report.

1 ☐ **2** ☐ **3** ☐ **4** ☐ **5** ☐ **6** ☐ **7** ☐ **8** ☐

8 Tick [✓] the gap-year experiences and locations that you think are being described in Exercise 6 and say why.

1 Marine research in New Zealand ☐
2 Tree planting in Canada ☐
3 Au pairing in Europe ☐
4 Farming in Australia ☐

Reason: _____

9 Read the report in Exercise 6 again. Are these statements true (T) or false (F)?

1 Few people think that a gap year is worthwhile. ☐
2 Voluntary work usually helps the environment. ☐
3 Generally a gap year is less rewarding for the person doing it than for the community where they work. ☐
4 You should choose something you haven't done before. ☐
5 The work itself may not be interesting but the overall experience is valuable. ☐

10 Read the advert. Then find and correct the mistakes in each section (1–6) in the email.

> Gap year abroad in conservation – join us on volunteering programmes in Australia and New Zealand. Would you like to explore a part of Australasia, work hard for the local and global environment and meet people from all walks of life? Find out more and apply today outlining your background and motivation to: Jake Simmonds.

11 Write a reply to the email in Exercise 10. Use the hedging expressions from Exercises 6 and 10, and the information in the box.

> Volunteers welcome: aged 17–60 and physically fit
>
> Projects: urban and remote (usually outdoors)
> Include: tree planting, erosion management and surveys (machines used)
>
> Projects: start four times a year with an orientation course (three days) in Auckland
>
> Free places: from September

> Dear Martin
>
>
>
> We look forward to receiving your application.
>
> Best regards
>
> Jake

TO: _____   FROM: _____
SUBJECT: _____

Dear Mr Simmonds

1 I would like to find out more about programmes with your organization, particularly conservation work in New Zealand. The advert <u>suggesting</u> volunteers are involved in work that benefits both the planet and the local community. ___suggests___

2 I have recently left high school and feel it's worth to consider taking a gap year before studying for a degree next year. My motivation is, firstly, to be part of an ecological project with a well-known organization. _____

3 Secondly, I would like to visit and work in a country where, in every likelihood, I will be able to learn new skills and develop an understanding of the local people and culture. I have always been fascinated by New Zealand. _____

4 I have heard that volunteers usually work in groups made up of different nationalities and age groups. Would it be right that this work would almost certain be hard both physically and mentally? _____

5 It will appear that working on a programme like this would be a thoroughly rewarding experience. I would appreciate receiving more details, particularly about the tree-planting projects: where they are and when exactly the progammes start. _____

6 It could be say that I'm hard-working and sociable and a team player, qualities I believe you are looking for. I look forward to hearing from you. _____

Yours sincerely

Martin Hews

YOUR IDEA

1 Read about each person's change of lifestyle. Complete the table.

1 **Aiko:** One of the biggest changes in my life has been how easy it is nowadays to get online. I used to work in an office and had to spend hours commuting from home. Now I can take my work with me wherever I go. As a writer, it's easy to keep in touch with my editor by email, I can do a lot of my research on the Internet, and of course submit my manuscripts electronically. These days I feel much freer – I am not tied to a desk or any one place, so I can set my own working hours. But most important of all, I am able to travel and experience different ways of life. That is such a great thing, as it means I am always exposed to new things and can include these experiences in my stories.

2 **Jan:** So many people do it every year, don't they? In January, usually after an overindulgent festive period, you see people joining gyms and fitness clubs. I used to be one of them too, but inevitably my enthusiasm dropped and a few months into the New Year I would stop going. But I found a solution – one that was obvious, now I think about it. I just made exercise a part of my everyday life, by walking a lot more instead of driving everywhere and doing little bits of exercise whenever I can, like some sit-ups or jogging on the spot. After a few months of making these small changes, I feel fitter and happier about myself. I also don't have to work out in a smelly gym anymore!

3 **Vanessa:** Something I'd been reading about a lot was the impact that what we eat actually has on the world. Did you know that the process of meat production causes so much waste and can damage the environment? So, I decided to become a vegetarian. It's not easy to make such a big change in your life, especially when your friends and family don't always understand. At first, I made the change gradually, only sticking to a vegetarian diet during the week, while still eating meat at the weekend. After a few months, no one questioned what I was doing any more, so I cut out meat from my diet completely. I feel a lot happier, even if this is only a small part of a very big issue in society.

	Aiko	Jan	Vanessa
a Who changed their routine so it was more flexible?			
b Who had to introduce their lifestyle change gradually?			
c Who has become more active?			
d Whose lifestyle change was motivated by a bigger problem in the world?			
e Who changed their lifestyle with technology?			
f Who made small everyday changes to their lifestyle?			

2 Write notes about your lifestyle, focusing on one of these areas. If you can, think of a change you have made to your lifestyle.

work	diet	exercise
hobbies	home and family	

_____

_____

_____

_____

_____

_____

_____

3 Answer the following questions about your lifestyle.

1 How would you describe your lifestyle or a change you have made to your lifestyle in one sentence?

_____

2 Who or what things are important for your lifestyle to work?

_____

3 What changes have you made to your lifestyle, if any?

_____

4 What prop could you use to illustrate your lifestyle?

_____

4 Practise talking about your lifestyle out loud. Remember to practise using props to ...
- stimulate the audience's curiosity.
- provide a visual focus.
- serve as an example.
- make your talk memorable.

ORGANIZING YOUR PRESENTATION

5 Match the four steps of a presentation with the examples of useful language (a–d).

1 Introduce yourself and your topic ☐

2 Say what aspect of your lifestyle you want to talk about ☐

3 Say who or what is important to make your lifestyle work ☐

4 Finish ☐

a I'm going to talk about a change in my lifestyle that relates to improving my memory.

b For me, it was great to have the support of my friends and family to make this change.

c Thank you for taking the time to listen.

d Hello. I'm Steven. It's great to have you here today for this talk.

YOUR PRESENTATION

6 Read the useful language on the left and make notes for your presentation.

1 Introduce yourself and your topic My name's … , and today I'm going to talk about my lifestyle. I'm … . Today's presentation is about my lifestyle.	
2 Say what aspect of your lifestyle you want to talk about The aspect of my lifestyle I want to talk about is … … is an important part of my lifestyle …	
3 Say who or what is important to make your lifestyle work In order to make my lifestyle work … The most important thing/person for me is … because …	
4 Finish Thank you for taking the time to listen. That's it from me. Does anyone have any questions?	

7 Film yourself giving your presentation or practise in front of a mirror. Give yourself marks out of ten for …

- using props to give examples.   ☐ /10
- following the four steps in Exercise 6.   ☐ /10
- using correct grammar.   ☐ /10

2 Image and identity

2.1 Who am I? Think again

TEDTALKS

HETAIN PATEL is an artist of Indian descent, who was born, raised and is based in the United Kingdom. His prolific works have been exhibited internationally in 75 group exhibitions, solo projects and performances. Yuyu Rau is a multi-faceted dancer who moved from Taiwan in 2006 and has lived and worked in England since then. Rau has performed with Patel in his work *Be Like Water* that challenges assumptions about what we look like and where we come from. She adds not just dance to the performance, but also another language, nationality and gender.

Patel has performed with his father to explore the issue of nature vs. nurture. In one piece called *To Dance Like Your Dad* they are seen doing and saying the same things in almost exact synchronicity. He uses popular cultural figures too. In 2015, he made a life-size sculpture of himself called *Letter to Spider-Man* in gratitude to his superhero.

In one of his most ambitious projects, the *Fiesta Transformer*, Patel worked with his father and an engineer to transform a Ford Fiesta car into a work of art that 'sits' like an Indian or like Spider-Man. In this way Patel explores how his identity was shaped by both his Indian origin and the influences of popular culture.

Hetain Patel

CAREER PATHWAYS

1 Read the text. Answer the questions.

1 Which cultures do Patel and Rau represent?
2 Where, how and how much has Patel exhibited?
3 How has he involved his father in his work?
4 What does the *Fiesta Transformer* installation tell us about Patel's identity?

TED PLAYLIST

2 Other TED speakers are interested in topics similar to Hetain Patel's TED Talk. Read the descriptions of four TED Talks at the top of page 15. In your opinion, which is the best title for this playlist, a, b or c?

a Finding yourself in words and culture
b Discovering and exploring identity
c Forging your own journey

3 Complete the six-word summary (1–4) that corresponds to each talk in the TED playlist. Use these words.

| constant | rhyming | soul | tales |

1 Articulating emotion in powerful _____ verse.
2 Multiple _____ matter and empower us.
3 Self isn't _____ , the infinite is.
4 A question of _____ not soil.

4 Match the verbs (1–5) with their collocates (a–e). Check your answers in the playlist descriptions.

1 to bubble   a the danger
2 to warn of   b the direction of
3 to channel   c the question of
4 to experience   d with energy
5 to reflect on   e first-hand

5 Which talk would you most like to see? Why? Watch the talk at TED.com.

▶ **Jamila Lyiscott: Three ways to speak English**

Jamila Lyiscott is a spoken-word artist, professor and student whose performance bubbles with energy and rhyme. She describes herself as a 'tri-lingual orator' and explains how she uses a different language in her three main communities: one with her friends, one at work in the classroom and another with her family. In the talk, she entertains and challenges us with her poetical exploration of language and identity.

▶ **Chimamanda Ngozi Adichie: The danger of a single story**

Chimamanda Ngozi Adichie is a novelist who grew up reading stories that were set in a cultural context very different to her own. Through her work, and in her own personal narrative, she explores how the stories we share have a powerful influence on how we understand other people and cultures. Having only a single story, she warns of the danger of creating damaging stereotypes and ignoring our individual and collective richness and complexity.

▶ **Julian Baggini: Is there a real you?**

In this entertaining talk, Julian Baggini relates this core question to the areas of science and philosophy. There's a reason we are different to things like a wristwatch or a cup of water, according to Baggini. Like these things, we're the sum of our parts and experiences, but we differ in that we have the added capacity of being able to shape ourselves and influence our environments. He suggests that it's a liberating prospect that we can – within certain limits – channel the direction of our development.

▶ **Pico Iyer: Where is home?**

Pico Iyer is one of the 220 million people today living in a country that is not his place of birth. He doesn't have straightforward answers to 'Where are you from?' or 'Where is home?', having experienced several cultures first-hand and lost his physical home through disaster. He reflects on the question of home through the juxtaposition of travel and home, movement and stillness, and the new and the familiar.

AUTHENTIC LISTENING SKILLS
Assimilation and voiced and unvoiced sounds

6 🎧 **1** **8** You are going to hear a podcast in which a member of the *Keynote* team talks about Pico Iyer's TED Talk *Where is home*? Listen to the sentences from the beginning of the talk. Circle each end-of-word consonant that is clearly sounded. Underline the ones that are silent or nearly silent.

1 Pico Iyer's talk resonated deeply with me on a personal level.
2 I was born in the south of England, but I've lived abroad much longer than I've lived in Britain.
3 This last statement seems to ring true for him, and it certainly does for me.
4 Pico Iyer is such a crisp, clear and calm presenter.

LISTENING

7 🎧 **1** **9** Listen to the full podcast. Choose the correct options to make true sentences.

1 Home for Iyer is *where you grow up / something you feel inside of you*.
2 What makes the talk animated are the pictures he *paints with his words / shows on the screen*.
3 The key moment he describes is *his house being burned down / moving to another country*.
4 He enjoyed staying in the monastery because he *is religious / loved the quiet it offered*.

8 🎧 **1** **9** Listen again. Answer the questions.

1 What does the podcaster have in common with Iyer?
2 What does Iyer mean by the 'great floating tribe'?
3 What did Iyer learn about his sense of home from the house fire?
4 What did he do in the monastery?
5 What does 'looking with new eyes' mean?

VOCABULARY IN CONTEXT

9 Read the extracts from the podcast. Choose the correct meaning of the words in bold.

1 Pico Iyer's talk **resonated deeply with me** ...
   a filled me with sadness ☐
   b had a strong effect on me ☐
   c made me very happy ☐
2 The **animation** comes from within Iyer ...
   a energy ☐   b movement ☐   c interest ☐
3 He makes the audience feel **compelled to** listen.
   a driven to ☐
   b encouraged to ☐
   c unmotivated to ☐
4 Iyer says home is [...] where you '**fashion** your sense of self'.
   a create ☐   b review ☐   c study ☐
5 He'd been **hankering after** stillness and silence.
   a avoiding ☐
   b interested in ☐
   c longing for ☐

2.2 Cyber crime

GRAMMAR Amounts and comparisons

1 Complete the definition. Use these words.

> defrauding   impersonating   obtaining   revealing   using

Phishing is:

- ¹_____ someone by ²_____ a real company online.
- ³_____ money dishonestly online.
- ⁴_____ a false email or web address in order to trick someone into ⁵_____ passwords or other sensitive information.

2 Look at the pie charts showing phishing targets in 2013. Then match the two parts of the sentences.

1 A little over a third ☐
2 A small number ☐
3 A little less than a quarter ☐
4 About half of targets ☐
5 About twice as many ☐
6 The vast majority of ☐
7 A sizeable portion of ☐

a target online games.
b e-shops are targeted as payment systems.
c online finance targets involve banks.
d involve email or online finance.
e online finance targets involves e-shops.
f target email services.
g involve social networks.

3 Complete the text. Use the phrases (1–7) from Exercise 2 and the pie charts.

¹_____ phishing scams involve trying to either steal money or obtain sensitive personal data from the victims. Phishers, like the more traditional fishing its name is based on, use bait to attract their victims. ²_____ cases cannot be recognized as fake even by expert computer users. ³_____ were email and online finance, as these are the sources of the most lucrative information for scammers: credit card details and passwords. Email services alone made up ⁴_____ of all targets. ⁵_____ involved social networking sites and only ⁶_____ targeted online games. ⁷_____ e-shops as payment systems were targeted and, as smartphone and tablet use has increased Internet use overall, so has phishing activity increased.

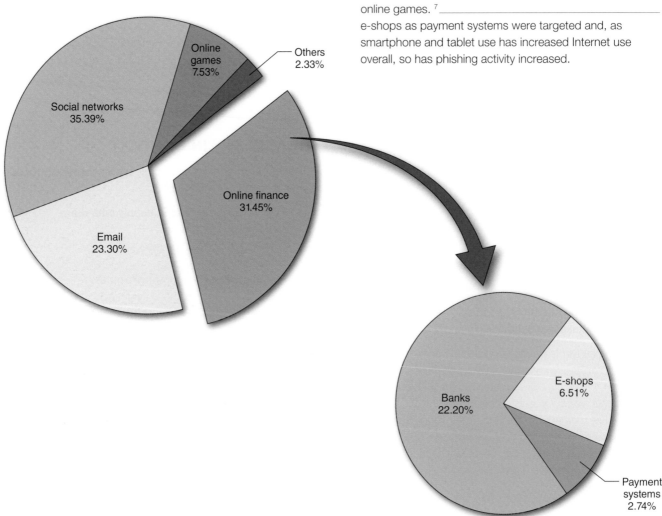

Social networks 35.39%
Online games 7.53%
Others 2.33%
Online finance 31.45%
Email 23.30%

Banks 22.20%
E-shops 6.51%
Payment systems 2.74%

4 Choose the correct options to complete the grammatical information about amounts and comparisons expressions. Look at the exercises above for examples.

1 **The vast majority of** and **a considerable number of** function as plural nouns and are always followed by *singular / plural* verbs.

2 **A small amount of** and **a small portion of** function as singular nouns and are always followed by *singular / plural* verbs.

3 **A sizeable portion of**, **a large amount of** and **a great deal of** function as singular nouns and are always followed by *singular / plural* verbs.

4 Expressions using fractions like **about half of** and **a little over a quarter of** can function as singular or plural depending on the nouns they modify. They are followed by *singular and plural / singular* verbs.

5 **A minority of** and **a handful of** function as plural nouns and are always followed by *singular / plural* verbs.

5 🎧1 10 Complete the sentences. Use these words and phrases. Then listen and check your answers.

are	deal of	does	don't
fifty per cent	a handful	is	small minority of
twice as many	vast majority of		

1 A great _____ unaccountable activity _____ evident.

2 There are _____ payments on your credit card statement this month as there were last month.

3 Unfortunately, only a very _____ criminals _____ caught.

4 The credit card company _____ cover the losses in all but _____ of cases.

5 The _____ victims _____ notice until it's happened.

6 We've had a _____ rise in reports in this last year.

6 Complete the sentences with these words and phrases so that they have a very similar meaning to sentences 1–5 in Exercise 5.

a considerable number of		a large amount of
double the number of	a tiny number	a handful of

1 _____ unaccountable activity is evident in the account.

2 There are _____ payments on your credit card statement this month as there were last month.

3 Unfortunately, only _____ criminals are caught.

4 The credit card company does cover the losses in all but _____ of cases.

5 _____ victims don't notice until it's happened.

PRONUNCIATION Weak *of*

7 🎧1 11 Read the sentences. Underline the weak *of* sounds. Then listen and check your answers.

1 Yes, 12, 14, 16 of March and 19 and 20 of March – all in the same week.

2 If you didn't make those payments yourself, you may well have been a victim of a phishing scam.

3 Unfortunately, only a very small minority of criminals are caught, but the credit card company does cover the losses in all but a handful of cases.

DICTATION

8 🎧1 12 Listen to someone talking about ID theft insurance. Complete the paragraph.

_____

the key to preventing phishing scams is awareness, caution and using up-to-date security. However,

_____

policies to protect us from identity theft too. Apparently, it's the fastest growing form of insurance according to the Insurance Information Institute.

_____

for a little less than $30. But,

_____

providers don't reimburse people suffering a loss, is it really necessary?

_____

suffering losses due to ID theft had to pay more than $1,000 themselves.

_____

with their service and offer peace of mind.

2.3 You are what you wear

READING

1 Match the dress code terms with the clothes (a–c). Read the article attached to the memo to check.

1 Formal ☐
2 Smart or business casual ☐
3 Casual ☐

a Trousers / jeans or skirt and shirt or T-shirt
b Suit and tie, jacket with trousers or skirt
c Trousers / skirt and neat but relaxed look; optional tie

2 Read the memo. Are these statements true (T) or false (F)?

1 The company's corporate identity has changed recently. ☐
2 The industry sector has become more formal in the last few years. ☐
3 The company was taken over in January. ☐
4 The new dress code is mostly business casual. ☐
5 A casual dress code includes sportswear. ☐

Dear colleagues

As you know, we've recently implemented the new corporate identity encapsulated by the acronym AIM:

Aim high

Insist on the best

Minimize risk and waste

Business dress code in our sector has relaxed and become less formal over the last couple of years. I would welcome this shift for our company too, particularly now that our new IT colleagues have joined us. This merger in January brought many changes to how we work but has also resulted in two dress codes: a casual one and a formal one. We've since grown together and have developed our joint culture and identity. I'd like this to be reflected in how we all look. After working closely with HR and the works council we have updated our dress code and aligned it with our new identity.

The new dresscode is being launched this month through meetings and posters as you will have noticed. In a nutshell this means:

* suits and ties are only necessary for very formal occasions and will be mentioned in meeting invitations
* jeans are now allowed as long as they are 'dark and smart'
* the general look for most people should be business casual

These terms are explained more in a short article below. I've embraced the new look already, as you may have noticed.

Dress code terms **explained**

Dress code exists to ensure everyone dresses suitably and appropriately and feels comfortable. Casual dress codes often create more misunderstandings than formal ones so here are a few guidelines to clarify the differences normally understood by the terms.

A *formal* dress code is the one that has been established the longest, with the modern-day suit dating back to the 1920s. A suit and tie is expected for men and a jacket with a skirt or trousers for women. In both cases dark shades of navy, black or brown are usually preferred. This has traditionally been the dress code of financial corporations. *Smart casual* is a little relaxed with ties being optional. Sweaters are also often worn instead of shirts or blouses. It's often the dress code of academia and conferences.

Business casual is a term that came in in the 1990s in America and Canada and spread to other parts of the business world and involves a neutral, relaxed but neat-and-tidy look. It was popularized in the late nineties when reportedly ninety-five per cent of American companies had a day in the week where wearing more casual clothes was allowed – called 'casual Friday' or 'dress-down Friday'. This trend started in Silicon Valley with the IT and start-up companies that were more casually dressed.

A dress code that is deemed *casual* can include trousers and jeans (although some business casual policies also allow smart jeans) and T-shirts. Although freedom is permitted, clothing should still be suitable for work and not include clothing usually worn at the gym, in a club or on the beach.

Please ask your line manager if you have questions. Together, let's make how we look better reflect how we work and who we are.

Thank you all for your co-operation.

Jan Rehmann

CEO Owen, Silk and Sullivan PLC

---

3 Read the texts again. Choose the correct options to complete the sentences.

1 AIM is the acronym that is used to *summarize / portray* the new corporate identity.
2 Employees should feel they dress *similarly / suitably* to each other.
3 Posters have been *displayed / demonstrated* already.
4 They hope to *centralize / consolidate* the message through the new policy.
5 Business casual is *appropriate for / approved by* most employees most of the time.
6 The CEO has *adapted / appropriated* her image accordingly.
7 Formal styles of clothes are *usually / uniformly* dark in colour.
8 Business casual *declined / started* in America and Canada.

4 🎧 **1 13** Listen to part of a department meeting. Complete the poster with these words and phrases.

dark and smart	hoodies and scruffy
pullovers	shirts and blouses
sportswear and slogan	suits and ties

Do wear …	Don't wear …
1_____ jeans	2_____ jeans
3_____, and jackets	4_____ except when requested
5_____, cardigans, T-shirts and tops	6_____ T-shirts or tops

VOCABULARY Describing dress

5 Match the words and phrases (1–8) with the meanings (a–h).

1 classic style ☐
2 looks trendy ☐
3 clashing clothes ☐
4 glamorous clothes ☐
5 unconventional ☐
6 scruffy jeans ☐
7 imaginative look ☐
8 tasteful suit ☐

a ones that don't fit together in either style or colour
b unusual for the culture, occasion or current fashion
c appears up-to-date and fashionable
d a look that is simple and beautiful and doesn't date
e ones that are not looked after and are untidy
f a style that is new and exciting
g one that is well-chosen and attractive
h ones that are fitting for a movie star

6 Complete the sentences. Use the words and phrases (1–8) from Exercise 5.

1 He's really interested in fashion and always _____ and with his _____ outfits, always offers surprises.
2 Having a _____ in your wardrobe makes attending formal events much less stressful.
3 He's so stylish that he even makes _____ look acceptable.
4 She always wears beautiful and _____ to events but last night she achieved a particularly _____ which really stole the show.
5 I can't stand _____. I don't like seeing too many bright colours together. I prefer neutral colours and in general, a _____ .

WORD FOCUS Clothing idioms

7 Match the clothing idioms (1–8) with the meanings (a–h).

1 to be in another's shoes ☐
2 to be given the boot ☐
3 to dress up ☐
4 to have something under one's belt ☐
5 to fit like a glove ☐
6 to pull up one's socks ☐
7 to take one's hat off to someone ☐
8 to roll up one's sleeves ☐

a to do better or try harder
b to wear something smarter than usual
c to have made an achievement
d to know what it feels like to be another person
e to be just the right size and shape for someone
f to be fired or dismissed
g to prepare to work hard at something
h to show admiration or respect for someone else's achievements

8 Complete the sentences with the correct form of the idioms (1–8) from Exercise 7.

1 With the new client there'll be even more work to do so we'll all have to _____ .
2 They're having a big fancy wedding. Everyone's really _____ .
3 You have to _____ . She's really turned the company around since she became CEO.
4 His new well-cut Italian suit _____ and it looks great.
5 The boss told him to _____ to keep up with the others in the team.
6 She's only nineteen and she's already got a degree _____ .
7 He insulted one of the key clients and was immediately _____ .
8 I wouldn't like _____ when the boss finds out.

2.4 I need to work on my image

MAKING SUGGESTIONS

1 Complete the suggestions about the situation below. Use the correct form of the verbs in brackets.

> A friend of yours is finding it difficult to return to work after a career break.

1 Have you considered _____ (start / own business)?
2 You might want to _____ (ask / professional advice).
3 If you don't want to spend money on a course, why not try _____ (read / self-help book)?
4 _____ (do course / get started) might be a good idea.
5 I would seriously consider _____ (rewrite / CV).

2 Complete the dialogues. Use these words and phrases.

> don't lose heart   have you considered that
> I would seriously consider   remember   you mustn't

1 A: I'm too old to learn new skills!
   B: _____ practising new skills will help you become more confident?
2 A: Who's going to be patient enough to teach me?
   B: _____ they are professionals and it's run by an expert coach.
3 A: I'd be embarrassed in front of the others.
   B: _____. You wouldn't be the only one to feel that.
4 A: I'm sure there would only be weaknesses and no strengths.
   B: _____ be so negative, look on the bright side.
5 A: I'd be sure to be one of the 22 per cent who wasn't successful.
   B: If I were you, _____ attending the course.

3 🎧 1 14 Match the two parts of the sentences. Then listen and check your answers.

1 Most of you might want to ☐
2 One other thing to consider ☐
3 You mustn't forget that ☐
4 If you feel nervous, why not try ☐
5 It might be a good idea to remember ☐
6 I would seriously consider ☐

a is making eye contact.
b breathing deeply?
c putting your papers on the table and not holding them.
d use more positive body language.
e that everyone feels nervous before an interview. It's not necessarily a bad thing.
f people can't help receiving a more positive impression if you smile.

PRONUNCIATION Sounding encouraging

4 🎧 1 15 Listen to the suggestions. Does the intonation rise (↑), fall (↓) or stay the same (–)? Which two sentences sound less encouraging? Why?

1 Have you thought about wearing something more comfortable that still looks smart? ☐
2 If I were you, I'd stress my language and IT skills more. ☐
3 You mustn't be so negative. Look on the bright side. ☐
4 Don't lose heart. Don't forget how much experience you've got. ☐
5 Why not try doing it again but more slowly? ☐
6 Don't give up. You're really improving. ☐

WRITING SKILL Being diplomatic

5 Read the feedback email from the coach. Circle the section(s) of the email that give(s) positive feedback. Underline the section(s) that give(s) suggestions and encouragement.

> Dear Erik,
>
> Thank you for your hard work on the course. I can really see that you've made progress, particularly with your shyness. I appreciated your positive contributions in group discussions.
>
> I was impressed by the way you worked on your body language and eye contact, in particular when you were talking about your last job in the second interview recording. I can really see an improvement. You also improved how you answered the questions. You were more focused and that made a better impression. However, as we said on the course, your general appearance needs to be a little smarter and a visit to the hairdresser could make a difference.
>
> If I were you, I'd keep trying to find a job in the hotel sector as you seemed to really enjoy the last job you had. Don't give up and don't forget that it wasn't the quality of your work that was the reason for the redundancy.
>
> We will keep in contact over the next few weeks. Please keep me informed of your interview experience and let me know if I can support you further.
>
> I wish you the very best of luck with your continuing job search.
>
> Best regards
>
> Amanda

6 Find and correct eight mistakes in the draft email.

> Dear Amanda
>
> 1 Thank you for your feedback. I appreciate it the time you took to consider the points.
> 2 I was impressive by the course and I learned a lot in a short time.
> 3 I found the interview practice that was recorded the more interesting, although it was difficult to do.
> 4 Some of the feedback isn't easy to took on, but it's important to hear it.
> 5 Your advice about to work in the hotel sector is very good.
> 6 I hadn't realized that appearance was so important. I'll a haircut have before my next interview.
> 7 Thank you for the interested course and feedback.
> 8 I look forward to be able to tell you I have a job!
>
> Best regards
>
> Erik

7 Complete the sentences. Use the information and the words in brackets to make them more diplomatic.

1 Someone who seems rather shy.
We're looking for someone *(a little) more confident*.
(confident)

2 Someone not familiar with computer programs.
We're looking for someone ＿＿＿＿＿＿＿.
(computer literate)

3 Someone is at an interview in very casual clothes.
We're looking for someone ＿＿＿＿＿＿＿.
(smart)

4 Someone is applying for a job requiring skills they don't have.
We're looking for someone ＿＿＿＿＿＿＿.
(marketing)

5 Someone gives unclear answers to questions.
We're looking for someone ＿＿＿＿＿＿＿.
(communication skills).

6 Someone who speaks poor French.
We're looking for someone ＿＿＿＿＿＿＿.
(French)

8 Put the words in italics in the correct order to complete the feedback email.

TO:		FROM:	
SUBJECT:			

> Dear Jane,
>
> Thank you for your hard work on the course. I can really see that you've made progress particularly [1] *at / considering / how / nervous / start / the / were / you*. I appreciated [2] *group / humour / of / relax / the / to / use / your*.
>
> I was impressed by [3] *board / feedback / on / the / took / way / you*, in particular the way [4] *managed / papers / you / your* in the second interview recording. I can really see an improvement. You also improved [5] *appearance / back / hair / tied / with / your / your* and that made a better impression. However, as we said on the course, [6] *need / still / practice / you*.
>
> If I were you, [7] *CV / I / rewrite / would / your* and consider [8] *an / course / IT / taking* to improve your prospects. Don't give up.
>
> I wish you the very best of luck with your continuing job search.
>
> Best regards
>
> Amanda

The proposal you will read in Exercise 2 is in answer to the following exam question.

> New employees have recently joined your company from abroad. They don't know your country very well. After a meeting, your manager has asked you to put together suggestions for a weekend away so you can all get to know each other in a relaxed environment away from the office. Ideas raised in the meeting include a weekend in the capital city, a weekend at a national park and a weekend at an activity centre. You have been asked to compare two possible weekends away, from this list or your own idea, and decide which would be most popular among your colleagues.
>
> Write your proposal in **220–260 words** in an appropriate style.

IDEAS

1 Tick (✓) the things you would expect to see in the proposal.

a   a sentence about why the proposal has been written ☐

b   a section about the benefits of a company weekend away ☐

c   a section about one possible weekend away ☐

d   a second section about a different weekend away ☐

e   another section covering a third weekend ☐

f   a sentence summarizing the recommendations in the proposal ☐

MODEL

2 Read the proposal. Match the four sections with four descriptions from a–f in Exercise 1.

1 ☐   2 ☐   3 ☐   4 ☐

3 Read the proposal again. Are these statements true (T) or false (F)?

1   The proposal includes research from after the meeting. ☐

2   A visit to Prague would be too expensive. ☐

3   If they visit the city, it will be easy for people to find things they like doing. ☐

4   The writer's company is based in an office surrounded by nature. ☐

5   At a national park, the team would still spend time with each other after dinner. ☐

[1]This proposal is intended to evaluate possible plans for a social weekend away in October, following the meeting held last Thursday. It also takes into account the opinions of those of my colleagues I have spoken to since then.

[2]**Prague**

At the meeting, one suggestion for a weekend away was for everybody to visit Prague. It would be relatively easy to organize, as there is a regular coach service from our town, and it would also be fairly cheap. However, while it is true that in the city everybody will be able to find something they are interested in, whether it is historical buildings or sporting events, it is likely that we will break into smaller groups if we visit Prague. Since the aim of the weekend is for the whole team to get to know each other better, I would suggest avoiding cities.

[3]**National park**

One major factor when selecting a destination for a company weekend away is the opportunity it gives us to experience something completely different from our urban office environment. By visiting a national park, our colleagues would be able to hike and spend time in the countryside, both of which they enjoy. In addition, staying in a guesthouse in the evening would give everyone the chance to cook together, and then play games or show off their musical talents.

[4]**Recommendation**

Based on the opinions of my colleagues, there is no doubt that a weekend in a national park would be preferable to time spent in Prague. I would therefore suggest that this is what is organized for the visit in October.

USEFUL LANGUAGE

4 Put the phrases in the correct order to create introductory sentences for a proposal.

1 of this proposal / a destination for / and to give reasons / the purpose / for my choice / is to recommend / a weekend away

2 has been written / and to decide / this proposal / suggestions for / which is best / a weekend away / to evaluate

3 possible destinations for / and to select / of this proposal for the company to book / the aim / a weekend away / is to outline / the best option

4 for the company weekend away / to summarize / and to suggest / is intended / a destination / this proposal / the outcomes of Thursday's meeting

5 Find and correct the mistake in each sentence.

1 The whole team would definite benefit much more from spending time outside.

2 We could do a tour of the castle, in addition visiting the cathedral.

3 Other major benefit of visiting an activity centre would be the choice of sporting activities available.

4 Spending time in the city should to offer something for everyone.

5 No only does a national park offer beautiful views, but it also gives you the chance to learn more about nature.

6 Complete the sentences. Use these words.

doubt	experience	highlight
mentioned	importance	reason

1 I know from my own _____ that a weekend at an activity centre can be very exciting.

2 I would like to _____ the drawbacks of a visit to the capital city.

3 Other problems _____ include the cost of trying to find accommodation at the weekend.

4 However, it is possible to give too much _____ to trying to keep everyone happy.

5 There is no _____ that some of my colleagues will want to know if they can bring their families with them.

6 For this _____ it is important to find somewhere that can accommodate young children.

7 Match the two parts of the summary sentences.

1 I am confident that if these recommendations are implemented, ☐

2 Following these recommendations will ensure that ☐

3 I feel sure that by

4 In conclusion, I would like to recommend that ☐

5 To sum up, there are ☐

a the weekend will be a success.

b clearly more benefits to visiting the city than an activity centre.

c visiting the activity centre, everyone will enjoy the weekend.

d the situation continues to improve.

e we spend the weekend at the national park.

PLANNING

You will answer the following question.

You have been talking to somebody from a local tourist information office. During your conversation you noted that some tourists are not very aware of your culture. As a result, you decide to write a proposal for tour companies suggesting where tourists could go in your area to learn about the culture and what typical features of your culture should be highlighted.

8 Plan your proposal. Write notes to answer these questions. Don't write full sentences yet.

1 What are the three or four most interesting or important aspects of your culture?

2 Where could tourists go to find out about them?

3 What headings will you use?

WRITING

9 Write a proposal to reply to the question in Exercise 8. In your proposal you should ...

- explain why you have written the proposal
- list three or four aspects of your culture which tourists could learn about
- explain where they should go to learn about them
- use neutral or slightly formal language.

Write **220–260 words** in an appropriate style.

ANALYSIS

10 Check your proposal. Answer the questions.

- **Content:** Does the proposal list places tourists could go to learn about your culture? Are the cultural features that should be highlighted clearly described? Is it 220 to 260 words long?

- **Communicative achievement:** Is it written in a neutral or formal style? Is it clear to the reader why you have chosen these aspects of your culture?

- **Organization:** Is the proposal logically organized? Does it use headings?

- **Language:** Does it use correct grammar and vocabulary? Is a good range of structures used?

3 Harmony

3.1 Making peace is a marathon

TEDTALKS

MAY EL-KHALIL was born in Lebanon and, after her marriage, relocated to Nigeria for many years and raised a family. El-Khalil started running to keep fit, even though it was unusual there in the late 1990s. She was often joined by curious local children, who at first ran barefoot and later with shoes that she had bought them.

In 2000, the family moved back to Beirut, where May El-Khalil continued to run until her fateful accident. During her long and painful recovery she put all her energy into creating the first international running event in Lebanon, the Beirut Marathon. Although she could no longer run, El-Khalil wanted others to experience the positive feelings of being part of an organized event where political differences can be put aside. Since the first race in 2003, the Beirut Marathon has grown each year to become what is now the biggest sporting event in the Middle East, thanks to El-Khalil's vision and determination. Through this work El-Khalil has won international recognition and numerous awards, including the AIPS Power of Sport Award in Lausanne and the Laureus World Sports Academy Lifetime achievement award in Abu Dhabi.

With its focus on bringing people together, the race caters for middle-eastern athletes but also international and elite runners; both roadrunners and wheelchair racers are welcome to take part. There's also a special race for

May El-Khalil

women only that takes place every spring to empower local women. May El-Khalil said in a CNN article after the Boston Marathon attack in 2013, 'In times of such uncertainty, it is more important than ever to remind people of what is good, and what is important: healthy competition, unity, prosperity, growth, joy and, most of all, peace'.

CAREER PATHWAYS

1 Read the text. Answer the questions.

   1 Who joined May El-Khalil on her runs and why?
   2 What qualities does El-Khalil have that made the Beirut Marathon such a success?
   3 Who takes part in the Beirut Marathon?
   4 What does El-Khalil see as the top priority in life?

TED PLAYLIST

2 Other TED speakers are interested in topics similar to May El-Khalil's TED Talk. Read the descriptions of the four TED Talks at the top of page 25. In your opinion, which is the best title for this playlist, a, b or c?

   a Using art to represent cultural diversity
   b Collaborating towards greater creativity
   c Working towards mutual understanding

3 Complete the six-word summary (1–4) that corresponds to each talk in the TED playlist. Use these words.

foreign	persuasion	poster	world

   1 Travelling that makes the _____ familiar.
   2 One _____ started a peace movement.
   3 Unusual forms of _____ bring change.
   4 Starting small for a peaceful _____ .

4 Match the verbs (1–5) with their collocates (a–e). Check your answers in the playlist descriptions.

   1 to break down   **a** weapons
   2 to build   **b** a movement
   3 to put down   **c** walls
   4 to gather   **d** understanding
   5 to start   **e** support

5 Which talk would you most like to see? Why? Watch the talk at TED.com.

▶ **Aziz Abu Sarah: For more tolerance, we need more … tourism?**

Palestinian entrepreneur and TED Fellow Aziz Abu Sarah is dedicated to the proposition that tourism can build peace. In his talk he tells us that while ignorance divides people, when you bring people together, walls are broken down and friendships made. He urges the one billion people who travel internationally yearly to interact with the communities they visit to build deeper understanding and mutual respect.

▶ **Ronny Edry: Israel and Iran: a love story?**

Israeli graphic designer Ronny Edry thought he was just posting another picture online for his Facebook friends when he shared a poster of himself and his daughter with the words 'Iranians … we ♥ you'; in fact his message reached far and wide and created social media communities on both sides of the political divide. He was so overwhelmed by the response that he started 'The Peace Factory', the online movement that shares images of ordinary people worldwide.

▶ **Jose Miguel Sokoloff: How Christmas lights helped guerrillas put down their guns**

Colombian ad executive Jose Miguel Sokoloff says he hasn't known a day of peace in his beloved homeland due to the country's long and violent lifetime of guerrilla wars. In response, Sokoloff has worked with government officials to launch an unorthodox, moving, and highly effective peace campaign designed to encourage guerrilla fighters to put down their weapons and return to their families and communities.

▶ **Jeremy Gilley: One day of peace**

In 1998, Jeremy Gilley had the crazy yet simple idea to create a global day of peace. In 2001, after years spent gathering support, 21 September was finally adopted unanimously by every head of state as the first ever 'Nonviolence Ceasefire' day. Since then each year this day has given small windows of opportunity to vaccinate millions of children in war-torn countries, for example. Over the years Gilley has visited 76 countries in order to spread his message of a global truce.

AUTHENTIC LISTENING SKILLS
Discourse markers

6 🎧 1 16 You are going to hear a podcast in which a member of the *Keynote* team talks about Ronny Edry's TED Talk, *Israel and Iran: a love story?* Listen to sentences from the talk. Match the five discourse markers in bold with the correct category below.

1 **Although** his English is far from perfect, Edry is a natural communicator.

2 He uses images **as well as** humour to tell his story warmly and directly.

3 **Actually,** the only filmic element this talk lacks is the major setback you usually get two thirds of the way through, to heighten the drama.

4 At one point early on Edry says, 'Everybody's crying now' – and, **to be honest**, I was too, within the first few minutes of the talk!

5 **All in all**, he communicates a simple but dramatic story about the power of images.

a Summing up   b Introducing additional information
c Introducing a surprising detail   d Balancing contrasting points   e Showing what the speaker thinks

LISTENING

7 🎧 1 17 Listen to the full podcast. Put the events in the order the podcaster described them.

a He received photos with messages from Iran.
b He posted a picture of himself and his daughter.
c The movement received global news coverage.
d He put up a poster of his wife and his friends.

8 🎧 1 17 Listen again. Then answer the questions.

1 Why do Edry's images make an impact, according to the podcaster?
2 In what way might Edry's story remind us of a film?
3 What kinds of friendships have developed as a result?
4 Why was Edry's story particularly moving for Stephanie?
5 What has she taken away from the talk?

VOCABULARY IN CONTEXT

9 Read the extracts from the podcast. Choose the correct meaning of the words in bold.

1 … which has had extraordinary **repercussions**.
   a consliquences ☐
   b challenges ☐
   c reasons ☐
2 … the major **setback** two thirds of the way through.
   a risk ☐
   b difficulty ☐
   c disaster ☐
3 … lots of **spin-off** Facebook movements.
   a identical (and unoriginal) ☐
   b new (but inspired by the previous) ☐
   c instant (but superficial) ☐
4 … without **preaching** or any political bias.
   a being unclear ☐
   b being aggressive ☐
   c telling people what to think ☐
5 We should all … **take a leaf out of Ronny Edry's book.**
   a follow Edry's example ☐
   b read what Edry wrote ☐
   c memorize what Edry says ☐

What's the magic number?

GRAMMAR Cleft sentences

1 Tick [✓] the statements from the advert that are cleft sentences.

Is PR for you?

1 If you are an excellent communicator and thrive in a competitive environment, Public Relations (PR) is for you. ☐

2 We'll show you how to connect customers with organizations and services through information and events. ☐

3 The thing about PR is knowing the sources and the market forces well. ☐

4 You'll learn about these with expert lecturers and relevant work placements. ☐

5 It's great communication skills that can make or break a career in PR. ☐

6 If you need help using the range of multimedia and communication channels available today, we'll work with you to improve your repertoire. ☐

7 It's creating the right message that is the real skill of PR. ☐

8 What PR people of the future need is familiarity with many different applications from press releases to Twitter. ☐

2 🎧1 18 Rewrite 1–8 as cleft sentences. Then listen and check your answers.

1 I've had enough of working on my own.
It's working _____ .

2 I haven't had any colleagues for twenty years.
It's been twenty years _____ .

3 I thought you liked the freedom and independence.
I thought it _____ .

4 I don't want to give up my freedom.
What _____ .

5 I've been thinking that I'd really like to go into partnership with someone else.
What _____ .

6 I need someone with good social media skills.
The person _____ .

7 I miss having someone to share ideas with.
The thing _____ .

8 You solve problems by talking about them with someone.
The way _____ .

3 🎧 **1 19** Put the words in italics in the correct order to complete cleft sentences. Then listen and check your answers.

M: I wonder if you can guess [1] *have / I / in / is / it / mind / that / who.*

J: Are you talking about me?

M: Exactly. I think the reason it [2] *benefit / both / from / is / that / we / work / would / would / well* a wider skills base.

J: Yes, good point! The thing [3] *is / lacking / media / skills / social / you're* and I need your fashion and lifestyle connections for my new project.

M: Actually, [4] *gave / idea / it's / me / project / that / the / your.*

J: Let's talk about it over lunch.

PRONUNCIATION Sentence stress in cleft sentences

4 🎧 **1 20** Listen and underline the words that are stressed.

1 It's great communication skills that can make or break a career in PR.
2 It's working on my own that I've had enough of.
3 I thought it was the freedom and independence that you liked.
4 Actually, it's your project that gave me the idea.
5 What I don't want is to give up my freedom.

GRAMMAR EXTRA! Cleft sentences for emphasis

5 Match the words or phrases in bold in sentences 1–4 with the emphasis they give (a–d).

1 **What we did was** join forces. ☐
2 **What happened was** I got fed up of working alone. ☐
3 **All / The only thing** the course focused on was teamwork. ☐
4 **It wasn't until** I went freelance that I realized how stressed I'd been. ☐

a Emphasis on time expression
b Emphasis on a limitation
c Emphasis on verb
d Emphasis on whole sentence

6 Rewrite the statements as cleft sentences.

1 Attending the PR course changed his career prospects completely.
   What _____ his career prospects completely. (emphasis on verb)
2 The co-founders started to disagree about everything and eventually the business collapsed.
   What _____ and eventually the business collapsed. (emphasis on whole sentence)
3 The marketing manager is only interested in the press releases.
   The only _____ the press releases. (emphasis on a limitation)
4 I'll make sure the trade fair dates are carefully co-ordinated with the launch.
   What _____ carefully coordinated with the launch. (emphasis on verb)
5 The reporter focused on the problems with the company.
   All _____ problems with the company. (emphasis on a limitation)
6 I changed companies and realized how competitive my previous colleagues had been.
   It wasn't _____ my previous colleagues had been. (emphasis on time expression)

DICTATION

7 🎧 **1 21** Listen to someone talking about PR skills. Complete the paragraph.

Public relations, or PR, _____ and increase brand awareness in the eyes of the public.

_____ and to whom. Nowadays, it's not just the press release that counts; _____, media and social media channels. And _____, according to a 2011 survey. _____ that about a third of reviewers react positively after a negative review is dealt with appropriately by the company in question.

3.3 Dare to be different

READING

1 Read the article *The story of Freakonomics*. Which statement best sums up the brand, a, b or c?

a Crazy economics ideas from the past tested out in modern day situations

b An economist's unusual take on everyday problems packaged in a readable way

c Understandable economics for non-academics with humour and a modern twist

2 Read the article again. Answer the questions.

1 How did the Freakonomics partners meet?
2 What does the brand include?
3 What unique point does each partner bring to the mix?
4 What do they have in common?

3 Read the blog post, *Thinking like a child*. Choose the correct options to make true sentences.

1 The blogger was looking for ways to think more *creatively / seriously* about things.
2 The Freakonomics partners make their living *daring to / trying not to* be different.
3 Stating the obvious is something we learn *to do / not to do* as we get older.
4 Work was *more effective / less effective* when the writer 'thought like a child'.
5 Overall the work experiment was *typical of / different to* the usual working week.
6 In the experiment the writer *stood up to / possibly went unnoticed by* the boss.

The story of Freakonomics

The Freakonomics brand started in 2005 with two young Americans. Stephen J. Dubner, a journalist, had been assigned to interview and write an article about Steven D. Levitt, the economist and university professor. Instead of taking a couple of hours to collect information for the profile, Dubner reportedly took three days. The article was very well received and they were offered a book deal. Their first book, which applied economic theory to unusual subject areas such as cheating in sumo wrestling, gave the brand its name 'Freakonomics'. It has since sold millions of copies worldwide and has been translated into 35 languages.

The book became a brand with a radio show, podcasts, blogs, four more books, and even a film. The podcast gets five million downloads a month. In 2015, the pair published their fifth best-selling book, *When to rob a bank*, a bound collection of their blogs. It marks ten years of their collaboration.

A key principle of the 'Freakonomic' philosophy is not to accept conventional wisdom but to try things out. The founders take their experimenting seriously and, for example, have a part of their website dedicated to gathering data on such things as whether tossing a coin to make a decision is as good a way as any of deciding something and they encourage visitors to the site to have a go.

The key to the success of their brand is the combination of Levitt and Dubner's different personalities. Levitt has a quirky way of looking at the world, everyday life and economics, and Dubner can tell a great story for a modern, lay audience. With their insatiable curiosity, quick wit and enthusiasm for finding things out, it's a match made in heaven.

Thinking like a child

'If you always think what you've always thought, you'll always get what you've always got.' Anon

Looking for new ideas, and in an attempt not to go with the flow, I wondered how I could think differently rather than as I've always thought. I listened to some podcasts I hadn't heard before by economist Steven D. Levitt and journalist Stephen J. Dubner, and came across an episode called 'Think like a child'. The Freakonomics pair like turning things on their head. Three main components are at the heart of thinking like a child. The first: *think small* is about not trying to tackle the bigger complex problems but thinking about the tiny questions and learning something from those. The second is *stating the obvious* – most adults stop doing this when they grow up and lose perspective. The third and final point is *injecting fun* – children do this automatically and adults don't tend to, unless they are making a joke.

So, I decided to take this advice literally and think like a child at work for a week. I injected fun by asking colleagues to tell a joke – the result was surprise and laughter. I stated the obvious in every meeting I attended – but unfortunately nothing spectacular happened. Through thinking small I concentrated on two main activities that had most impact in my work. I would even stick my neck out and say it was a more productive week than I've had for a long time. I wonder if my boss noticed.

VOCABULARY Conformity and non-conformity

4 Match the verbs (1–6) with the nouns (a–f) to make expressions about conformity and non-conformity.

1	to rock	**a**	the tide
2	to go with	**b**	the line
3	to stick your	**c**	the flow
4	to swim against	**d**	it safe
5	to toe	**e**	the boat
6	to play	**f**	neck out

5 Complete the definitions of three verbs of conformity and non-conformity.

1 If you blend _____ , you become similar to others around you, in a way that makes you unnoticeable.

2 If you fit _____ , you are accepted by others around you, because you become similar to them.

3 If you stand _____ , you are noticeable by being different to others.

6 Complete the sentences with the correct form of the expressions from Exercises 4 and 5.

1 It's a company that always *swims against the tide*; they are the ones always starting new trends, taking risks rather than _____ .

2 The new administrator _____ to the new work environment straight away. It was as if he'd worked there for years.

3 He'd always been a bit of a rebel and never really wanted to be like everyone else or _____ at school. It wasn't until he went to university that he settled down and started _____ .

4 She really _____ in the meeting and spoke so authoritatively that no-one knew what to say.

5 He's a great boss and really believes in his team. If it comes to it, he is prepared to _____ for people.

WORDBUILDING Heteronyms

7 Heteronyms are words that look the same but have a different meaning and pronunciation. Match the heteronyms (1–6) with their meanings (a–f).

1 present and present
2 bow and bow
3 close and close
4 content and content
5 minute and minute
6 wind and wind

a a strong breeze and to coil something
b a kind of tie and to bend from the waist
c one of sixty in an hour and very small
d being happy and the topic of something
e a gift and to give an award
f near and the opposite of to open

8 🎧 **1 22** Complete the sentences with the words (1–6) from Exercise 7. Then listen and check your answers.

1 a The _____ was blowing so hard they had difficulty walking.
b Can you _____ the cables up to keep them out of the way?

2 a The _____ of the presentation was perfect for the sales meeting.
b The customer wasn't _____ with the outcome; she wanted a full refund.

3 a Have you got a _____? I'd like to have a word about that complaint.
b There was a _____ flaw in the paintwork on the new car, so they gave us a discount.

4 a Please _____ the window. It's starting to rain.
b They're still very _____ friends despite living in different countries.

5 a The groom looked dashing in dinner jacket and _____ tie.
b When meeting royalty you should _____ or curtsey.

6 a They gave her a lovely leaving _____ on her last day.
b He said that he wanted to _____ the team with a certificate for their achievement.

WORD FOCUS *play*

9 Match the expressions in bold with the correct definitions.

1 Be careful! You're **playing with fire** by making him that angry. ☐

2 I'm not sure exactly what's expected, we'll just have to **play it by ear**. ☐

3 I wish he'd stop **playing games** and tell me what the problem is. ☐

4 If you **play your cards right** I think you might be in with a chance of promotion. ☐

5 He said he had to make a few phone calls. I think he's just **playing for time** before he makes a decision. ☐

6 I know he's being unreasonable but I suggest you just **play along with** his ideas. It'll make everyone's life easier. ☐

a hiding your real feelings and trying to get what you want in an indirect way
b behave in the right way
c improvise and be spontaneous about it
d doing something dangerous that could cause problems later
e delaying on purpose because of some other objective
f pretend to agree in order to get what you want or avoid an argument

3.4 Which one gets your vote?

DEALING WITH DISAGREEMENT AND REACHING CONSENSUS

1 Match the functions (1–4) with the groups of phrases (a–d).

1 Disagreeing by asking a question ☐
2 Disagreeing by expressing uncertainty ☐
3 Reframing the disagreement ☐
4 Hedging (softening your own opinion) ☐

a
  I don't know about you, but …
  Maybe it's just me but …
  … I guess you could say

b
  So, here's the real question: … ?
  We could look at this from a different perspective.
  I think one way of looking at this is …

c
  I may be wrong, but …
  I can't say for certain that …
  Hmmm, I'm not so sure …

d
  Would you want that?
  Do you really want … ?
  Can you seriously picture … ?

2 🎧 **1 23** Complete the sentences. Use these words. Then listen and check your answers.

agree	condition	don't	proposal	right
suggest	your take	view	views	

1 Do we have any _____ on … ?
2 So, why _____ we choose … ?
3 I'll agree to the _____ so long as …
4 _____ . Absolutely.
5 What's _____ , Helen?
6 I'd accept the local idea … on _____ that we all _____ .
7 What's your _____ , Ant?
8 I'd like to _____ that we …

3 Rewrite the responses using a more polite option from Exercise 1.

1 A: What do you think about donating to an animal home?
  B: Not a good idea. (uncertainty)
  Hmmm, *I'm not so sure it's a good idea.*

2 A: What's your view on choosing one charity to work with every year?
  B: I think it's better to share out what we give. (hedging)
  I don't _____ .

3 A: If we stick to one organization, we'll build up better co-operation.
  B: That will restrict us in the future. (question)
  Do we _____ ?

4 A: Why don't we choose something abroad?
  B: I think it's more complicated with a money transfer. (uncertainty)
  I may _____ .

5 A: How can we agree on this?
  B: We must think about our core values. (reframe)
  We could _____ .

6 A: I'd like to give to an environmental organization. What's your view?
  B: The whole company won't agree to support the environment (question)!
  Can you _____ ?

PRONUNCIATION Stress in expressions of disagreement

4 🎧 **1 24** Read the phrases of disagreement. Underline the words you think will be stressed. Then listen and check your answers.

1 I don't know about you, but I think it's better to share it out.
2 Do we really want to be restricted?
3 Why don't we choose the special needs school?
4 I may be wrong, but I think it's more complicated.
5 We could look at this from a different perspective.
6 Hmmm, I'm not so sure I agree.
7 I'll agree to the proposal so long as we choose something else next year.
8 Can we resolve this by agreeing that we invite Childtrust to meet with us?

WRITING SKILL Encouraging cooperation

5 Complete the email with these phrases.

as you know	had second thoughts
I'd like to thank	I'm afraid I may not
let me know	may not be

TO: _____ FROM: _____
SUBJECT: _____

Dear everyone,

To follow up on today's meeting,
¹ _____ you all for your input. I think
we are close to a consensus on this.

² _____ have pointed out clearly
enough that we'll need to vote on this topic and get
everyone's agreement before proceeding.

Since the meeting, I've heard that some of you have
³ _____ about the final option we
discussed.

⁴ _____ , we've arranged to meet the
charity in question to become better acquainted. I'd
like to suggest we also meet with the school that
Jenny put forward to make a more informed choice.

A consensus ⁵ _____ quick to
achieve but, if necessary, we'll find more time to
discuss it after meeting both parties.

If you have any other concerns, please
⁶ _____ .

Best wishes

Ant

6 Read the email again and answer the questions.

1 What's the main purpose of the email?
2 What happened after the meeting?
3 What's Ant's suggestion?

7 Choose the correct options to complete the sentences.

1 *I guess / I'm afraid* I'll be out of the office this afternoon
so I can't tell you personally.
2 I *wonder if / wish if* we could have another meeting
about this.
3 Could we *find probably / possibly find* another time to
discuss this?
4 The first solution *may not be / mustn't be* popular with
customers.
5 *I suggest / If we can* co-ordinate our plans, it'll be more
efficient.

8 Read this email sent to Ant after the meeting. Add four
phrases to make it sound more polite and cooperative,
using the words in brackets.

TO: _____ FROM: _____
SUBJECT: _____

Dear Ant

Sorry to write to you about this.

I wanted to talk to you personally after the meeting
but there wasn't time.

I ¹ _____ reconsider the environmental idea.
(wonder)

I ² _____ the fact that both options we have
are focused on children. (second thoughts)

³ _____ add another charity to meet
in person but make the issue environmental?
(possibly)

I've come across an organization that works to
green our living spaces and involves local schools.

⁴ _____ a phone call later, please let me
know. (have)

Best wishes

Richard

9 Write an email from another of Ant's colleagues after
the meeting. Use the notes and make it polite and
cooperative using phrases from Exercises 5, 7 and 8.

Didn't explain myself well in the meeting.
Second thoughts.
Said I'd accept the local idea but want to discuss it more.
More worthy cause?
We didn't think things through enough.

TO: _____ FROM: _____
SUBJECT: _____

Dear Ant

Best wishes

Helen

YOUR IDEA

1 Read the descriptions about where three people come from. Match the descriptions with the summaries (a–c) below.

1 Emmanuel: As an African living in Europe, it hasn't always been easy to feel at home. The culture is very different. I come from a small village, and what happens there centres first of all on your family and then the local community. There is a very strong sense of togetherness; families will always sit down for meals together and there are lots of activities for people living in the area to get involved with. It's not really the same here. I don't often see people sitting down to have lunch or dinner together at home. Instead people eat out a lot. Music was also a big part of my life back home, but here it doesn't feel the same. Maybe in a few more years I will start to feel like I belong here. ☐

2 Flávia: This is such a diverse part of the world and with a lot of history. Europeans came to my country many years ago, looking for their fortunes. Naturally, they came across the indigenous people who already lived here, and there were a number of conflicts. But there were also examples of where the native and the colonizing peoples got on and even in some cases men and women from the two settled down and had families. Mixed relationships were a big deal back then and it sometimes caused problems within families, but I am very grateful for where I come from. I don't feel completely European or South American, but rather a mixture of the two. I try to keep these differences alive in my family today, teaching my children both our local languages and Spanish. I hope they appreciate coming from different places as much as I do. ☐

3 Arthur: I'm very proud of where I come from. It's not a big or important place, but it is significant in my life. Nowadays, I don't think people feel the same way about where they come from. Maybe that's because it's so easy to move around and live in other places. That's not something I've done. I was born in the local hospital, I work just down the road, and this is my home. I honestly wouldn't move anywhere else. ☐

a I have roots in several different cultures.
b I have stayed in the same place my whole life.
c I feel different to the people around me.

2 Write notes about where you come from. Try to write about both the place where you live now and anything you know about where your family is from.

_____
_____
_____
_____

3 Organize the information from your notes. Write sentences on these areas.

My area _____
_____

My family's background _____
_____

4 Practise your talk out loud. Try to …

- use relaxed body language so that people can relate to you.
- include relevant stories about yourself or people you know.

ORGANIZING YOUR PRESENTATION

5 Match the five steps of the presentation with the examples of useful language (a–e).

1 Introduce yourself and say what your talk is about ☐
2 Talk about the area you live in ☐
3 Talk about where your family is from
4 Make statements or comparisons about where you come from ☐
5 Thank the audience for listening ☐

a So, we're from the Caribbean, but what's actually interesting is that we found we had distant relatives here. Our ancestors came from England and travelled to Jamaica in the 1700s.
b Our way of life here isn't as relaxed as it was in Jamaica. The streets are busy and everyone seems to be in a rush. But there is a lot more opportunity here, so although I am proud of where I come from, this is now my home.
c Thank you so much for listening! Any questions?
d Hi! My name's Alicia. Today's talk is about my background and where I come from.
e The area where I live is quite diverse – walking down the street you will come across people from many different places. My family moved here about five years ago.

YOUR PRESENTATION

6 Read the useful language on the left and make notes for your presentation.

1 Introduce yourself and say what your talk is about My name's …. Today's presentation is about …	
2 Talk about the area you live in The place where I live is … My home is …	
3 Talk about where your family is from My family is … We came here … We have roots in …	
4 Make statements or comparisons about where you come from Life here is … There are some differences like … Some similarities are …	
5 Thank the audience for listening Thank you so much for listening … It's been great to … Thank you. Does anyone have any questions?	

7 Film yourself giving your presentation or practise in front of a mirror. Give yourself marks out of ten for …

- using relaxed body language.   ☐ /10
- including relevant stories about yourself or people you know.   ☐ /10
- following the five steps in Exercise 6.   ☐ /10
- using correct grammar.   ☐ /10

4 Challenges

4.1 How I beat stage fright

TEDTALKS

JOE KOWAN is an artistic type; he writes and performs songs and he's a senior graphic designer at State Street Corp. He started off studying music but changed to psychology and fine arts at Binghampton University. Kowan is also quite 'crafty': his website's name is CraftyGangsta and his pseudonym on the latest of his three albums is J-Krafty. Judging by his song where he sings: 'I'm good with my hands if you know what I mean, embroidered my sweater and bedazzled my jeans' he is clearly comfortable with glue guns, glitter and cameras. What he's not comfortable with, however, is speaking in public. So how did he confront his demons enough to give a TED Talk when he suffered so badly from stage fright?

As it turns out, he's not just crafty in the artistic sense, he also found a crafty way to use the stage to help him with his fear. He responded to a call for employees at his workplace to give talks at the TED@StateStreet event and he decided that the subject of his talk would be his own stage fright. It turned out to be a shrewd career move, although it might seem bizarre to talk and sing about stage fright in front of a sizable audience and cameras. After being selected to give the talk, he practised and was coached extensively. Every time he rehearsed – about one hundred times, he says – it must have desensitized his own fear a little more and helped him to overcome it. The enthusiastic applause shows how well his talk was received: it also became a talk of the week and has been watched over one million times.

Joe Kowan

CAREER PATHWAYS

1 Read the text. Answer the questions.

   1 In what ways is Joe Kowan artistic?
   2 What is the second way Kowan has been 'crafty'?
   3 How did he prepare for the talk?
   4 How was the TED Talk good for his career?

TED PLAYLIST

2 Other TED speakers are interested in topics similar to Joe Kowan's TED Talk. Read the descriptions of four TED Talks at the top of page 35. In your opinion, which is the best title for this playlist, a, b or c?

   a Changing our perceptions
   b Fear is good for you
   c Don't be afraid of fear

3 Complete the six-word summary (1–4) that corresponds to each talk in the TED playlist. Use these words.

fear	future	potential	stress

   1 Self-assurance that can reveal creative _____ .
   2 Practice takes the _____ from danger.
   3 Visualizing our _____ with our fears.
   4 Thinking positively about _____ builds resilience.

4 Match the verbs (1–5) with their collocates (a–e). Check your answers in the playlist descriptions.

   1 to unlock   a extreme dangers
   2 to face   b strong arguments
   3 to remain   c creative potential
   4 to work out   d the meaning of our fears
   5 to put forward   e calm

5 Which talk would you most like to see? Why? Watch the talk at TED.com.

▶ **David Kelley: How to build your creative confidence**

David Kelley started out as a digital designer and is now chair and professional innovator at the design firm IDEO. He feels that his life mission is to help people and organizations unlock their creative potential. He believes that even the most committed non-creatives can learn to build – or rebuild – confidence in their own creativity. His work has been inspired partly by his own creative passion and partly by some serious contemplation of what he'd most like his legacy to be.

▶ **Chris Hadfield: What I learned from going blind in space**

Retired colonel Chris Hadfield always wanted to be an astronaut and he made his dream come true. He captivates us with tales of the beauty of space and also talks candidly about the extreme dangers that astronauts face while on space missions. His true story about going blind on a spacewalk shows how astronauts can remain calm in the face of their worst fears by preparing for them. Astronauts practise everything thousands of times to be ready when things go wrong, without which he would have quite literally been lost.

▶ **Karen Thompson Walker: What fear can teach us**

Karen Thompson Walker tells us a gripping story to bring home what our fears can teach us if we pay attention to them. She shows us how our fears are often visions of what might happen; visions created by our imagination. She uses the story of some sailors stranded at sea to illustrate that our fears are a way of imagining possible futures and that working out the meaning of our fears can help us cope with them or make better decisions.

▶ **Kelly McGonigal: How to make stress your friend**

The health psychologist Dr Kelly McGonigal confesses that recent research has caused her to change her mind about stress and in her animated talk she puts forward strong arguments to convince us to change our minds too. McGonigal believes that it's not stress itself but rather the way we perceive stress that causes us harm. Her work translates scientific research into practical strategies for good health, success and happiness.

AUTHENTIC LISTENING SKILLS
Collaborative listening

6 🎧 **1 25** You are going to hear a podcast in which a member of the *Keynote* team talks about Kelly McGonigal's TED Talk, *How to make stress your friend*. Look at the data about the two studies. Listen and complete the data. Which data is from study one (1) and which from two (2)? Compare your answers with a partner.

1 1,000 _____ ☐ 4 30% _____ ☐
2 30,000 _____ ☐ 5 43% _____ ☐
3 Five years _____ ☐

LISTENING

7 🎧 **1 26** Listen to the full podcast. Are these statements true (T) or false (F)?

1 Kelly McGonigal sees stress as something to be avoided. ☐
2 The podcaster says we sometimes achieve more in stressful situations. ☐
3 McGonigal says that helping others can sometimes increase stress. ☐

8 🎧 **1 26** Listen again. Answer the questions.

1 What is the aspect of stress that makes us sick?
2 What does the podcaster learn about the effects of social contact?
3 According to Sonia, how is the science made easy to understand?
4 What does Sonia see as the problem with having such busy lives?
5 Who is she going to recommend this talk to and why?

VOCABULARY IN CONTEXT

9 Read the extracts from the podcast. Choose the correct meaning of the words in bold.

1 I've definitely seen how sometimes people can ... really **excel**, when they face stressful situations.
   a win ☐
   b fail ☐
   c do very well ☐
2 Again, they first **established** the stress load ...
   a set up and carried out ☐
   b made sure ☐
   c found out about ☐
3 The body ... becomes **more resilient** to stress ...
   a tougher ☐
   b fitter ☐
   c more vulnerable ☐
4 Although the talk is scientific in parts, ... she makes it **accessible** with pictures and examples.
   a really complex ☐
   b easy to understand ☐
   c very interesting ☐
5 The speaker's ... presentation style ... challenges them to think beyond their current **assumptions**.
   a beliefs ☐
   b speculation ☐
   c negative impressions ☐

GRAMMAR Approximation

The faster the better?

Would reading faster enable you to work and action emails quicker? Would it be worth the time spent to learn how to? According to research, most of us read [1] *approximately / odd* 250 to 300 words per minute. Speed-reading courses claim to teach people to read [2] *as few as / as many as* 1,200 words per minute. That is [3] *roughly / as little as* four times as many. Does that mean we could work [4] *as many as / as much as* four times faster?

The concept of speed reading has been around for [5] *as little as / about* 60 years but recently, with data being more accessible and bountiful, reading for speed has become more interesting. A Google search for speed-reading courses shows up [6] *just* over / *as few as* 51 million hits. Reading at an average speed, we take [7] *or thereabouts / around* one to two minutes to read a page or an email. Even if we only doubled this speed it would make us more efficient at work.

Harry Potter and the Deathly Hallows by JK Rowling contains [8] *nearly / as much as* 200,000 words and an average reader needs eleven hours [9] *more or less / sort of* to read the book. Reportedly, avid Harry Potter fans can read it in around four hours. In 2007, Anne Jones read this Harry Potter book in 47 minutes and one second and read [10] *some / as much as* 4,251 words per minute to make that world record. Imagine how quickly she would get through a full inbox!

1 Read the text. Choose the correct options to complete each sentence.

2 🎧 **1 27** Listen to a project proposal meeting. Are these statements true (T) or false (F)? Listen and check your answers.

1 The project proposal approval will probably take approximately a week. ☐
2 There must be over twenty project proposals. ☐
3 The training department submits as few as four or five proposals a year. ☐
4 Speed reading could make them about twice as efficient. ☐
5 There are just over fifteen on the waiting list. ☐
6 They've asked for about four days for the project. ☐

3 Complete the sentences to describe the <u>most positive</u> outcome, a, b or c.

1 Buy your ticket soon. If you buy it in advance it can cost …
  a as little as £30. ☐
  b at least £30. ☐
  c just over £30. ☐
2 I can't quite remember but I think the project itself was completed in …
  a around a week. ☐
  b at least a week. ☐
  c under a week. ☐
3 Word has been spreading, there are … registrations.
  a as few as 80 ☐
  b as many as 80 ☐
  c just over 80 ☐

4 I've had ... ten job offers as a result of my new profile.

   a as many as ☐

   b fewer than ☐

   c at least ☐

5 It's been running for ...

   a just over fifty years. ☐

   b just under fifty years. ☐

   c fifty years or thereabouts. ☐

6 It's improved productivity by ... twenty-five per cent.

   a as little as ☐

   b nearly ☐

   c some ☐

4 🎧 **1 28** Match the questions with the answers. Then listen and check your answers.

1 How many books do you read a week? ☐

2 Do you get many emails a day? ☐

3 Was that speed-reading app free, by the way? ☐

4 How long does it take you to check your emails? ☐

5 Did the app tell you your reading speed? ☐

6 Have you read the finance report yet? ☐

7 How many people attended that course you went to last week? ☐

8 How do they think productivity has improved since they ran the course? ☐

a Oh, by as much as 15 per cent, they say.

b It did! It's just over 350 a minute at the moment.

c More or less all morning most days.

d Nearly 25. A few extra joined at the last minute.

e No, it cost about a fiver, but it's really good.

f Roughly one and a half, but it depends on the week.

g Yes, sometimes as many as a hundred.

h Yes, and it took me approximately two hours to read.

5 Complete the sentences with the missing adjectives with the *-ish* suffix.

1 I'd say he's t_____, definitely over 1.80 metres.

2 A: Has that Thai restaurant near your office just opened?
   B: It's been open a couple of months, so I guess it's n_____. It's good. You should try it.

3 I don't know how old she is exactly. She's not just out of university and she's quite experienced, perhaps th_____.

4 There's an evening meeting at work so I'll be home l_____ again, sorry.

5 I didn't like the picture. It was rather c_____. It looked like the painter was about ten!

6 It's a l_____ journey; about three and a half hours I would think – depending on traffic of course.

6 Complete the sentences with these words and phrases.

| a kind of | odd | other things |
| something like | sort of | stuff |

1 Esperanto is an invented language, not a natural one. It's a mix of lots of other languages with only a thousand-_____ native speakers worldwide.

2 A sat nav is _____ smart phone for the car. It helps you find where you're going.

3 A lanyard is _____ a key ring but longer. You have them at conferences and for company IDs.

4 An e-reader is a device that can store lots of readable _____.

5 A shredder is an office machine that destroys documents and _____ that are sensitive, so no one can read them afterwards. It's important for data protection.

6 A tracker is a _____ watch; it collects and shows information about what your body does over the course of 24 hours.

PRONUNCIATION Approximations

7 🎧 **1 29** Read the sentences. Underline the words you think will be stressed. Then listen and check your answers.

1 Yes, sometimes as many as a hundred.

2 No, it cost about a fiver but it's really good.

3 It did! It's just over 350 a minute at the moment.

4 More or less all morning most days.

5 Oh, by as much as fifteen per cent, they say.

6 Yes, and it took me approximately two hours to read.

7 Nearly 25. A few extra joined at the last minute.

8 Roughly one and a half, but it depends on the week.

DICTATION

8 🎧 **1 30** Listen to someone talking about the brain. Complete the paragraph.

The brain is the most complex organ in the body. _____

_____

cm^2 That is kind of like a double page of a newspaper. The human brain _____

_____

a small cauliflower. It makes up around 2 per cent of what the body weighs but it uses _____

_____

the body. It's made up of as many as 100 billion neurons and the senses send the brain _____

_____

Most of the processing is automatic but _____

_____

second of information. Research shows that the brain can make new connections, grow and adapt even with increasing age.

READING

1 Look at the brand names (a–d) and think about how each product or service got its name. Then answer the questions (1–4).

Which brand name …
1 describes a cracking sound?
2 describes a bird talking or singing?
3 is a person's name?
4 is a word made up of parts of other words?

2 Read the article about creating a good brand name. According to the writer, are these criteria essential (E), non-essential (N) or it doesn't say (DS)?

1 it should contain a sense of fun ☐
2 it should be easy to say ☐
3 it should describe what the product is ☐

Twitter

Vodafone

Crunchie

Hoover

4 it should reflect the quality of the product ☐
5 it should be easy to remember ☐
6 it should be original ☐

The name **game**

When I tell people what I do for a living, their reaction is often the same: 'Wow, that sounds like the coolest job ever!' or 'You actually get paid to do that?'. I'm a naming consultant, which means I help companies to find names for their companies or individual products: to give verbal expression to a brand. A verbal identity is a powerful thing. It can make otherwise ordinary products into an attractive proposition. Take Paperchase Products Ltd., the UK-based company selling stationery, launched in 1996. Stationery is not something we usually associate with fun and excitement, but the name gives that impression. Of course a name in itself doesn't guarantee the longevity of a brand. Paperchase became an international success because of its eye-catching product designs too. To have staying power the products themselves must be good quality. There are plenty of brands whose names in themselves are not particularly exciting – BMW, Dyson, Adidas – but which have over time become synonymous with something desirable.

Brand names fall into several categories. Those which use acronyms or initials, like IBM (International Business Machines) or parts of words, like Nabisco (National Biscuit Company); those which are descriptive: Microsoft, Toys R Us or Pizza Hut; those which use the company founder's name – Armani, Kimberley-Clark – or the company's location – Fuji, Cisco; and those which are evocative or allude to a benefit of the product or brand. Kindle, the name of Amazon's e-reader, is a good example of this. Literally, 'kindle' means to set something alight, but we more often use it metaphorically in phrases like 'kindle your interest' or 'kindle your imagination', so it works perfectly for a bookseller.

So what's the trick for a naming consultant like me in hitting on a winning name? What you'll notice with all of the above names is that they're easy to get your tongue around and have a certain ring to them. Those are the two golden rules: your name should be easy to pronounce and it should be memorable. KitKat is one of the world's best-selling chocolate bars. It started life as 'Rowntree's Chocolate Crisp' and no one is entirely sure where the name KitKat came from. It doesn't describe the product or its benefits – if it did it would be more likely to describe cat food. But it's a short, catchy word (note the use of alliteration with the letter K) and once the product gained favour with consumers, the name stuck.

So it's linguistic magic that I'm looking for (me and usually several other competitors that have been given the task of coming up with a name). Apart from my imagination, I use a number of tools: a thesaurus, a rhyming dictionary, foreign language dictionaries and even a Scrabble word finder on the Internet. One problem I have to get round is finding names that haven't been used before, which is easier said than done these days. There are solutions to this. One useful one is to drop a vowel here and there, as in the Scottish drink 'Irn-Bru' (a word play on Iron Brew) or the photo-sharing website 'Flickr'. It's all about playing with words and sounds. If, like me, you're into that, then yes, it *is* the coolest job ever.

3 Read the article. Find two-word answers to each of these questions.

1 What is the writer's job title?   A _____ _____ .

2 What does a name give to a brand?   A _____ _____ .

3 What did the name 'Paperchase' bring to the brand? _____ and _____ .

4 What do BMW, Adidas and Dyson's products have in common? _____ _____ .

5 What is Toys R Us an example of?   A _____ _____ .

6 What two types of meaning of 'kindle' did the writer describe?   The _____ and the _____ meaning.

7 Why does the name 'KitKat' work?   It's _____ and _____ .

8 Other than books, what does the writer use to think of names?   Her _____ and the _____ .

VOCABULARY Obstacles and opportunities

4 Match the phrases (1–8) with their meanings (a–h).

1 sell like hot cakes	**a** tackle the problem
2 come up against a brick wall	**b** express your worries
3 be an obstacle	**c** sell very well
4 meet with opposition	**d** not be welcomed or liked
5 address the issue	**e** have a dramatic impact
6 get a cool reception	**f** have your progress blocked
7 make a splash	**g** find others are against you
8 voice one's concerns	**h** be a barrier to progress

5 Complete the sentences. Use the correct form of the words and phrases from Exercise 4. Use the negative form if necessary.

1 Their new smartphone _____ from the press. One magazine only gave it one star out of five.

2 We feel that the toy is unsuitable for the age range (4–8 years) it is targeted at and we have _____ to the advertising standards authority.

3 The makers of the film really wanted to _____ when the film came out so they organized a giant free open-air screening in Central Park.

4 You can try to persuade him if you want to. When I tried, I _____ .

5 JK Rowling's first adult novel _____ , thanks to the success of her Harry Potter series.

6 The move to get people using the stairs instead of the lift initially _____ , but after a while employees began to see the benefits to their health.

7 Money _____ . I'm only concerned in getting the job done quickly and well.

8 We have to _____ of why so many parents are choosing to educate their children at home.

WORDBUILDING Suffix -able

6 We use the suffix *-able* to make adjectives which talk about ability or capability. Look at the example. Replace the information in bold with a construction containing an adjective with *-able*. Note that if the idea is negative you will also need to put the prefix *un-* at the front of the adjective.

1 BMW, Adidas and Dyson make good quality products which **people desire**. *are desirable*

2 I think **we can solve the problem** if we put our minds to it. _____

3 The weather in England **changes a lot** – sunny one day, raining the next. _____

4 **Most young people can't afford to buy a flat in London**. _____

5 It's a lot of work to do in a week but I think **I can manage it**. _____

6 My new boss is about the same age as me. She is nice and **very easy to approach**. _____

7 Last year we had a holiday in Cologne. **I'll never forget the firework display we saw on the Rhine**. _____

WORD FOCUS Irreversible word pairs

7 Sometimes two words that are commonly used together have to be used in a particular order, for example *here and there* (not *there and here*). Match 1–8 with a–h to make irreversible word pairs.

1 black and	**a** pieces
2 sick and	**b** sound
3 peace and	**c** cons
4 bits and	**d** white
5 wear and	**e** tear
6 pros and	**f** quiet
7 safe and	**g** soul
8 heart and	**h** tired

8 Complete the sentences with irreversible word pairs from Exercise 7.

1 I can't concentrate in a noisy office. I need to have _____ .

2 A certain amount of _____ is usual with furniture like this after two years.

3 That was an amazing performance. You really put your _____ into it.

4 What are the _____ of having an e-reader? Is it really worth the investment?

5 I'm glad you finally got home _____ .

6 If you don't believe me, take a look at the contract. It's all written there in _____ .

7 You go on and I'll catch you up. I just have a few _____ to finish here first.

8 I wish she'd stop complaining about her job. I'm _____ of hearing how awful it is!

4.4 I thought it would be easy

ASKING FOR CLARIFICATION AND REPETITION

1 🎧 **1 31** Listen to the dialogue. Which topic is being discussed, a, b or c?

a Explaining how to use a computer program
b Explaining how to use a teleconferencing tool
c Explaining how to use a games console

2 🎧 **1 32** Match the two parts of the sentences. Then listen to check.

1 Could you just ☐
2 I didn't quite catch ☐
3 Can you explain why ☐
4 You've lost ☐
5 Are you saying that ☐

a me a bit, sorry.
b go over that last bit again?
c I can set things up beforehand?
d what you said.
e I would need to do both?

3 🎧 **1 33** Complete the sentences. Use these words and phrases. Then listen and check your answers.

did you missed that	just being with you	mind giving would you

1 I'm not _____. Would you _____ it to me one more time?
2 OK. Yes, I see. That's great. _____ say we can all write things there? That'll be great for brainstorming.
3 _____ mind backing up for a second? I _____ last bit – I was trying out the whiteboard.
4 There's a delay but it's clear. I'm probably _____ a bit slow, but how can you check the sound when the meeting's in progress?

PRONUNCIATION Intonation in questions

4 🎧 **1 34** Read the questions. Does the intonation rise (R) or fall (F) at the end of each sentence? Listen and check your answers.

1 Could you just go over that last bit again? ☐
2 Are you saying that I can set things up beforehand? ☐
3 Can you explain why I would need to do both? ☐
4 Would you mind giving it to me one more time? ☐
5 Did you say we can all write things there? ☐
6 Sound still OK? ☐

WRITING SKILL Instructions

5 Match the two parts of the sentences.

1 Please don't feed the cat ☐
2 Don't forget to put the bins out on Monday evening ☐
3 Lock the door ☐
4 Lock up the bikes ☐
5 Water the garden ☐
6 Bring in the post ☐

a if it's hot.
b because there have been a lot of thefts recently.
c so the box doesn't get too full.
d more than a small tin as he's on a diet.
e otherwise it doesn't stay shut.
f as they collect them the next morning.

6 Complete these instructions with a reason.

1 Don't let the cat sleep on the beds _____ (own bed).
2 Water the house plants _____ (need it).
3 Close the shutters at night _____ (security reasons).
4 Let the neighbours use the lawnmower _____ (share tools).
5 Leave the key with the neighbours _____ (next guest / get in).

7 Choose the correct options to complete the instructions.

1 *Beware if you / Beware of* parking on the main road; it's not always free of charge.
2 *I'd be grateful if you would / I'd be grateful* please clean the fridge before you leave.
3 *Bear in mind that / Bear with me that* the bins are collected really early so you need to put them out the night before.
4 *I've got one request / I've request* – that you set the burglar alarm before leaving the house.
5 *Just to be sure about / Just to be on the safe side,* don't leave any windows open and double lock the door.
6 *Be sure to / Be careful not to* leave any food out of the fridge as the cat will steal it.

8 Complete the instructions from a work colleague. Use these words and phrases.

| bear in mind | be sure to | beware of shutting |
| I'd be grateful | just to be on the safe side | |

TO: _____ FROM: _____
SUBJECT: _____

Dear office guest,

You are welcome to use my desk and computer when I'm away. I hope you enjoy the peace and quiet and the view of the chestnut tree. There are a few things you should bear in mind about how things work:

1 _____ the blinds when the window is open. I did that once and damaged them and they were expensive to replace.
2 _____ turn off the printer when you're not using it, it uses a lot of electricity. If you need more ink cartridges there are some on top of the cupboard.
3 _____ the office next door is quite noisy sometimes. It's a doctor's and they seem to get a lot of small children as patients.
4 _____, don't forget to lock up each day.
5 _____ if you watered my plant and left the rubbish outside the room for the cleaner in the evening.

Best wishes

Rachel

9 Look at the information below. Write an email similar to the one in Exercise 8, giving reasons for the instructions you are leaving.

- Lock / unlock the phone with number 4546
- Water the plant
- Check for viruses and updates

TO: _____ FROM: _____
SUBJECT: _____

Dear

Best wishes

The report you will read in Exercise 2 is in answer to the following exam question.

> Your manager is worried that employees in your company are suffering from information overload as they are spending an increasing amount of time dealing with email each day. In preparation for a presentation at the next staff meeting, your manager has asked you to write a report suggesting ways to make email communication more efficient.
>
> Write your report for your manager in **220–260 words** in an appropriate style.

IDEAS

1 Tick (✓) the things you would expect to see in the report.

- **a** examples of situations where information overload is a problem ☐
- **b** recommendations for further action ☐
- **c** a sentence summarizing what should be done as a result of the report ☐
- **d** the purpose of the report and how the information was gathered ☐
- **e** headings to help the reader understand the structure of the report ☐
- **f** a formal greeting ☐
- **g** a description of how the presentation will be structured at the meeting ☐

MODEL

2 Read the report. Match the five sections with a description (a–g) from Exercise 1.

1 ☐   **2** ☐   **3** ☐   **4** ☐   **5** ☐

3 Read the report again. Are these statements true (T) or false (F)?

- **1** The problems and solutions were all suggested by the report writer. ☐
- **2** Too many employees receive emails which are not relevant to them. ☐
- **3** A wide range of topics are sometimes covered without the subject line being changed. ☐
- **4** 'Reply all' is the most efficient function to use when sending emails within the company. ☐
- **5** At times, employees should telephone their colleagues rather than relying on email. ☐

USEFUL LANGUAGE

4 Put the words in the correct order to make phrases that can be used to recommend further action.

1 of / result / as / this / a
2 it / hoped / that / is
3 my / it / belief / that / is
4 would / against / I / advise
5 would / it / to / advantage / our / be / to
6 it / not / beneficial / would / be / to

---

[1]The purpose of this report is to make recommendations aimed at reducing the amount of time necessary for dealing with email communication each day, taking account of suggestions from colleagues within the company.

[2]**Main issues**
[3]The following areas were highlighted by the majority of the people I spoke to:

1. Emails are often sent to many more people than necessary, particularly if the 'reply all' function is used.
2. Email threads can become confusing, with many different topics being discussed in a single chain of emails.
3. Some projects are being held up because one person is waiting for another to deal with the relevant emails.

Recommendations
[4]Firstly, before sending an email, one colleague recommended that employees think carefully about who needs to read it. They should only send it to the relevant recipients, and avoid using 'reply all' unless absolutely necessary.

Only one topic should be covered in each email thread, and the subject line of the email should clearly show what this is for ease of reference. When a discussion about a new topic is started, the subject should be changed to reflect this.

Finally, it is important to consider whether it would be more efficient to send an email or make a telephone call to keep a project moving. We recommend that colleagues phone each other whenever possible as issues are more likely to be dealt with quickly if they are discussed than if an email is sent.

[5]We are confident that if these recommendations are followed, the time spent dealing with emails will be considerably reduced.

5 These sentences refer to sources of information for reports. Complete the phrases in **bold** with a preposition.

1 **The majority of people I spoke** *to* expressed a desire for fewer emails to be sent.

2 This report is written **light of responses to a questionnaire** conducted last week.

3 We compiled this report **taking account feedback received** over the previous quarter.

4 **According the majority of respondents,** there is a need for managers to reduce the amount of messages they send.

5 This report aims to suggest ways to communicate more effectively **based feedback collected from our staff**.

6 The recommendations in this report are **the result of a survey conducted our colleagues** to find out their needs.

6 Match the two parts of the sentences. Use the phrases in **bold** to help you.

1 We are lucky that our company **had the** ☐
2 Communication can also be improved **by way** ☐
3 Only employees who do not regularly speak to customers should be **exempt** ☐
4 Email templates should be **made available** ☐
5 Our telephone help centre is **in serious** ☐

a **of** regular smaller meetings in place of large ones.
b **need of** faster, more efficient IT support.
c **foresight to** streamline its communication systems a few years ago.
d **from** further training.
e **to** those who regularly write formulaic messages.

7 Complete the sentences. Use these words.

address	conduct	impact
lead	measure	option

1 This time next year, management should _____ another survey to find out what still needs to be done.
2 Organizing further training would be the best _____ based on what we know so far.
3 If we do not _____ problems of cultural awareness soon, we are likely to lose some of our foreign customers.
4 Adopting a new communication system will have an _____ on our finances for the next quarter.
5 This would be another potential way to _____ the impact of reducing time spent on dealing with emails.
6 If we do not update the system soon, it could _____ to further misunderstandings with customers.

PLANNING

You will answer the following question.

> You have just attended a course about how companies can reduce their impact on the environment. In preparation for a meeting, your manager has asked you to write a report covering the points below:
>
> What negative impacts does our company currently have on the environment?
> What can we do to reduce these?

8 Plan your report. Write notes to answer these questions. Don't write full sentences yet.

1 What is the purpose of the report?
2 Which two or three impacts on the environment will you describe?
3 What suggestions do you have for reducing the company's impact in these areas?
4 What headings will you use?

WRITING

9 Use your plan to write a report to answer the questions in Exercise 8. In your report you should ...

- write the purpose of the report and how the information has been gathered.
- list negative impacts the company has on the environment and suggest ways of reducing the company's impact in each case.
- state what should happen as a result of the report.
- use headings to organize the report.

Write the report for your manager in **220–260 words** in an appropriate style.

ANALYSIS

10 Check your report. Answer the questions.

- **Content:** Does the report describe two or three areas in which the company has a negative impact on the environment, plus suggestions for how to reduce this impact? Is it 220 to 260 words long?
- **Communicative achievement:** Is the text objective? Is it clear what should be done as a result of the report? Is the report written in neutral or formal language?
- **Organization:** Are the sections logically organized? Does it use headings to highlight important points?
- **Language:** Does it use correct grammar and vocabulary? Is a good range of structures used?

5 Inspiration

5.1 I'm not your inspiration, thank you very much

TEDTALKS

STELLA YOUNG's TED Talk is like she was: feisty, funny and intent on challenge and change. She said about herself: 'I am a strong, fierce, flawed adult woman. I plan to remain that way in life, and in death.' She believed passionately that disabled people are often limited by the environment in which they must function, and by other people's perceptions of disability – but not by disability itself. She was born in 1982 in Victoria, Australia, with the condition called brittle bone disease – *Osteogenesis imperfecta*. From an early age and somewhat controversially, she started calling herself a 'crip', short for cripple – a usually offensive term to describe someone who is physically disabled; she claimed it made her feel strong and powerful. As a teenager she surveyed shops on her local high street to ascertain how disability-friendly they were. Later she studied journalism and became a qualified teacher, although she preferred to educate society as a whole rather than just a class of pupils. This she did through as many mediums as possible; with her columns, blogs and Twitter posts, via her comedy show *Tales from the Crip* and by speaking on radio and TV. She also collaborated with the Australian government and did a tour for the US government, to spread a different message about disability.

Stella Young

She died well before her time, at the age of thirty-two. Sadly, she was never able to read the moving letter she wrote to her eighty-year-old self, in which she promised to '… grab every opportunity with both hands, to say yes as often as I can, to take risks, to scare myself stupid …'. But her passion to change lives continues through a campaign started in her honour called *Stella's Challenge* which aims to change social attitudes to disability.

CAREER PATHWAYS

1 Read the text. Answer the questions.

1 How did Stella Young describe herself?
2 Why was the nickname 'crip' controversial?
3 How did Young apply what she studied?
4 Name three of her achievements.

TED PLAYLIST

2 Other TED speakers are interested in topics similar to Stella Young's TED Talk. Read the descriptions of four TED Talks at the top of page 45. In your opinion, which is the best title for this playlist, a, b or c?

a No limits to creativity
b Disability in sports
c Changing perceptions positively

3 Complete the six-word summary (1–4) that corresponds to each talk in the TED playlist. Use these words.

if	overcoming	multiple	wheelchair

1 _____ I can, you can too.
2 A _____ user underwater challenges preconceptions.
3 Enabled not disabled by _____ limitations.
4 _____ perspectives boost understanding and empathy.

4 Match the verbs (1–5) with their collocates (a–e). Check your answers in the playlist descriptions.

1	to make	a	the Arts
2	to promote	b	in someone else's shoes
3	to highlight	c	on track
4	to get back	d	someone think
5	to put yourself	e	the silver linings

▶ **Maysoon Zayid: I got 99 problems … palsy is just one**

The Arab-American comedian, writer and actor Maysoon Zayid, is both fascinating and funny on the TED stage, making us laugh and making us think as she tells us about her life growing up in New Jersey as a part of several minorities – she's Palestinian, Muslim, and a disabled woman. Despite her physical challenges, her father always encouraged her to walk, dance and live like her sisters and like everyone else. Hearing about her achievements, we get a sense that he was right to do so.

▶ **Sue Austin: Deep sea diving … in a wheelchair**

Sue Austin is a multimedia and performance artist and the founder of *Freewheeling*, which aims to promote Disability Arts. In her talk she challenges the usual ideas of disability: limitation, fear and restriction. She explains that she experiences freedom, motion and possibility through wheelchairs, and, in particular, her underwater wheelchair which in turn influences her art. She creates new and positive associations when she shows thrilling footage of herself exploring the seabed, which allows us to share some of the exhilaration and joy she feels.

▶ **Amy Purdy: Living beyond limits**

Amy Purdy is a pro snowboarder and competitor on *Dancing with the Stars*, despite having lost her legs when she was only nineteen. Her movingly honest talk finds and highlights the silver linings in an awful stroke of fate. She tells us about the dark time after she lost her legs and her decision to become the 'author of her own life'. It took some rewriting to get back on track, but she found the drive and creativity to dream and snowboard again. She has since won two World Cup gold medals in snowboarding and co-founded a non-profit organization to involve young people with disability in action sports.

▶ **Raghava KK: Shake up your story**

Raghava KK is an artist and writer. In his talk, he presents his charming iPad book *Pop-it* and demonstrates how by shaking it the characters, and thus the perspective, changes. The rationale behind his innovative idea is that developing many views on life builds empathy and creativity. If we have more empathy we can more easily imagine putting ourselves in someone else's shoes. With *Pop-it* he encourages us to shake up our personal points of view too.

5 Which talk would you most like to see? Why? Watch the talk at TED.com.

AUTHENTIC LISTENING SKILLS Elision

6 🎧 1 35 You are going to hear a podcast in which a member of the *Keynote* team talks about Maysoon Zayid's TED Talk *I got 99 problems … palsy is just one*. Underline six examples where you don't hear the consonant at the end of a word.

1 When I first watched Maysoon Zayid's TED Talk, …
2 She begins by forthrightly saying that she isn't drunk but has cerebral palsy …
3 By answering the unasked question in everyone's minds, she clears the way for what she has to say.
4 The main content of her talk covers how she grew up in New Jersey with three older sisters …
5 She went to the same schools as her siblings …

LISTENING

7 🎧 1 36 Listen to the full podcast. Answer the questions.

1 How does the podcaster describe Maysoon Zayid?
2 What do you think the unasked question is?
3 What did Zayid do when the acting didn't work out for her?
4 What effect has Zayid's talk had on Laura?

8 🎧 1 36 Are these statements (T) true or (F) false? Listen again and check your answers.

1 Maysoon Zayid's parents treated her differently to her sisters. ☐
2 Laura found the first part of Zayid's talk particularly funny. ☐
3 With her reference to parking problems, Zayid makes jokes about the advantages of being disabled. ☐
4 Laura was particularly upset that people were so unkind to Zayid at school. ☐
5 Zayid's attitude and the positive mantra are good examples to get us to push ourselves a bit. ☐

VOCABULARY IN CONTEXT

9 Read the extracts from the podcast. Choose the correct meaning of the words in bold.

1 I was in complete **awe** over what an inspirational, vibrant and funny person she was.
  a admiration ☐ **b** delight ☐ **c** shock ☐
2 She begins by **forthrightly** saying that she isn't drunk.
  a uncertainly ☐ **b** directly ☐ **c** timidly ☐
3 By answering the unasked question in everyone's minds, she **clears the way for** what she has to say.
  a clarifies ☐ **b** removes any obstacles to ☐
  c emphasizes ☐
4 She found her **niche** in comedy …
  a particular role ☐ **b** profession ☐ **c** goal ☐
5 What a **cowardly** act to make comments like that …
  a weak ☐ **b** nervous ☐ **c** brave ☐

5.2 If only I'd studied harder ...

GRAMMAR Unreal past

1 Complete the text about job dissatisfaction. Use these words.

had	sooner	wished	worked	would

Are you satisfied with your job? In a survey of 1,673 workers by an American non-profit research group, it was found that 52 per cent of workers in the USA were dissatisfied at work in 2014. Most employees ¹_____ they had more job security. What about you? Do you wish you ²_____ more job security? 60 per cent reported they ³_____ rather work with people they liked. And do you think to yourself 'If only I ⁴_____ with friendlier colleagues'? 41 per cent said they would ⁵_____ do work that interested them than paid them more. Is that the same for you?

2 Choose the correct options to complete the sentences.

1 If you *would be / were* dissatisfied in your job, what would you do?

2 Suppose you *have studied / studied* part-time and were happier, what would you do then?

3 If it *didn't get / wouldn't get* better, what would you do?

4 I *would take / had taken* a course instead, if there was one on offer.

5 What would you do if you *offered / were offered* a job volunteering in another country?

6 He said he *'d talked / 'd talk* to his boss about promotion if he ever got offered a job elsewhere.

7 If I'd updated my CV and wasn't happy at work, I *applied / 'd apply* somewhere else.

8 If you retrained to do something that suited you better, what would you *do / did*?

9 If he wasn't happy at work, he *'d do / did do* nothing about it.

10 If she decided to take that course, what would she do after she *would complete / completed* it?

3 Use the prompts to write unreal past sentences.

1 Supposing / you / dissatisfied at work, / apply for / a new job?

_____

2 If he / have / problem / at work, he / not / talk / boss.

_____

3 If I / want / job abroad, I / update / CV.

_____

4 I wish / boss / offer me / a transfer. If / he / do / take it.

_____

5 If / look for / new job, post / CV / online.

_____

6 It's high time / you / more responsibility, / you / talk / boss / promotion opportunities.

_____

4 🎧 **1 37** Complete the sentences about wishes and regrets. Then listen and check your answers.

1 He sends his regards. He wished he
_____ you too. (see)

2 If we hadn't had that setback with the project, I
_____ . (go)

3 He always said he _____ with people than computers. (rather / work)

4 I wish I _____ to be a teacher when I had the chance. (train)

5 If only we _____ six weeks' summer holiday like him! (have)

6 I'd rather _____ all that marking.
(not / have)

5 Match the questions with the responses.

1 Do you mind if I contact Tim? ☐
2 Supposing you don't get the job? ☐
3 Can we interview candidates this week? ☐
4 Don't you wish you hadn't turned that job down? ☐
5 Would you mind checking the proposal with the boss? ☐

a I'd rather not think about that yet!
b I'd rather we waited a bit if possible.
c Not really, but I'd rather you didn't mention it.
d I'd rather not until we are a bit further along with the planning.
e I'd rather you didn't. I'd rather get in touch with him myself if you don't mind.

GRAMMAR EXTRA! Inversion in conditionals

6 Rewrite the sentences with inversion.

1 If I had known there were so many interns, I wouldn't have advertised externally.
Had I known *there were so many interns, I wouldn't have advertised externally.*

2 If I'd realized he'd worked here before, I'd have offered him the position.
_____
_____

3 If she updated her CV, she would have a better chance of success.
_____
_____

4 If I attended more often, I'd be able to follow the meetings more easily.
Were I to attend more often, I'd be able to ....

5 If she hadn't had that idea, she wouldn't have set up her own business.
_____
_____

6 If he accepted the job abroad, he wouldn't go back to university.
Were he to accept,

7 If I hadn't failed that interview, I wouldn't have done the course that led to this job.
Had I not failed
_____

8 If we employed more women and some younger people, we'd have more diverse ideas.
Were we to employ women & some younger people

7 Complete the text about job dissatisfaction with the correct form of the verb in brackets.

1 _____ (know) how dissatisfied I would be, I would not have begun working in this industry.

2 Were I in the position to retrain, I _____ (take) the opportunity.

3 _____ (have) my boss not had such ambitious expectations, I would not have to work such long hours.

4 _____ (be) it not for the fact that my children are at college, I would work less or change my job.

5 Had I known about it earlier, I _____ (take) the project work when it was offered.

6 _____ (be) I in a position to relocate, I would certainly do it.

DICTATION

8 🎧 **1 38** Listen to someone talking about early retirement. Complete the paragraph.

Supposing _____ ?
That's a good question. Well, leaving the salary considerations for now, _____ _____ .

However, I would miss doing something worthwhile and the contact with people, so _____ _____ .

I'd always rather work with people in some way. _____ _____ .

Actually it's not a bad idea – _____ _____ ;

after all I studied special needs education. _____ _____ _____

at the end of my career. I always _____ _____ ,

so maybe I can even combine the two.

5.3 I've got it!

READING

1 Match the terms (1–3) to the definitions (a–c). Read the first paragraph of the article to check.

1 Ideation ☐
2 Brainstorming ☐
3 Blue-sky thinking ☐

a Spontaneous discussion to generate ideas or solve a problem.
b Creating ideas that are not limited in any way.
c The whole process of creating new ideas.

Brainstorming ideas about brainstorming

A

'Brainstorming' was a term first coined by Alex Faickney Osborn, a creative theorist, in 1953. Nowadays most people are familiar with using brainstorming techniques as a way to gather ideas. Most of us brainstorm regularly both alone and collectively. Blue-sky thinking, as the name suggests, is freer and unconstrained by practicalities, while ideation is the term for the whole process from initial idea to implementation.

B

Two heads are supposed to be better than one, yet how often have we attended meetings to brainstorm something and we haven't been able to come up with anything? Ideas can't always be conjured up on demand. Sometimes it's the topic, sometimes it's the company and sometimes, for some reason, everyone just draws a blank. It can be very frustrating to be stuck for ideas collectively, embarrassing even. However, there are tools and techniques that have been developed to help ideation and to bring some discipline into the fuzzy realm of idea creation.

C

Tony Buzan invented Mind Maps in the 1960s as a way of remembering things, but they also serve well as brainstorming tools to picture ideas and the connections between them. There are Mind Mapping software tools you can use or they can be drawn freehand – so they are available to everyone. Working on a Mind Map together as a group can be a great starting point and an effective way to generate and record ideas. However, some people are put off by their non-linear nature and just can't work out how to use them effectively; others are fine at the beginning but get stuck just when a Mind Map can be a really useful tool that shows synergies that hadn't been apparent before.

D

Another tool is a brainstorming card deck, called the 'ThinkPak'. This is a deck of cards printed with symbols and prompts designed to facilitate the generation of ideas. Michael Michalko is a creative thinker and expert who developed the pack, having collected many thinking techniques and approaches throughout his career. The idea is that everything new is a combination, addition or modification of something that already exists. The cards then provide the impulse to re-visit something and think about it again. There are two sets in the pack: one to generate and one to evaluate ideas. There are nine cards used to generate ideas, where each one gives a simple instruction to change one element at a time – for example, substitute something, adapt something, magnify something or reverse something and so on. Then another set with eight different models is used to evaluate the ideas. One basic model for evaluation is PMI – plus, minus and interesting, i.e. categorizing ideas into positive, negative and thought-provoking ones. The cards enable members of a group to focus on different elements individually before passing them on for additions by others.

E

As far as modifying existing ideas goes, Seth Godin actively encourages people to steal his. In one of his blog posts he says; 'Ideas can't be stolen, because ideas don't get smaller when they're shared, they get bigger'. He encourages people to take an original idea, credit the person whose idea it is and then change or add to it to make it better. He claims that it's the connection between ideas where the real innovation lies and that there's no connection without sharing. So don't wait for an idea to occur. Go out and steal, credit and improve on one instead.

2 Read the article. Match each heading (1–5) with the correct paragraph (A–E)

1 Struggling for ideas ☐
2 Springboarding from other people's ideas ☐
3 Visualizing connections ☐
4 A game of cards ☐
5 Brainstorming is born ☐

3 Read the article again and answer the questions.

1 Why is brainstorming not always easy?
2 What are the advantages and disadvantages of Mind Mapping?
3 How does 'ThinkPak' work?
4 What is PMI?
5 Why does Seth Godin not mind his ideas being 'stolen'?

4 🎧 1 39 Listen and make changes to the notes (1–4) to make true statements.

1 The meeting wasn't successful in finding a new idea for packaging.
2 Bob had the idea for packaging cards to focus their ideas.
3 The packaging was redesigned by the team in the meeting.
4 Having total freedom helps new ideas form.

VOCABULARY Having ideas

5 Match the verbs (1–6) with the nouns (a–f) to make expressions about ideas.

1 to draw — ₃ a for ideas
2 to dawn — ₄ b come up with something
3 to be stuck — ₆ c the faintest idea
4 to be able to — ₅ d to someone
5 to occur — ₁ e a blank
6 to not have — ₂ f on someone

6 Complete the sentences with the correct form of the expressions from Exercise 5.

1 The first time I was asked for my opinion in a meeting like that, I _drew a blank_. I couldn't think clearly and come up with anything sensible.
2 He didn't _have the faintest idea_ how to use the new software; he really needed some training.
3 It only _occurs to_ her afterwards that it wouldn't work in practice unless they adapted it even more for the Asia market.
4 It only _dawned on_ them when they realized it would need massive investment.
5 He's so creative; he can always _come up with_ up good ideas in every meeting.
6 With a creative team like that you'll never be _stuck for ideas_.

WORDBUILDING *off* and *up*

7 Phrasal verbs with *off* and *up* often have the sense of completing an activity. Complete the sentences with the correct form of these verbs.

add up	call off	dress up	follow up
give up	pay off	save up	take off

1 That idea of his really _____. Now every department is doing it.
2 I didn't know you were a vegetarian. When did you _____ eating meat?
3 It's a very formal event so you'll have to _____ for it. Have a look at the pictures from last year.
4 The seminar they attended on teamwork really _____; they have far fewer conflicts these days.
5 We had to _____ the teleconference as too many participants were absent.
6 His accounts didn't _____ so he had to redo them.
7 We were taught to _____ on contacts made at a trade fair by calling them the week after the event.
8 He's _____ his overtime payments over the last two years to buy a new car.

WORD FOCUS collocations with *idea*

8 Underline the verbs (a–h) that <u>don't</u> collocate with *an idea/ideas*.

a to gather
b to occur
c to dream up
d to conjure up
e to strike
f to reject
g to contribute
h to visualize

9 Underline the adjectives (a–h) that <u>don't</u> usually collocate with *idea*.

a an innovative
b an original
c a crazy
d a sharing
e a brilliant
f a unique
g a worthwhile
h an ugly

10 Replace the verbs and adjectives in bold with words from Exercises 8 and 9. How many different combinations can you make without changing the meaning?

1 I've **thought of** 52 **very good** ideas and he's **said no to** all of them!
2 He always **brainstorms unusual** ideas but not always in time for the meeting!

5.4 Anyone got a bright idea?

BRAINSTORMING AND CHOOSING THE BEST IDEAS

1 🎧 **1 40** Choose the correct options to complete the brainstorming phrases. Then listen and check your answers.

1 a *Let's / Why not* try to put together a plan for the training event.

  b We *need to / mustn't* come up with a theme and a keynote speaker.

2 a I really *fancy / suggest* the idea of holding part of it outdoors.

  b Anyone got any *objections / obstacles* to 'New technology' as a theme?

3 a That *would be / will be* a great idea.

  b Yes, I'd go *around / along* with all of those.

4 a *Any / Some* thoughts on a speaker?

  b The same *goes / is* for the speaker.

5 a *Anyone / Someone* got a bright idea about format?

  b *Which / Why* ideas can we reject?

6 a An outdoor event *won't be / may not* be practical.

  b *That's / It's* also true of any event, really.

7 a We *should / must* probably opt for technology rather than teamwork or communication.

  b *Let's go / Let's got* with the technology theme.

2 Match the functions (a–g) with the pairs of phrases (1–7) from Exercise 1.

a Making suggestions ☐

b Choosing ideas ☐

c Comparing ideas ☐

d Showing enthusiasm and agreeing ☐

e Abandoning ideas ☐

f Encouraging contributions ☐

g Stating objectives ☐

PRONUNCIATION Softening negative statements

3 Rewrite the comments about a training event by softening the negative statements. Use a negative verb form and a more positive adjective.

1 Outdoor events are more unpredictable than indoor ones. (quite)

Outdoor events aren't quite as predictable as indoor ones.

2 The speaker got rather negative feedback, didn't he? (such)

_____

3 I heard the caterers were unfriendly. (especially)

_____

4 The atmosphere was cold. (particularly)

_____

5 I thought the speaker was boring, actually. (that)

_____

6 The room was really cold. (quite, enough)

_____

4 🎧 **1 41** Listen and check. Write the word that is stressed in each sentence.

1 _____ **4** _____

2 _____ **5** _____

3 _____ **6** _____

5 For each comment in Exercise 3 write a suggestion to improve the situation.

1 Let's _____ .

2 Why don't we _____ ?

3 We should _____ .

4 Any thoughts _____ ?

5 Let's _____ .

6 I really fancy _____ .

WRITING SKILL Abbreviations

6 Read the processes involved in organizing a training event. Put them in the order they would usually happen.

a Set up the room ☐
b Book the speaker, room and caterers ☐
c Decide on the aims and the programme ☐
d Invite the participants ☐
e Establish the budget ☐

7 Match the abbreviations (1–10) with the meanings (a–j).

1	dept.	a	that is: specifically
2	etc.	b	as soon as possible
3	mgt	c	approximately
4	e.g.	d	August
5	i.e.	e	department
6	asap	f	and so on
7	Aug.	g	including
8	Re:	h	for example
9	approx.	i	regarding
10	incl.	j	management

8 Read the minutes from a brainstorming meeting. Answer the questions.

1 What were the lessons learned from last time?
2 What is the overall aim of a training event?
3 What fun activity has been chosen?

---

11 August Department meeting minutes

The topic of the meeting was the spring training event.

- We discussed lessons learned from last year: a smaller room and a better speaker (interesting topic) and caterers would improve things.
- We organized who is doing what.
- The management team have set the budget at €450 to include a speaker.
- Team brainstormed ideas for a speaker. Lisa is to get approximately four recommendations, and meet and book speaker to fit with overall aims.
- Training event is to improve department communication through technology skills – should be a practical and interactive element with participants bringing smartphones and so on. (Mention in invitation.)
- Invitation to go out as soon as possible after speaker is booked.
- We talked about an ice breaker, for example, a communication quiz. Martin to organize.
- We voted for a fun activity afterwards with karaoke being the most popular. Gerry to organize.
- Regarding food, there was plenty of discussion. Jason to book caterers (he knows a good one) and room.

---

9 Complete the to-do list and notes from the meeting discussed in Exercise 8. Use the abbreviations from Exercise 7.

To-dos and notes:

1 Meeting minutes, 11 _____
2 _____ team have set the budget at €450, _____ speaker.
3 Lisa to get _____ four speaker recommendations
4 Event aims to improve _____ communication
5 Invitation to go out _____ after speaker booked.
6 Remind trainees to bring smartphone, _____ .
7 Martin to organize ice breaker, _____ quiz
8 _____ caterers: Jason to book + room.
9 Fun activity _____ karaoke to be organized by Gerry.

---

10 Write an email after the event from the abbreviated notes using the model below.

- Re: event ☺☺
- thx 4 yr hard work last few wks
- dpt aims met
- theme / speaker ✓ incl.–lots of tech info
- approx. 10 people thx speaker personally
- catering etc. v gd
- weather so gd lunch outside poss
- thx 2 all involved

TO:		FROM:
SUBJECT:		

Dear everyone

_____

_____ . It really paid off!
We can honestly say _____ .
Sensible choices of _____ .
In fact, I even heard that _____ .
_____ were well chosen
The weather didn't disappoint either. In fact,
_____ .

All in all, a complete success _____ .

Best wishes

Sam

YOUR IDEA

1 Read the advice about preparing for job interviews. Match each piece of advice with its title (a–c).

1 I read an article the other day that said we form opinions about other people as soon as we meet them – maybe in as little as seven seconds – so it is important to make those first moments count. Pay attention to your body language. You don't want to appear unfriendly by having a closed posture and crossed arms. Keep your shoulders back and stand tall. Smiling helps you appear much more approachable. These elements of body language are important to consider when you arrive for the interview and you want to get people on your side right from the beginning. ☐

2 The way you look often gives clues about your professionalism and the respect you have for people around you. So it's definitely not a good idea to turn up to an interview with your hair looking untidy and wearing torn jeans. Dressing appropriately for an interview shows respect for the person that will be interviewing you. Of course, this depends on the job that you are being interviewed for, but to be on the safe side, pick a plain suit and don't wear too many accessories, like pocket handkerchiefs or chunky jewellery. Avoid anything flashy; you want your potential boss to focus on you and not the clothes you are wearing. ☐

3 When getting ready for an interview, it's important to know a bit about the job and company, so make sure you take the time to look into this. It's easy nowadays to find out this kind of information by doing a simple Internet search. That way you'll be ready if you are asked about your interest in working for the particular company. But don't forget that you will also have the opportunity to ask questions – so think about what you want to know, and how to ask about it politely. ☐

a What to wear
b First impressions
c Do your research

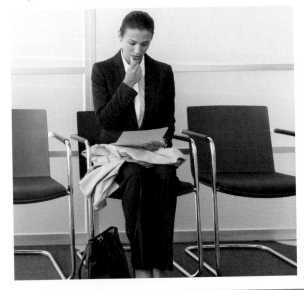

2 Write notes about a situation where you had to overcome a challenge. This might relate to your work, studies or personal life. Some examples of challenges like this are job interviews, preparing for an exam or meeting new people at a social event.

_____

_____

_____

3 Answer these questions about your challenge.

1 What part of your life does your challenge relate to?

_____

2 Why was it such a challenge for you?

3 How did you get through your challenge?

4 In what way did your family and/or friends help you?

4 Practise talking about your challenge out loud. Try to …
- memorize the first few and last few sentences of your talk.
- maintain a steady pace – don't rush and don't forget to breathe.
- make eye contact with members of the audience and engage with them directly.

ORGANIZING YOUR PRESENTATION

5 Match the five steps of a presentation with two examples of useful language (a–j).

1 Greet and welcome the audience ☐ ☐
2 Introduce yourself ☐ ☐
3 Introduce your challenge ☐ ☐
4 Explain how you overcame the challenge ☐ ☐
5 Thank the audience and finish the presentation ☐ ☐

a My name's Alex Smith.
b It was tough, but I managed to …
c Hello. It's great to have all of you here today.
d Thanks so much for your time and attention.
e A few years ago I had to …
f A big thank you for taking the time to listen.
g I'm Clara Wright.
h What helped me do this was …
i A warm welcome to you all.
j Something that was really difficult for me was …

YOUR PRESENTATION

6 Read the useful language on the left and make notes for your presentation.

1 Greet and welcome the audience Hello. I'm pleased to see all of you … It's great to have you all here … Let me give you … A very warm welcome to you all.	
2 Introduce yourself My name's … I'm …	
3 Introduce your challenge A few years ago I had to … Something that was difficult for me was … A challenge I faced was …	
4 Explain how you overcame the challenge It was tough but … What helped me was … Eventually I managed to …	
5 Thank the audience and finish the presentation Thanks for your … A big thank you for … Thank you so much for …	

7 Film yourself giving your presentation or practise in front of a mirror.
Give yourself marks out of ten for …

- maintaining a steady pace. ☐ /10
- engaging with the audience. ☐ /10
- following the five steps in Exercise 6. ☐ /10
- using correct grammar. ☐ /10

6 Solutions

6.1 How to make filthy water drinkable

TEDTALKS

MICHAEL PRITCHARD was born in 1967 in the UK and studied Business Administration and Political Science at the University of Redlands in California, USA. He started his career as an entrepreneur and co-founded his first company in 1998. Pritchard has also established himself as an inventor, with one of his most significant inventions being the *Lifesaver* bottle, which took him eighteen months of trial and error to develop.

The water bottle isn't his only patent. Michael Pritchard holds over a hundred others that relate to water, aerosols and oil. He appeared on the BBC TV series *Dragons' Den* in 2009 with the *Anyway spray* – a spray bottle that can spray at any angle. His safe water innovation system is exhibited in science museums in the UK and the USA. Most importantly, *Lifesaver* is saving lives all over the world and Michael Pritchard's ambitious mission is to end water poverty. His company not only produces the 750ml bottles seen in the TED Talk but they also cater for larger needs: 18.5-litre jerry cans, suitable for a family of four for two and a half years, and large 750-litre mobile water tanks – or bowsers – that can provide up to 12 litres a minute and are ideal for communities. The products are used by humanitarian organizations like the Red Cross and Oxfam, the British Army, and the Malaysian government as well as gap-year travellers. His website and blog show him involved in constant relief action in the far-flung corners of the world most in need. It is such work that led to him being awarded an MBE (Member of the British Empire) in 2013 for services to innovation for water poverty. As he says 'Everyone deserves safe drinking water' and there are still 1.1 billion people worldwide without it.

Michael Pritchard

CAREER PATHWAYS

1 Read the text. Answer the questions.

   1 How long did it take to create the Lifesaver bottle?
   2 How many other inventions has he come up with?
   3 Which product is suitable for families?
   4 What earned him an MBE?

TED PLAYLIST

2 Other TED speakers are interested in topics similar to Michael Pritchard's TED Talk. Read the descriptions of four TED Talks at the top of page 55. In your opinion, which is the best title for this playlist, a, b or c?

   a Energy to create and innovate
   b Good ideas transferred to new territories
   c Saving lives simply, quickly and cheaply

3 Complete the six-word summary (1–4) that corresponds to each talk in the TED playlist. Use these words.

affordable	lifesaving	public	premature

   1 Safe, sustainable and _____ cooking technology.
   2 _____ babies kept alive and warm.
   3 Soap – a simple _____ health intervention.
   4 A network of fast, _____ volunteers.

4 Match the verbs (1–5) with their collocates (a–e). Check your answers in the playlist descriptions.

   1 to transform   **a** partnerships
   2 to embrace   **b** a programme of change
   3 to set up   **c** the problem
   4 to champion   **d** a motorcycle (with sth)
   5 to kit out   **e** ideas into inventions

5 Which talk would you most like to see? Why? Watch the talk at TED.com.

▶ **Amy Smith: Simple designs to save a life**

Amy Smith is an MIT engineer who transforms ideas into inventions. She specializes in finding inexpensive solutions to issues in developing countries. Her enlightening talk focuses on a core issue for people in developing countries: cooking safely with affordable and sustainable resources. Currently a shocking two million people die annually from cooking-fire fumes. With her team of students she's discovered alternative safe fuels that are easily accessible to local people in countries across the globe.

▶ **Jane Chen: A warm embrace that saves lives**

TED Fellow Jane Chen is a social entrepreneur who has spent many years working for health in the developing world, for example, improving infant mortality in India. Currently one in five premature babies there do not survive, partly because local women and midwives don't have access to expensive incubators. Jane Chen's talk introduces us to 'Embrace', a low-cost micro-environment for these babies that provides sustained warmth in a low-tech way that quite literally embraces the problem.

▶ **Myriam Sidibe: The simple power of hand washing**

The public health expert Dr Myriam Sidibe sets up partnerships with governments, companies and communities across the globe to improve health. Her straightforward message: promoting hand washing in order to prevent the spread of diseases such as diarrhoea, cholera and flu. She urges us all to keep our hands clean and champions the biggest hand washing programme in the world.

▶ **Eli Beer: The fastest ambulance – a motorcycle**

An ambucycle is a motorcycle kitted out for quick emergency medical work. Its advantage? It can arrive more quickly at the scene of an emergency than an ambulance. Eli Beer is the man who came up with this idea. As a teenager he volunteered as an emergency medical technician (EMT) and became convinced of the need for an even faster response than ambulances could manage. In his informative and heart-warming talk he explains how he founded an organization of like-minded medic volunteers. His non-profit organization, the United Hatzalah of Israel, helps hundreds of thousands of patients survive.

AUTHENTIC LISTENING SKILLS Signposts

6 🎧 **1 42** You are going to hear a podcast in which a member of the *Keynote* team talks about Amy Smith's TED Talk, *Simple designs to save a life*. Read the sentences and underline the signposting expressions.

1 I'd like to start by telling you about what particularly impressed me about this talk and why.

2 The first thing is Amy Smith is an engaging speaker, inspiring and passionate about using her resources, the resources available in a developed country, to make the world a better place.

3 Now that I've explained a little bit about her, I'll move on to describe what she said that was new for me … over two million people worldwide die annually from indoor cooking-fire fumes. Isn't that heart-breaking?

4 I'd like to tell you what the solutions are a little later.

5 OK, now for the work she tells us about in her talk. It really felt like people making a difference, a worthwhile investment.

LISTENING

7 🎧 **1 43** Listen to the full podcast. Are these statements true (T) or false (F)?

1 Amy Smith recruits engineers from high schools. ☐

2 The team is using modern technology to find solutions for local problems. ☐

3 They created something necessary out of waste. ☐

4 The same process worked in India. ☐

8 🎧 **1 43** Listen again. Answer the questions.

1 Why was the podcaster particularly impressed by the talk?

2 Why did he find it horrifying?

3 What statement does Amy Smith make about farmers?

4 How do the solutions help people live with dignity?

5 What about the talk made Nick feel hopeful for the future?

VOCABULARY IN CONTEXT

9 Read the extracts from the podcast. Choose the correct meaning of the words in bold.

1 I watched this TED Talk after reading the **synopsis**.
   a reviews from others ☐   **b** brief summary ☐
   c interactive transcript ☐

2 … I had no idea of the number of people dying due to **respiratory** illnesses from indoor cooking-fire fumes.
   a breathing-related ☐   **b** eye-related ☐
   c stomach-related ☐

3 … I **take it for granted** that I can easily and safely cook a meal for my family each day.
   a underestimate ☐   **b** don't appreciate ☐
   c treat it as special ☐

4 This material, unlike charcoal, does not cause **deforestation** like traditional wood cooking fires …
   a the clearing of forests ☐   **b** forest farming ☐
   c increasing tree growth ☐

5 Having **dedicated**, innovative individuals working towards a better world really made me feel hopeful …
   a intelligent ☐   **b** energetic ☐   **c** committed ☐

What a waste of time!

GRAMMAR Purpose

1 Complete the text. Use these words and phrases.

| avoid | for | not in order to | so as to | so that | so |

As much time as the Buddha?

An approach to time management

The Buddha had time is a book about how to
¹_____ the suffering involved in managing time
– it's not religious but it does make you think about the
meaning of life. The title explains the essence of the book:
that we lead hectic lives without enough time. The Buddha,
in stark contrast, has time and always has had. The author,
Thomas Hohensee, uses the metaphor ²_____
make sensible and sometimes unexpected arguments. He
explains how we can learn ³_____ manage our time
but to live with as much ease and as little stress as possible.

Unexpectedly one of the 'evils' isn't time itself but greed,
greed for things, ⁴_____ situations and for people
being how we want them to be. We want to have it all,
instantly and as much as possible. We strive to manage our
time and we believe the future can be un-hectic if only we
manage it ⁵_____ . However, the past, present and
future aren't perfect and the sooner we can accept this fact
the better off we will be. Martin Scott, a time management
consultant, says it's not necessary to have everything for a
happy life; two priorities at a time are sufficient
⁶_____ you can concentrate on the important things
in life. What those things are is in another chapter …

2 Choose the correct options to complete the sentences.

1 We hurry through life *in order to / in order that* have more
   time.
2 Hurrying *avoids / prevents* us from seeing the meaning of
   life.
3 We should manage time *so as to / so to* have more time.

4 *In order to / So that* explain the idea, he uses the
   metaphor of the Buddha.
5 We should try to be less perfect *so that / for* we can be
   less stressed.
6 To *avoid / prevent* having too many priorities, limit them
   to two.

3 Write an answer to each question (1–8) stating a purpose. Make the answers sound as natural as possible.

1 Why does he do so much sport? (so as to / good work-life balance)

He does so much sport so as to have a good work-life balance.

2 Why does she go to a different office in the afternoon? (so that / meditate)
I think _____

3 Why do you turn your phone off at work? (so / interrupted)
I _____

4 Why do some people only check email twice a day? (in order / more focused)
I believe _____

5 Why do we keep that door clear? (for / emergencies / fire door)
I understand _____

6 Why does she take an earlier train than we do? (so as to / seat)
She _____

7 Why did you go back via Italy? (so that / visit a client)
I _____

8 Why does he need the computer? (in order to / work at home tomorrow)
I think _____

4 Match the two parts of the sentences.

1 Use first names ☐
2 Keep to deadlines ☐
3 Stay on topic in meetings ☐
4 Inform the project leader in advance about absence ☐
5 Think positively and expect the best ☐
6 Celebrate milestones when possible ☐

a to avoid time wasting.
b so as to reschedule if necessary.
c in order to build rapport quickly.
d so that team members receive work on time.
e for a sense of achievement and success.
f so as not to start a negative spiral.

5 Complete the sentences with *prevent* or *avoid*. Use the correct form of the verbs.

1 By running the seminar themselves they _____ paying high training costs.
2 Effective time management _____ him from having high levels of stress.
3 He _____ delegating work tasks and insists on having complete control over a situation.
4 The emergency meeting certainly _____ the customer from ending the contract.
5 The admin team worked so they could _____ taking unnecessary extra steps in the process.
6 He _____ speaking Spanish on the phone because he was embarrassed to speak it in front of his colleagues.

GRAMMAR EXTRA! Idiomatic ways to express purpose

6 Match the idiomatic phrases expressing purpose (1–8) with their meanings (a–h).

1 on purpose
2 with a view to
3 accidentally on purpose
4 for the sake of
5 at cross-purposes
6 for the good of
7 as a means to an end
8 sense of purpose

a for the purpose of
b looks casual but is deliberate
c deliberately
d as a way to get something desirable
e with a goal to
f with conflicting aims
g mission in life
h very good intentions of

7 Complete the sentences with the idiomatic phrases (1–8) from Exercise 6.

1 He's currently the sales manager and he's going on a management training course _____ him replacing a CEO one day.
2 After her gap year they noticed she had a new _____ about her.
3 He doesn't like being _____ with any of the staff and strives to clear any issues up in a timely fashion.
4 _____ the shareholders, they cut further costs in the business including making some staff redundant.
5 He attended the trade fair _____ and was soon working for a competitor in a higher position.
6 She missed the train _____ so as to avoid travelling on such a full one.
7 I think you forgot your sports kit _____ so you wouldn't have to go to the gym!
8 There had to be some management changes made _____ the company.

DICTATION

8 🎧 1 44 Listen to someone talking about time management myths. Complete the paragraph.

Time management itself is a myth. _____ _____, but this is rarely possible. Everyone has the same number of hours in the day. Fundamentally, it's naïve of us to think that we can _____ .
The best way to manage time is to avoid doing things _____ . In other words, dropping habits and hobbies you don't like _____ . Making a 'to-do' list _____ , but making a note _____ , can be productive. Ultimately, it's not about managing time itself; it's about managing what you do with your time _____ .

6.3 Thinking outside the box

READING

1 Read the beginning of the interview. Tick (✓) the statements about Deutsche Post DHL that are correct.

  1 Deutsche Post DHL is the largest courier company in the world. ☐

  2 Its headquarters are in Berlin. ☐

  3 It operates in 220 countries worldwide and employs 480,000 employees. ☐

  4 It went public in 1998. ☐

New worlds and new markets

Walter, you've worked for Deutsche Post DHL for over forty years. Can you tell us about the company first, in a nutshell?

'Well, it was originally government owned and split into different divisions in 1990 for banking, postal services and telecommunications. It went public in 2000 and has grown to a global company operating in 220 countries and employing 480,000 people. Its headquarters are in Bonn and it's the biggest courier service in the world.'

2 Read the rest of the interview and match the questions (a–d) with Walter's responses (1–4).

  a Did your idea lead to a promotion, or some recognition?

  b What was it like working there?

  c It's hard to imagine. Can you give us some examples of this entrepreneurial spirit?

  d If you look back, can you identify a point in time where you took up an opportunity?

1 _____

'There are a couple but the most memorable was autumn 1989 in Germany, where many changes were taking place. The Berlin Wall had just come down and the country was reuniting. I was working in Hamburg as a controller, a number cruncher, if you like. One evening my boss asked for help with a huge backlog of Quelle's mail-order catalogues. Those were the days before the Internet, you understand. The problem was that there was a strike on so 500,000 catalogues weren't reaching their customers who were eager to shop. I puzzled over it and in the morning, I had a detailed plan to deliver by taxi. My boss promptly executed it. Over the next three days, all of the catalogues were delivered. Problem solved. A success!'

2 _____

'Better than that, it led to a new mindset. My boss became the boss in Dresden and he asked me to join him. I didn't hesitate! With the opening of the markets in the eastern part, there was a huge demand for western products. Working there, we developed an entrepreneurial spirit and way of thinking that I wouldn't have had otherwise. I learned you have to take some risks sometimes, which isn't always easy for a German. Everything we'd done so far wouldn't work, the rules had changed and sometimes there weren't any rules. There was no real infrastructure, there were no buildings and there was no equipment or workers – or not enough of them. Nothing really worked but business was booming. We had to start completely from scratch, without a rulebook.'

3 _____

'I'll give you three. The first problem was manpower to sort all the parcels. After the Wall came down there were 10,000 Russian soldiers stationed in Dresden, with nothing to do. We offered them sorting jobs cash-in-hand. They worked gladly and hard. Problem number two was equipment. We asked all the West German post offices for anything that they didn't need: conveyor belts, sorting bins, cages, and anything else useful. It was all sent over – a kind of recycling. There was no one who could help with solutions – you had to think for yourself. We found new premises and delivery vehicles – 500 in total – we rented from the west. The third problem was delivery staff; we looked for and employed local people to deliver; they had three days' training and then they worked.'

4 _____

'It was like being a pioneer in the Wild West in a way; after the Wall came down everyone looked for opportunities to make money. It was pure capitalism really, but very exciting building up the infrastructure. For me personally, it was one of the best times in my career – rolling up my sleeves and having to think outside of every box every single day.'

3 Read the interview again and answer the questions.

1 What was the problem with the catalogues?
2 What solution was offered? Did it work?
3 What was the reward?
4 What kind of thinking was required?
5 What did managers like Walter have to do?

4 Write the solutions that were found to 1–5. Read again to check.

1 Russian soldiers _____
2 Unwanted postal machinery _____
3 Vehicles _____
4 Delivery staff _____
5 Infrastructure _____

5 Find the words in the interview that match the definitions (1–6).

1 A list of things waiting for attention or action that should have been taken. _____
2 A way of ordering something over the phone or by letter. _____
3 When employees stop working to protest about pay and/or conditions. _____
4 Very keen on doing something. _____
5 The attitude of someone who makes deals and generates business. _____
6 The first to go somewhere or do something new and important. _____

VOCABULARY Solution collocations

6 Match the two parts of the sentences.

1 She didn't solve ☐
2 The team eventually managed to sort out ☐
3 He never overcame ☐
4 It was impossible to imagine how he'd done it, but eventually they got to the bottom ☐
5 When Claire and Sally met in person they managed to clear up ☐
6 He spent a good part of his research trying to crack ☐
7 I wish we'd learned to think ☐
8 It didn't take long to find ☐

a his fear of heights.
b the problem in the mechanics.
c the misunderstanding they'd had over the phone.
d a solution this time.
e outside the box at school.
f the financial mess left by the previous manager.
g of the mystery.
h the riddle of the disappearing fish until she saw the cat.

WORDBUILDING Phrases with do

7 Complete the sentences. Use these words and phrases.

did her a good turn	does their bit	did the trick
do a double take	do it blindfolded	do me a favour
do you any harm	didn't do him justice	

1 Going for a run really _____ , I've just had a great idea.
2 She's done the same task so many times that she could _____ .
3 Can you _____ ? I've misplaced his number. Can you send it again?
4 If everyone _____ , we'll be finished in no time.
5 The review really _____ . He was actually brilliant!
6 Did you see him _____ when he saw the car she was driving?
7 Well, she helped me, so I _____ too and told her about the flat.
8 Don't worry, it's only herbal tea. It won't _____ , it may even do some good!

WORD FOCUS chance

8 Complete the definitions with these words and phrases.

| fat | jump | leave | outside | stand a | take | the off |

1 a tiny possibility = an _____ chance
2 let fate take its course = _____ something to chance
3 with the hope/possibility that = on _____ chance
4 do something despite there being a risk = _____ a chance on someone/something
5 little likelihood / no way = _____ chance
6 accept an opportunity with enthusiasm = _____ at the chance
7 have a hope of success = _____ chance

9 Complete the sentences with the correct form of the phrases from Exercise 8.

1 She's got a _____ of passing the exam – she hasn't done enough work.
2 He heard he was on the shortlist and therefore _____ of getting the job.
3 I disagree; we need to plan ahead and not _____ .
4 It's well worth _____ her because even though she's young, she's very keen to learn.
5 She was really excited when she was offered the opportunity to work in Spain and immediately _____ .
6 I'm just ringing _____ you can shed some light on the test results.
7 There is an _____ of getting a seat on the next plane to New York.

6.4 What are our options?

DISCUSSING OPTIONS

1 🎧 **1 45** Listen to the conversation. Match each question or statement (1–7) with its response (a–g).

1 What shall we do now?
2 Well, what are our options?
3 Don't you know where we are either, George?
4 We could go back till we recognize where we are.
5 Let's give it a try anyway.
6 Maybe we should consider looking for the other teams.
7 Wait! Maybe we should try going the other way at the tower.

a You mean retrace our steps? Good idea.
b I think you're right. It's worth a try.
c Oh, I'm not too sure about that. Won't we just get more lost doing that?
d Why don't we keep calm and think of a plan?
e Sorry, no idea.
f Maybe we should consider calling for help.
g Yes, OK, let's try it.

2 🎧 **1 45** Try to complete the sentences from memory. Then listen again and check your answers.

1 What a crazy idea _____ .
2 We could go back _____ .
3 If we had phones _____ .
4 Let's take _____ .
5 I think we _____ .

3 Complete the phrases for each function using the prompts to help you.

1 Considering options:
  a (could / retrace) _____ .
  b (not / do / try / retrace) _____ ?
2 Talking about possible outcomes:
  a (worth / try) _____ .
  b (got / lose) _____ ?
3 Raising doubts:
  a (not / sure / that) _____ .
  b (not sure / work) _____ .
4 Deciding to take action:
  a (let / try) _____ .
  b (let / give / try) _____ .

PRONUNCIATION Stress: content and function words

4 🎧 **1 46** Underline the word or words you think will be stressed in each sentence. Then listen and check your answers.

1 It's certainly worth a try.
2 I'm not too sure about that.
3 I'd rather keep looking.
4 Let's take stock.
5 If we had phones we could ring.
6 We could go back till we recognize it.

WRITING SKILL Online advice forum

5 Match the problems (1–6) with the solutions (a–f).

1 My colleagues do the same work as me but always seem to finish more quickly.

2 Over the last month my back has become more painful.

3 My boss expects me to answer emails and calls in the evenings and at weekends.

4 As the office has become more electronic my skills are more and more outdated.

5 We have a new customer who is French and we have to answer the phone and emails in French.

6 My colleagues say what they think privately but don't say anything in meetings.

a You need to have your chair adjusted properly.

b You need to ask your boss for support with the technology.

c You need to get some training from colleagues or go on a special course.

d You are too concerned with details. Check your work only once.

e You can suggest presenting topics collectively at meetings.

f You should try and set limits. Try agreeing to check only once a day.

6 Add polite phrases to soften the solutions (a–f) from Exercise 5. Use <u>two</u> of these words in each solution.

it	consider	have	find
find	may	might	possibility
probably	should	the	will

1 You _____ need to get a new chair or have yours adjusted properly.

2 You _____ asking your boss for support so you can communicate.

3 You _____ to get some training from colleagues or the company.

4 You will _____ quicker to work without checking things so much.

5 You could think about _____ of presenting topics collectively.

6 You _____ if you talk to the boss, she / he may agree that you only need to check once a day.

7 Choose the correct options to make true sentences.

1 *Don't be afraid / I'm afraid* to admit you are not able to use computer programs.

2 *Consider / Considering* asking for French lessons.

3 *Think about / Consider about* finding out about ergonomic office guidelines.

4 You *may have to / might probably have to* discuss what situations need urgent weekend attention.

5 Think about *the possible / the possibility* of working with a colleague to learn from them.

6 You *might like / might like to* talk about it with your colleagues privately.

8 Complete the advice about dealing with weekend and evening messages with sentences a–c.

a It could be that you have agreed to some availability after hours, but it's not been necessary until now.

b But you could try to find a way of limiting it somehow.

c It sounds as though you may need to approach your colleagues to discover the extent of the issue.

TO:	FROM:
SUBJECT:	

Dear Tom,

You aren't alone with this problem. I'm getting an increasing number of emails about staff being required to reply to messages after hours.

In your email you say that being available is now expected, however, you don't say whether you are the only one or if all staff are expected to be available. ¹ _____ Before approaching your line manager, you might want to check the details of your contract. ² _____ . If you do talk to him / her, it may be a good idea to do so with a colleague present. Consider accepting some calls and texts after hours if it is important for the business. ³ _____ . You could bring up the possibility of having a rota so that only one colleague is 'on' each evening / weekend.

Good luck

Marjorie

9 Write an email giving advice to a colleague having trouble keeping up with technology. Include the bullet points and softeners. Make it less formal and shorter.

• Ask your boss for training

• Be prepared to invest in a course yourself

• Ask colleagues for some informal support

• If colleagues need support too bring it up in a department meeting

TO:	FROM:
SUBJECT:	

Dear

Best wishes

The review you will read in Exercise 2 is in response to the following exam question.

> **The Grand Theatre**
> We would like to increase the number of comedians featured at our theatre and we need your help! Write us a review of a comedy show you have seen telling us why you enjoyed it and who the show would be suitable for. Your favourite comedians may appear on our stage soon!
>
> Write your review in **220–260 words** in an appropriate style.

IDEAS

1 Tick (✓) the things you would expect to see in the review.

a a recommendation saying who the show would be suitable for ☐

b one or two things the writer didn't like about the show and why ☐

c a biography of the comedian(s) ☐

d when and where the writer saw the show ☐

e a summary of the show's theme or main points ☐

f positive points from the show with reasons ☐

g a description of what makes a good comedy show ☐

MODEL

2 Read the review. Match the five sections with a description (a–g) from Exercise 1.

1 ☐   **2** ☐   **3** ☐   **4** ☐   **5** ☐

¹In June last year I had the pleasure of watching Bill Bailey's latest show, *Qualmpeddler*, at the Theatre Royal in Newcastle. ²In the show, Bailey describes some of the issues (qualms) he has with modern life, ranging from celebrity culture to politics, from our use of language to the way we treat animals. The 'peddler' part of the title is about how he is trying to 'sell' us his ideas.

³One of the highlights of the evening was his story about an owl he and his team came across while eating at an exotic restaurant in China. They rescued it and released it into the wild. The story was accompanied by surreal pictures of Bailey and the owl shown on the screen, mostly taken at night. It may not sound funny, but the way Bailey told the story was full of jokes and cliffhangers, leaving you wanting more.

No Bill Bailey show is complete without him showing off his piano playing skills, and this was no exception. By playing a famous TV theme tune at different speeds he changed it from a triumphant tune to one which was slow and melancholic or one like a Jewish folk song. The joy of his comedy often lies in these contrasts between our expectations and the surprises he produces. ⁴The only downside was the speed at which some of the changes between sections of the show took place – it was hard to keep up at times.

⁵Bill Bailey is a must for anyone who enjoys thought-provoking comedy or who enjoys hearing music being twisted into new and interesting combinations.

3 Read the review again. Are these statements true (T) or false (F)?

1 Bill Bailey based his comedy show on problems he has experienced. ☐

2 The reviewer didn't enjoy a story about an animal. ☐

3 Images were used to help tell the story. ☐

4 Bailey is a talented musician. ☐

5 The reviewer found the show easy to follow throughout. ☐

USEFUL LANGUAGE

4 Put the phrases in the correct order to create introductory sentences.

1 *were joined by / for a concert of / On Saturday the New York Philharmonic / in Central Park / opera favourites / tenor Andrea Bocelli*

2 *– in fact, 60,000 people / at the BMW Welt Auditorium in Munich / I certainly wasn't alone / saw Coldplay / in my choice of concert / perform last night*

3 *one of my dreams, / To see Madonna perform / when I saw her concert in Prague / has long been / and, in November last year, / I achieved that dream*

4 *jazz pianist Herbie Hancock / the Barbican Theatre in London, / When I heard that / I knew / was playing at / I had to be there*

5 *at the Glastonbury Festival in 2015 / to see them perform / The Who / As part of their farewell tour, / were the final act / and I was privileged enough*

5 Match the basic description (1–6) with a more advanced way of expressing the same idea (a–f).

1 His music makes you want to dance. ☐
2 The audience enjoyed it. ☐
3 You could lose yourself in the music. ☐
4 I listened to their music a lot when I was younger. ☐
5 The words are interesting, not just the tune. ☐
6 Her concert was fun to watch. ☐

a It was a real crowd-pleaser.
b There is more to his songs than just the melody; the lyrics have a real depth.
c No party would be complete without a few of his songs.
d It was difficult not to feel overcome by the music.
e The singer's performance was engaging and entertaining.
f The band's music played a huge part in my childhood.

6 Complete the sentences to add emphasis. Use these adjectives and adverbs.

huge	remarkably	severely	simply
ultimate	wonderful		

1 From start to finish, the concert was _____ magnificent.
2 The whole concert had a _____ effect on me.
3 It's the _____ way to experience rock music.
4 Even though they have been _____ criticized, I still wanted to see them live.
5 The melody is _____ moving.
6 I have to say that they did a _____ job with the costumes.

7 Choose the correct options to complete the recommendations.

1 I would definitely *recommend / avoid* going to see Maná to anyone who is a fan of Spanish pop music.
2 *All in all, / In general,* Tom Jones is a singer who has something to offer everyone, from the youngest to the oldest audience members.
3 This piece should not only appeal to seasoned concert goers *but also / in addition* to those who have never been to a classical concert before in their lives.
4 *Although / Despite* Darren Hayes is a talented singer, I'd say that his concerts are best for those who know some of his music.
5 I *challenge / predict* even the most serious listener not to be smiling and tapping their feet by the end of her concert.

PLANNING

You will answer the following question.

> We are looking for concert reviews to feature in the culture section of the tourist information office website for our area. Send us a review explaining what kind of concert you went to and what aspects of it you most enjoyed. You should also suggest one way in which you think the concert could have been improved.

8 Plan your review. Write notes to answer these questions. Don't write full sentences yet.

1 Which concert will you write about? Where and when did you go to it? How will you summarize it?
_____

2 What aspects of the concert did you most enjoy?
_____

3 How could the concert have been improved?
_____

4 Who would you recommend the concert to? Why?
_____

WRITING

9 Write a review to answer the question in Exercise 8. In your review you should:

- write who the performers were and where and when the concert was
- describe the best parts of the concert experience
- suggest one way that the concert could have been improved
- say who this type of concert would be most suitable for

Write your review in **220–260 words** in an appropriate style.

ANALYSIS

10 Check your review. Answer the questions.

- **Content:** Is it clear who you saw, when and where? Does the review describe the good and bad points of the concert? Is it 220 to 260 words long?
- **Communicative achievement:** Is it clear to the reader why the concert was enjoyable?
- **Organization:** Is the review logically organized? Are the ideas connected?
- **Language:** Does it use correct grammar and vocabulary? Is a good range of structures used?

7 Imagination

7.1 Taking imagination seriously

TEDTALKS

'I try to imagine my goal as a reality, and then work backwards to figure out all the steps I need to take to make it so,' says **JANET ECHELMAN**. This imagination dreamed up, for example, *Unnumbered Sparks*, a 745-foot net sculpture which would billow in the wind and come alive at night with light and digital designs powered by the public. Her career has been as fluid and varied as her art. Although originally rejected by seven universities, she has since studied art at Harvard University, and has an MA in counselling psychology. She has been awarded residencies, grants and scholarships in Europe and Asia, including the Fullbright Senior Lectureship and the Guggenheim Fellowship. When she began painting she listened attentively to her inner voice; she drew and wrote using her less dominant hand to access creative ideas that might otherwise never come into being. A stroke of fate changed her chosen media from paint to fibre; the knotting and sculpture she now does requires both hands.

She has exhibited prolifically across the globe and the awards she has won have been for architecture and structural engineering as well as in art and design. She's worked with and learned from fishermen, engineering firms, software engineers, industrial weavers and experts to bring what she imagines to life. For example, to make *Unnumbered Sparks*, which was designed and built to celebrate TED's thirtieth year, she collaborated with Aaron Koblin, another TED speaker and a digital media artist. The huge, interactive structure was suspended outside the Vancouver Conference Centre where TED 2014 was held, making something truly original that brought together the man-made, the natural and the public.

Janet Echelman

CAREER PATHWAYS

1 Read the text. Answer the questions.

  1 How does Janet Echelman use her imagination in her work?
  2 What is distinctive about *Unnumbered Sparks*?
  3 What did she study at university?
  4 What does she use to help access her creativity?

TED PLAYLIST

2 Other TED speakers are interested in topics similar to Janet Echelman's TED Talk. Read the descriptions of four TED Talks at the top of page 65. In your opinion, which is the best title for this playlist, a, b or c?

  a Storytelling and technology
  b Art and imagination's limitations
  c Stories and art that stretch the imagination

3 Complete the six-word summary (1–4) that corresponds to each talk in the TED playlist. Use these words.

between	carpet	everywhere	pushing

  1 An imaginative artist's magic _____ ride.
  2 _____ the envelope of boundless creativity.
  3 Depicting everything and _____ in paper.
  4 Imagination lies _____ truth and lies.

4 Match the verbs (1–5) with their collocates (a–e). Check your answers in the playlist descriptions.

  1 to colour   **a** disbelief
  2 to push   **b** characters and stories
  3 to depict   **c** someone on a fantastic journey
  4 to launch   **d** boundaries
  5 to suspend   **e** one's life experiences

5 Which talk would you most like to see? Why? Watch the talk at TED.com.

▶ **Raghava KK: My 5 lives as an artist**

Raghava KK is an artist who's lived and travelled around the world, changing his art along the way. His life experiences have driven his artistic reincarnations and in turn these reincarnations have coloured his life experiences. As cartoonist, painter, realist, thinker and family guy, he's been both media darling and media outcast. His honest and vulnerable talk details all five of Raghava KK's artistic chapters so far, warts and all, and contains all the drama, emotion and colour of a Bollywood film.

▶ **James Cameron: Before Avatar … a curious boy**

James Cameron is a director of blockbuster films like *Titanic, Avatar* and *Terminator*, as well as an underwater explorer and science-fiction fanatic. His curiosity has led him to explore the world and these three passions. In his personal talk he tells us how film-making puts stories and pictures together to push boundaries to create a new reality.

▶ **Béatrice Coron: Stories cut from paper**

Béatrice Coron glides onto the TED stage in a full-length paper-cut cape that contrasts dramatically with her plain black clothing beneath, providing a stunning demonstration of her work as a papercutting artist. Coron uses scissors, paper and other materials to depict characters, stories and entire worlds in amazing and imaginative detail.

▶ **Mac Barnett: Why a good book is a secret door**

Mac Barnett believes that children are in many ways the most imaginative and serious of all readers, and he writes books that launch them on fantastic journeys: to worlds that include, for example, trading phone messages with pet blue whales. He's an award-winning writer with a penchant for the zone where disbelief is suspended and fiction can escape the page and enter the real world.

AUTHENTIC LISTENING SKILLS Inferring meaning from context

6 🎧 2 1 You are going to hear a podcast in which a member of the *Keynote* team talks about James Cameron's TED Talk, *Before Avatar … a curious boy*. Complete the sentences. Then listen and check your answers.

1 This talk has personal _____ for me and not only me, but for any professional.
2 Everyone has some degree of motivation for choosing what they do for a _____ and in this talk James Cameron revealed some personal reasons why he made particular film choices.
3 James Cameron has an easy, confident way of talking, without relying on emotional outbursts and high-pitched statements for his audience's _____ .
4 This confidence may come in part from Cameron's phenomenal business success, but I think it's also based on his _____ in what he does.
5 This belief is impersonal and fact-based, in other words, he disconnects his ego from his work when he talks about it, and he isn't the block-buster _____ but a man doing a job and living a life.

LISTENING

7 🎧 2 2 Listen to the full podcast. Are these statements true (T) or false (F)?

1 James Cameron uses a lot of exciting visuals in his talk. ☐
2 Doruk describes Cameron as having been fascinated by nature as a child. ☐
3 Cameron was always keen to learn about and explore unknown worlds. ☐
4 His dream was to go scuba diving in California. ☐

8 🎧 2 2 Listen again and answer the questions.

1 What two areas was Cameron especially interested in as a child, which influenced his later work?
2 When making *Titanic*, how did he legitimately use the film's production to realize a personal dream?
3 What technology did Cameron want to use in *Titanic* and why?
4 What does Doruk see as the message of the talk?

VOCABULARY IN CONTEXT

9 Read the extracts from the podcast. Choose the correct meaning of the words in bold.

1 I found that Cameron's way of talking was especially **compelling** because of his lack of ego …
   a memorable ☐ **b** undeniable ☐
   c interesting and exciting ☐
2 He was also an **avid** reader of science fiction and read for at least two hours a day.
   a secret ☐ **b** quick ☐ **c** keen ☐
3 He would spend time drawing – as a **creative outlet**.
   a exercise ☐ **b** means of expression ☐
   c hobby ☐
4 … making a film about it was the perfect **vehicle** to do this.
   a disguise ☐ **b** way ☐ **c** car ☐
5 This was the part that particularly **grabbed me** …
   a caught my attention ☐ **b** made me laugh ☐
   c puzzled me ☐

7.2 The power of daydreaming

GRAMMAR The continuous aspect

1 Match the headings 1–5 with sections A–E of the text.

1 Daydreaming makes you forget what you [ ]
   ¹*did /were doing*.
2 Daydreaming turns off other parts of the brain. [ ]
3 You daydream less as you get older. [ ]
4 Daydreaming makes you more creative. [ ]
5 Your brain, not your mind, ²*controls / is
   controlling* your daydreams. [ ]

2 Choose the best options (1–8) to complete the text.

Five surprising facts about daydreaming
By Christine Dell'Amore, National Geographic

Here are some interesting facts about daydreaming you
³*may not have known / may have not been knowing*.

A

Daydreaming is often about anticipating the future, dreaming
of what you ⁴*will be doing / are doing*, notes Peter Delaney, a
psychologist at the University of North Carolina, Greensboro.
Later in life, daydreaming decreases as the future shrinks.

B

If people are asked to daydream about the past, for
instance, they tend not to remember what they ⁵*were
working on / worked on* before the daydream started.

C

Our brain has two key systems: an analytic part that helps
us make reasoned decisions, and an empathetic part that
allows us to relate to others. Our mind uses one system at
a time and ⁶*is requiring / requires* the energy from the other
one to complete the task at hand.

D

The physical and the conscious are like different aspects
of the same thing, like the software and hardware of
a computer. As we learn new things the connections
between nerve cells ⁷*are constantly changing / constantly
change*.

E

When daydreaming, the brain accesses information that
was dormant or out of reach, notes Eugenio M. Rothe, a
psychiatrist at Florida International University. It may make
an association between bits of information that the person
⁸*had never considered / had never been considering* in that
particular way.

3 🔊 **2 3** Complete the conversation with the correct
continuous form. Then listen and check your answers.

A: ¹ _____ (you / daydream) when I came in?
B: Oh dear. Yes, I was. Actually, I ² _____ (think)
   about my holiday next week.
A: I heard we daydream less when we get older. Do you
   think there's anything in it?
B: ³ _____ (you / be) cheeky and saying I'm too old
   to daydream?

A: Of course not! I ⁴ _____ (not imply) anything of
   the sort. I ⁵ _____ (just / wonder).
B: I ⁶ _____ (daydream) since I was at school, though.
A: Yeah, I ⁷ _____ (always / get caught)
   daydreaming, too, especially in French. It was so boring.
   What made you start daydreaming this time?
B: Not sure. Maybe it's to do with the report
   I ⁸ _____ (read) all morning!
A: Oh, that report's next on my to-do list. I ⁹ _____
   (probably / daydream) myself soon.

4 Complete the sentences with the correct continuous form of the verbs in brackets, using contracted forms where you can. More than one answer may be possible.

1 He _____ (work) in the research team for two years before he was asked to lead it.
2 They _____ (come) over from head office to meet the new manager, once she's settled in.
3 We _____ (go) to Greece on holiday ever since I can remember.
4 I _____ (work) in the garden when the news of the disaster broke.
5 You could tell he _____ (not / listen); he was still working out the finances in his head.
6 She _____ (exhibit) in Australia and New Zealand later in the year; she's a very sought after artist.
7 He _____ (dream) of going abroad when the chance for an exchange came up.
8 She _____ (hope) to do some research into cognitive processing next year.

5 Choose the best options to end each sentence.

1 I'm working in London *for the summer / since 2004*.
2 She's waiting for the response from her interview *last week / next week*.
3 He hadn't ever been sailing *last year / before last year*.
4 They were planning to arrive this evening, *until they've been delayed / but there's a strike*.
5 By then she'll be living in Spain – *she's moving this week / she moved last week*.
6 They were just signing the contract *when they heard the news / when they were leaving*.
7 They're implementing the project in Sweden *every year / before the end of the year*.
8 She's been attending training courses there *ever since I can remember / last year*.

6 Choose the best answer (a, b or c) for each question.

1 How long have they been renting out their place on Airbnb?
   a Last week they started.
   b About a year now.
   c More regularly.
2 Is there someone staying there now?
   a I'm not sure, you'd have to ask them.
   b There's someone who will stay every June.
   c No, no one stayed last week.
3 Will anyone be using it over the holidays or can we stay there again?
   a Their parents won't stay.
   b That would be nice, wouldn't it? We'll have to see.
   c I think so.
4 Were you still living at home or were you there when there was that huge storm?
   a Yes, I did.
   b Yes, I stayed there.
   c Yes, I was there. It was awful actually.

5 How long had they been renting it for before we went there?
   a Not long, about six months.
   b In 2013.
   c Six months previously.

GRAMMAR EXTRA! Adverbs of certainty

7 Complete the sentences with the correct adverbs of certainty.

1 We'll *probably / maybe* be renting a car for the whole summer.
2 Future generations will *maybe / definitely* be living longer.
3 Most of us will *probably / surely* be living in megacities in 30 years' time.
4 We'll *perhaps / undoubtedly* be shopping online more over the next decade.
5 Businesses will *maybe / certainly* be using and sharing more through open source in the future.
6 Higher life expectancy means people will *definitely / perhaps* be needing more support and services in coming years.
7 There *most probably / maybe* won't be many mono-ethnic workforces in existence over the next 20 years.
8 People will *surely / maybe* start to take better care of the environment in the near future.

PRONUNCIATION /ŋ/ sound

8 🎧 **2 4** Underline the words that have a /ŋ/ sound. Then listen and check your answers.

1 How long have they been renting their place on Airbnb?
2 Is there someone staying there now?
3 Will anyone be using it over the holidays or can we stay there again?
4 Were you still living at home or were you there when there was that huge storm?
5 How long had they been renting it for before we went there?

DICTATION

9 🎧 **2 5** Listen to someone talking about getting a good idea. Complete the paragraph.

Well, they say that daydreaming makes you more creative. I remember one time _____ the details of a presentation. _____ in the final section and needed a way of bringing them together. _____ and nothing had worked. Then _____ but actually _____, daydreaming and sort of allowing my mind to freewheel. Suddenly there it was, _____.
It just popped into my head from nowhere. The perfect solution.

READING

1 Read the introductory paragraph. Match each term (1–6) with the best definition (a–f).

A personal vision behind each event

With an emphasis on global cuisine and a passion for incorporating plentiful Vermont fresh food and products, Susanna's Catering provides a fully-insured service that combines outstanding quality ingredients, a wealth of experience, bold imagination and impeccable service for any size event in the greater Stowe, Vermont region. Susanna is a member of the Vermont Fresh Network and can provide a tailor-made service to perfectly orchestrate your special event.

1	global cuisine	a	back-up in case of loss or damage
2	Vermont Fresh Network	b	original ideas
3	fully-insured service	c	foods and recipes from around the world
4	bold imagination	d	planning an event to suit the individual client
5	impeccable service	e	community that produces locally grown food
6	tailor-made service	f	smart and friendly staff

2 Read the interview and complete the questions (1–5) with five of the phrases from Exercise 1.

3 Read the interview again. Are these statements true (T) or false (F)?

1 The chef has worked on water and land internationally. ☐

2 The client's idea drives the menu creation. ☐

3 Clients start by looking at pictures of dishes online to create their own menu and then meet someone from Susanna's Catering. ☐

4 Most of the food is sourced from abroad. ☐

5 Highlights from Susanna's travels contribute to the mix. ☐

6 Staff have to learn about the food they serve in order to train new recruits. ☐

Interview with the chef

In what way can the food served by Susanna's Catering be called ¹ _____ **?**

Susanna Keefer is the chef and founder of Susanna's Catering. She says that her food is locally sourced but globally inspired and delicious. She grew up in the UK, has worked on hotel canal boats in France, sailed the seven seas as a private chef on yachts and travelled extensively in Asia and Australia. Based for the last twenty years in Vermont, USA, she has been catering for weddings and many other events. Beginning as a start-up out of her own kitchen, she now employs eight full-time staff and rents business premises.

How important is the ² _____ **to the success of the event?**

Every customer event is a culinary work of art designed to fulfil the expectations of the client and their guests. Each menu is original and made to order. Everything starts with the client – almost half are referrals, repeat customers or have been guests at other events. In the first consultation on the phone or in the tasting kitchen, Susanna and the client get to know each other and Susanna finds out about the event and the client's vision and expectations. She listens carefully to how they see the food fitting the overall concept.

Where does the local ³ _____ **come in?**

Great food engages all the senses, and the vision for each party is how the guests can enjoy it best. When a clear idea has been established, Susanna starts to add her own ideas. Working with illustrated lists of appetizers, starters, main courses and desserts, dishes and ingredients are selected that appeal. The menu is developed after taking any dietary considerations into account, such as vegetarians, or people with gluten or nut allergies. Susanna's Catering is a member of a local organization of farmers, producers and chefs whose aim is to promote rural identity and locally grown food. Most of the ingredients she uses are locally sourced and many are organic.

Where can we see Susanna's ⁴ _____ **in action?**

She says: 'The inspiration and imagination comes from everything I've experienced and collected from my travels. I can still see things in my mind's eye, remember the smell, taste and feel of things: markets in France, seafood in South Africa, spices in India, cakes and sweets in the Caribbean. The exciting thing is to bring the right elements from abroad to flavour and complement the rich local produce we have here. That's the magic.'

How does ⁵ _____ **add to the experience?**

The chef and catering team tease out some details from their clients that are personal; for example, if it's a wedding, where a couple met or where they go on holiday, and bring it out in the menu in some way. Nowadays people often marry and celebrate across cultures rather than within them. Stationed buffets create islands of the individual cultures, like a street food cart from India with all the dishes presented on it, or an English afternoon-tea table. These things make the event more interactive and exciting. The service staff are a tightly knit team and know everything about the food, so they can provide additional information as they serve the meals and help bring the whole experience alive – with a smile.

VOCABULARY Expressions with *mind*

4 Match 1–8 with a–h to complete the expressions with *mind*.

1 to put	**a** of mind
2 to bear	**b** your mind's eye
3 to blow someone's	**c** your mind to it
4 to give someone peace	**d** minds
5 to keep	**e** someone's mind
6 to ease	**f** something in mind
7 to be in two	**g** an open mind
8 to see something in	**h** mind

5 Complete the sentences with the correct form of the expressions from Exercise 4.

1 If I don't _____ , I'll never finish this presentation before the deadline.

2 Please _____ when applying for positions that due to the high demand we are not able to reply to unsuccessful candidates.

3 He was _____ about accepting the promotion; it was more responsibility but it would require relocating.

4 The high salaries of the board members and CEOs can _____ if you compare them to what a normal worker earns!

5 It can be difficult to _____ about the candidates; it's easy to be influenced by factors such as your first impressions and personal preferences.

6 It would _____ to know that you are going to be able to get the figures ready in time for my meeting.

7 If you can _____ the finish line _____ when you run a marathon it makes it easier.

8 He was leading a difficult project but working with a reliable team _____ .

WORDBUILDING Verbs with two past participles

6 Write the infinitive of the verb. Then match each past participle with its meaning (a or b).

1 *hang* hanged — **a** put a picture on the wall
     hung — **b** killed with a rope around the neck

2 _____ been — **a** travelled to and returned from
     gone — **b** being no longer present

3 _____ costed — **a** calculated the cost for accounts
     cost — **b** was priced at

4 _____ laid — **a** was horizontal at night
     lied — **b** not told the truth

5 _____ shined — **a** produced light
     shone — **b** polished (of metal or leather)

7 Complete the sentences with the correct past participle from Exercise 6.

1 It seemed as though I had barely _____ my head on the pillow when the alarm rang.

2 My grandfather has always _____ his shoes and pressed his shirts himself.

3 He's not here. He's _____ to head office to attend the training programme.

4 He had _____ to the Personnel Manager about his absence and so was given a warning about not telling the truth.

5 They have _____ all projects completed this year to help calculate the budgets for next year.

6 He's _____ to Italy several times but he still can't speak the language.

7 If I'd known how much it had _____ , I wouldn't have asked him to get it.

8 The last time a person in Britain was _____ was in 1964.

9 She had _____ her jacket on the back of the chair but only remembered it later.

10 The moon has _____ brighter than ever tonight. Is it a supermoon?

WORD FOCUS *eye*

8 Match the idioms (1–6) with the meanings (a–f).

1 to keep an eye on	**a** to see something without special equipment
2 to be up to one's eyes in	**b** to become aware of the truth of
3 to see something with the naked eye	**c** to be very attractive or unusual
4 to open one's eyes to	**d** to be overwhelmed by the quantity of
5 to be eye-catching	**e** to do something easily
6 to do something with your eyes shut	**f** to look after

9 Complete the sentences with the correct form of the idioms from Exercise 8.

1 Can you _____ the new intern until I get back and make sure she's got enough to do and answer any of her questions?

2 The company logo _____ really _____ . Everyone noticed it straight away.

3 On a clear day you can _____ the cathedral _____ from the top floor of the building.

4 I don't know anyone who isn't _____ work, do you?

5 He's driven that road so often he could almost _____ it _____ .

6 That documentary really _____ the issues for women in developing countries.

7.4 That doesn't seem possible

SPECULATING

1 Nicky didn't arrive at work today. Why might she be missing from the office? Write explanations using the prompts and the words in brackets.

1 I / she / holiday (expect) ☐
_____

2 I / she / training course (imagine) ☐
_____

3 She / ill (must) ☐
_____

4 One of her children / ill (might) ☐
_____

5 She / stuck in traffic (probably) ☐
_____

6 She / overslept (may) ☐
_____

2 🎧 2 6 Listen to a conversation about why Nicky isn't at work. Tick (✓) possible reasons in Exercise 1 that you hear and write the exact words of three additional speculations.

1 _____
2 _____
3 _____

3 🎧 2 7 Listen to the explanation and complete the sentences using the prompts in brackets.

1 She called us using someone else's phone so … (she / can't / her phone / with her)
_____
_____

2 There were no casualties so … (everyone / must / left the building / in time)
_____
_____

3 They couldn't re-enter the building so … (it / likely / serious fire)
_____
_____

4 She's suffering from shock so … (I / guess / need a day off)
_____
_____

5 They were up all night so … (the children / probably / tired)
_____
_____

6 The firemen … (bound / find cause / by now)
_____
_____

PRONUNCIATION Contraction with *have*

4 🎧 2 8 Do you think *have* is contracted or not in these sentences? Listen and check your answers.

1 They must *have / 've* been really worried.
2 How dreadful. They may *have / 've* had to leave quickly in the middle of the night.
3 They might *have / 've* been worried the fire would spread to their building.
4 I imagine they can't *have / 've* had much with them, just what they might *have / 've* grabbed.
5 Sounds lucky, the fire and smoke are likely to *have / 've* spread really fast.
6 I expect the boys would *have / 've* probably enjoyed watching the firemen, as long as everyone was safe.

5 🎧 2 9 Put the words in the correct order to make phrases for agreeing or disagreeing with a speculation. Use appropriate contractions. Then listen and check your answers.

1 be / right / can / not / that
_____

2 onto / think / you / I / something / there / are
_____

3 convinced / am / not / I / entirely
_____

4 certainly / way / that / looks / it
_____

5 does / that / at / all / likely / me / to / seem / not
_____

6 seems / that / a / explanation / likely
_____

WRITING Neutral reporting

6 Put the letters in the correct order to complete the sentences with neutral reporting words.

1 *deeporrytl* = said to be true by someone else

He _____ left two hours ago, but we've not heard from him.

2 *eleiveb* = have a strong feeling something is true

We _____ that dissatisfaction is the main reason for absenteeism.

3 *licma* = say something is true

She tried to _____ that her lateness was due to a train delay but it turned out to be untrue.

4 *plaarenpty* = it has been heard, but there's no evidence

_____ salaries are going to increase next year but at the moment it's just a rumour.

5 *aisd ot* = some people think it's true

Checking email just twice a day is _____ improve productivity at work.

6 *geaedlly* = it has been rumoured to be true

The CEO is _____ retiring earlier than planned, I heard on the grapevine.

7 *ecpualtions* = discussion of ideas

There is a lot of _____ about the reasons for his resignation. He needs to set the record straight.

8 *yb lal cunacots* = it's widely believed to be true

Working life is _____ becoming more, not less, stressful.

7 Read the article. Choose the correct options to complete the text.

[1]*Speculation / Believe* is mounting for the upcoming annual inter-departmental relay run. Each department elects a team of five to run the twenty-kilometre course, but, as tradition dictates, members of each team are not announced until the day of the race. A source close to the author [2]*said to / reportedly* witnessed the Research and Development department's team practising, which seemed to include the whole department. This [3]*claimed / is believed* to be either a tactic or a case of keeping as many options open as possible. The R&D department are [4]*speculation / by all accounts* strong contenders for winning, having finished in the top three for the last three years. The marketing team are [5]*said to / apparently* be this year's favourites due to the low average age and the high number of marathon runners in the department. The top management have [6]*allegedly / claimed* been keeping to a strict diet to better their chances. Kitchen staff [7]*claim / believe* to have removed all but the healthiest choices from the menus. Elsewhere, large mysterious boxes have arrived, [8]*apparently / said* containing exercise bicycles so department meetings can be conducted while improving fitness simultaneously. The countdown has started.

8 Read the report of the event and correct one mistake in each sentence.

1 The day of the race dawned with much excitement by each accounts.

_____

2 Management claiming to have been called away on business but managed to attend at the last minute.

_____

3 Kitchen staff alleged weren't competing at all and then surprised everyone by finishing third.

_____

4 The IT department, who are belief to dislike sport, walked much of the course with good humour.

_____

5 The Communications team are say to be generally unfit, but daily training paid off.

_____

6 As predicted, the winning team were R&D, despite much speculate as to who would actually run.

_____

9 Use the notes and the words in brackets to write another short report for the company magazine that will go to customers as well as staff.

1 Manufacturing companies not fit – trying reverse trend. / (reportedly)

Manufacturing companies are reportedly not the fittest but we're trying to reverse the trend.

2 When employees physically fit – positive effect business. (allegedly)

_____

3 Top management – this the reason start annual relay race five years ago. (quoted as saying)

_____

4 The race strengthens corporate identity, provides year-long entertainment, fun. (by all accounts)

_____

5 Tactics build throughout year – departments bond through training outside working hours. (speculation)

_____

6 Almost certain R&D department win every time, as this year. But some surprises in innovative tactics and other positions. (said)

_____

7 Total 250 employees, friends, family attend race summer party – weather, drinks and snacks provided. (apparently)

_____

8 Possibly highlight corporate year. (believe)

_____

YOUR IDEA

1 Read the paragraphs about *Using your imagination*. Match the paragraphs with the photographs (a, b, c).

1 My sister and I were little terrors, honestly. I'm not sure how Mum and Dad put up with us. We were always building things using our bed sheets. I remember one time we made this massive structure between our beds – we shared a bedroom, you see. We used our pillows and duvets to make walls. Then we would defend our 'fort' from everybody, including our parents! ☐

2 I think it's a phase that everyone goes through when they're young. You have wild dreams about what you're going to be when you grow up. I think it's a key thing for children to use their imagination like this and have crazy ambitions, however unlikely they are. My parents were great. They bought a load of dressing-up stuff for me. I would always put on an astronaut costume and pretend that I was going into space! ☐

3 I'm a big believer in the importance of being creative and imaginative. I think it's vital in order to develop fully as a human being. I get quite annoyed by the focus at school on children learning facts and preparing for tests. That's why I decided to set up a storytelling club for the children at my school. Every Wednesday, after the last lessons of the day, a group of teachers and students get together in one of the lounge areas we have – in the library or common room – and we tell each other stories. It's brilliant! ☐

a

b

c

2 Write notes about a time when you use, or have used, your imagination. If you can't think of something from your own experience, write about someone you know. Think of several ideas so you can choose the best one.

_____

_____

_____

_____

3 Choose one thing from your list. Answer these questions about it.

1 Where and when do/did you do it?

_____

2 Who do/did you do it with? Or is it something you do/did alone?

_____

3 How does/did it make you feel?

_____

4 Practise talking about using your imagination. Try to …
- include yourself in the talk as part of the story.
- use your own natural voice – imagine you are having a conversation with the audience.
- stay physically relaxed – move as you normally would but not so much that it is a distraction.

ORGANIZING YOUR PRESENTATION

5 Match the four steps of a presentation with two examples of useful language (a–h).

1 Greet and welcome the audience, and introduce yourself ☐☐

2 Tell a story or set a scene about using your imagination ☐☐

3 Talk about the benefits of using your imagination ☐☐

4 Thank the audience and finish the talk ☐☐

a Hi, I'm Tim Robson. It's wonderful you can all be here today.

b When I was younger, …

c It's so important for developing your creativity.

d I've always loved creating …

e Hello, and thanks for coming along. My name's Charlotte Smith.

f Thank you for taking the time to listen.

g There is proof that children who play make-believe games are better at problem solving.

h Thank you so much for listening today.

YOUR PRESENTATION

6 Read the useful language on the left and make notes for your presentation.

1 Greet and welcome the audience, and introduce yourself Hi, I'm … . It's wonderful you can all be here today. Hello, and thanks for joining me. My name's … Welcome, everyone. I'm …	
2 Tell a story or set a scene about using your imagination When I was younger, … I always used to … We would often …	
3 Talk about the benefits of using your imagination People say that … It's possible to … It's so important for … Using your imagination …	
4 Thank the audience and finish the talk Thank you so much … Thank you for …	

7 Film yourself giving your presentation or practise in front of a mirror. Give yourself marks out of ten for …

- including yourself in your talk. ☐ /10
- using your voice naturally. ☐ /10
- staying physically relaxed during your talk – not moving around too much. ☐ /10
- following the four steps in Exercise 6. ☐ /10
- using correct grammar. ☐ /10

8 Working together

8.1 Build a tower, build a team

TEDTALKS

It might be more appropriate to sketch a picture than to write a text about the designer and author, **TOM WUJEC**; he's such a visual thinker and communicator. He was born in Canada where he still lives and works. Although he now works in the fields of design and visual thinking, he originally studied Astronomy and Psychology at the University of Toronto. He worked first at McLaughlin Planetarium in Toronto as a producer, lecturer and writer. His next career step took him to the Royal Ontario Museum, where he was Creative Director and he designed and built interactive exhibits for the museum's diverse collection of fossils and dinosaurs, and modern discoveries. Wujec says that it was during his time at the museum that he really learned to think in images, although he'd been a student of visual thinking for many years. He now teaches these skills to others.

TED has played a key role in Tom Wujec's professional career since he attended his first TED conference in 1994. In addition to giving seven TED Talks, he's also been a visual artist and host at TED conferences, and he lists TED among his clients. He is the author of four books on design and creativity and is working on his fifth, *Wicked Problem Solving*. Currently, he's a fellow at Autodesk where he once designed and marketed their software and design products – one of which won an Academy Award. When asked in an interview what makes him tick, he said that he's a passionate learner, insatiably curious and loves to share ideas in a visual, tangible and persistent way.

Tom Wujec

CAREER PATHWAYS

1 Read the text. Answer the questions.

  1 Why does the writer suggest it could be appropriate to describe Tom Wujec's ideas pictorially?
  2 What might be seen as surprising about what he studied?
  3 What work led him to think visually?
  4 How has he been involved with TED?
  5 What was he working on at the time of this article?

TED PLAYLIST

2 Other TED speakers are interested in topics similar to Tom Wujec's TED Talk. Read the descriptions of the four TED Talks at the top of page 75. In your opinion, which is the best title for this playlist, a, b or c?

  a Forging new networks
  b Collaboration drives innovation
  c Making change happen faster

3 Complete the six-word summary (1–4) that corresponds to each talk in the TED playlist. Use these words.

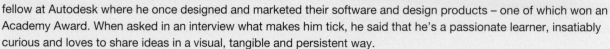

| collaboration | complex | create | origin |

  1 Coffee shops: _____ of new innovations.
  2 Leading innovation to _____ collective genius.
  3 Producing positive outcomes from close _____ .
  4 Making _____ systems work with checklists.

4 Match the verbs (1–5) with their collocates (a–e). Check your answers in the playlist descriptions.

  1 to come up with   a insights
  2 to gain   b connect in unexpected ways
  3 to urge people to   c a positive mindset
  4 to make a case for   d a checklist
  5 to devise / implement e new ideas

5 Which talk would you most like to see? Why? Watch the talk at TED.com.

Steven Johnson: Where good ideas come from

Steven Johnson examines how coffee houses may have been the hub of some of history's most significant innovations in science and technology. He uses fascinating examples to reveal that it is not a single 'Eureka moment', but a series of events and connections that contribute to making a breakthrough discovery. Johnson believes it's as important to share and connect new ideas as it is to come up with and protect them.

Linda Hill: How to manage for collective creativity

Linda Hill shares the insights she's gained from a decade's work observing creative processes at leading companies in twelve different industries. She's a business professor who uses ethnographical methods to study leadership in innovation. Using well-known companies as case studies, she presents surprising and paradoxical findings in skilful and memorable ways.

Kare Anderson: Be an opportunity maker

Kare Anderson is a columnist for *Forbes* who writes about research-based methods for, and benefits of, becoming more deeply connected. In her talk, she urges us all to connect in unexpected ways for the greater good. Using examples from her own experiences, she makes a powerful case for a positive collective mindset.

Atul Gawande: How do we heal medicine?

A surgeon and a public health journalist, Atul Gawande takes the question of 'How can we get good at doing what we do?' and answers it on many different levels. He explains how relatively simple changes can help us manage complex problems successfully. He describes innovations he has introduced in his own hospital, such as devising and implementing checklists for surgical teams, that have had a huge impact on the reduction of death rates.

AUTHENTIC LISTENING SKILLS
Understanding contrastive stress

6 🎧 2 10 You are going to hear a podcast in which a member of the *Keynote* team talks about Atul Gawande's TED Talk, *How do we heal medicine?* Listen to the extracts from the podcast. Underline the pairs of contrasting words or phrases that are stressed.

1 Gawande is able to take a step back from the detailed work of his job as a practising doctor to look at medicine as a whole.
2 He sets out to provide clarity to problems that show bewildering complexity.
3 … in 1970 the average hospital visit required care from two full-time clinicians. By the end of the twentieth century the number had risen to fifteen.
4 Gawande's message is an important one: medicine is broken but there are answers to its problems so it can be fixed.

LISTENING

7 🎧 2 11 Listen to the full podcast. Answer the questions.

1 What does the podcaster like about the way the information is presented?
2 According to Daniel, what does Gawande identify as the source(s) of complexity?
3 Which industries informed Gawande's solutions for managing complex systems?
4 What is Daniel's personal interest in medicine?

8 🎧 2 11 Try to complete the sentences from the podcast. Then listen again and check your answers.

1 Progress in medicine means _____ procedures and _____ drugs are available.
2 Three statistics show that the systems are failing: _____ heart patients and _____ stroke patients don't get appropriate care and _____ get sick while in hospital.
3 The three skills Gawande describes are: _____ , _____ and _____ .
4 Gawande discovered _____ when studying other high-risk industries.
5 When he implemented them in some hospitals, they _____ in every case and cut death rates by _____ .

VOCABULARY IN CONTEXT

9 Read the extracts from the podcast. Choose the correct meaning of the words in bold.

1 I like to see the **bigger picture** on …
   a whole situation ✓   b the visual aspects ☐
   c the facts ☐
2 … the number of **clinicians** required now and in the past …
   a doctors who do research ☐   b staff who work in pharmacies ☐   c doctors with patient contact ☐
3 In the next part of the talk, he outlines the **methodology** to find these solutions using three skills: …
   a principles used ☐   b medical philosophy ☐
   c personal beliefs ☐
4 … Gawande decided to look at other high-risk industries to see how they **tackled** complex systems.
   a observed ☐   b dealt with ✓   c forced ☐
5 … my daughter, who's eleven, was **diagnosed with** a rare genetic condition called cystic fibrosis.
   a identified as having ☐   b caught by ☐
   c developed ☐

GRAMMAR Cause and result

Teambuilding workshop

Our small team of six don't work together as well as we could, a recent audit revealed. We were rather surprised; we thought we were good at collaborating. As part of the audit recommendations, we all took part in a facilitated workshop which included various team-building activities. The first session involved ¹_____ *b* _____, which was to identify the strengths and weaknesses of our collaboration. The boss had a personal aim which was to participate and observe the team's iterative process in action while doing a task that had a clear outcome. Later we would identify some key issues that needed changing. Only time will tell whether the

²_____ *c* _____ will improve our overall collaboration and productivity. During the teambuilding workshop itself we worked inside and outside in various formations. Although some of the team, including myself, were initially quite sceptical, it built rapport and we enjoyed ³_____ *a* _____ in a competitive task. We were very motivated to be the winning team! The ensuing feedback session proved to be very enlightening and has helped us tighten our processes. We'll work towards eliminating steps we agree are no longer necessary and communicating more closely. I would recommend taking part in this workshop – it enabled us to focus on our work as a team and it was enjoyable.

1 Complete the text with the phrases (a–c).

   a achieving short-term targets
   b setting a clear goal
   c successful completion of targets and goals

2 Rewrite these sentences about the team-building event using the cause and result phrases in brackets.

   1 Our small team of six don't work together as well as we could, a recent audit revealed. (result in / revelation that)
     A recent audit _____ .

   2 As part of the audit recommendations, we all took part in a facilitated workshop. (to be the consequence of)
     Taking part in *facilitated workshop was the consequence of.*

3 The boss participated and later proposed changes in some key areas. (lead to / proposals) *a proposed*
   The boss's observations *led to changes ...*

4 Although some of us were initially quite sceptical, the workshop built rapport. (foster)
   Despite our *sceptism* .

5 The ensuing feedback session has helped us tighten our processes. (contribute to)
   The feedback session *contributed to us tightening our process*

6 We'll work towards communicating more closely. (bring about / communication)
   The workshop will *bring about* .

3 Choose the correct options to complete the sentences.

1 The team-building activity *was due to / brought about* a relaxed atmosphere and some fun.
2 The team with no manager won, which *caused / resulted from* some disappointment to management!
3 The tasks *are the result of / gave rise to* a useful context in which to assess collaboration.
4 An increased appreciation of everyone's contribution *stemmed from / brought about* the successful workshop.
5 Stronger rapport in the team *resulted in / resulted from* working and laughing together in the workshop.
6 A lack of communication *contributes to / arises from* some work tasks having to be done twice and others being neglected.
7 The facilitator *killed / fostered* better communication through debriefing and progress reporting.
8 Ultimately the workshop *resulted in / arose from* decisions to redefine working groups and optimize processes.

GRAMMAR EXTRA! *so / such … that +* clause

4 *So* and *such* are intensifiers used in combination with *that* to indicate a result. Write two sentence beginnings (use *so* in a and *such* in b). Keep the meaning the same. You may have to change or add some words.

1 (Bad storm) … the police and fire brigade were out dealing with fallen trees and flooding most of the night.
  a *The storm was so bad that*
  b *It was such a bad storm that*
2 (Cheap flights) … the New York trip has become considerably more realistic.
  a _____
  b _____
3 (Large order) … we'll have to employ some temporary staff to manage it.
  a _____
  b _____
4 (Good presentation) … he was promoted.
  a _____
  b _____
5 (Workshop a success) … she held an extra one.
  a _____
  b _____
6 (Travelling rush hour time-consuming activity) … the company started flexitime and home-working days to deal with it.
  a _____
  b _____
7 (Serious setback caused by IT problems) … they had to extend the project deadline by a week.
  a _____
  b _____

8 (Many complaints)… they had to remove the product from the shelves.
  a _____
  b _____
9 (Very popular product) … we had to increase orders.
  a _____
  b _____

PRONUNCIATION Voicing in final consonants

5 🎧 2 12 In each pair, underline where there's a shorter vowel sound before an unvoiced final consonant. Then listen and check your answers.

1 worksho**p**   workroo**m**
2 share**d**   shu**t**
3 lac**k**   la**g** behind
4 wor**k**   wor**d**

6 🎧 2 13 Listen and repeat. In each sentence underline the final consonant sound in bold that is voiced.

1 It was brought about by ba**d** manageme**nt**.
2 Plea**s**e cut u**p** your old credit card on receipt of your new one.
3 She asked me to co**m**e bac**k**.
4 He wasn't able to produ**c**e any I.**D**.

DICTATION

7 🎧 2 14 Listen to someone talking about a way to achieve big goals. Complete the paragraph.

When I have to achieve big goals, and _____

'eating an elephant model'. Creighton Abrams, a US army general, came up with it and, _____ .

The fact that the originator was in the army _____ .

Given the elephant's large size, the idea is that _____ .

Otherwise, reaching a big goal might seem unobtainable _____

Last year, before moving premises, we agreed to throw away any unwanted papers and files. _____

enormous task successfully was to deal with it bit by bit. _____

and cleared the way for the move. As Abrams said: 'When eating an elephant, take one bite at a time'.

READING

1 Are these statements true (T) or false (F)? Read the article and check.

1 Bhutan broke a World Record in 2001. ☐
2 Bhutan is a small country in the Himalayas. ☐
3 It's a well-known trekking destination. ☐
4 Football is the national sport in Bhutan. ☐

2 Read the article again and answer the questions.

1 What kinds of motivation are described?
2 What made the team one of the weakest in the world?
3 What did the players say about being bottom of the league?
4 How does the country restrict modern influences?
5 Why does Bhutan measure Gross National Happiness?
6 Why didn't they have a strong national team after the early 80s?

Motivating Bhutan's national **football team**

If you were coaching the players in a national football team that was bottom of the world league, how would you motivate them? Would you pay them bonuses for every goal? Or would you make everyone feel they had something to contribute? Do you believe in external or extrinsic motivators like money and fame, or in internal or intrinsic motivation coming from the task itself and wanting to do it well? Up until recently, Bhutan was bottom at place 209 in FIFA's ranking, with a reputation of being one of the weakest teams in the world. They are relatively new to the game, having only started playing internationally in 1982. Since then they have only won four times in 33 years. In 2000, they broke the Guinness World Record for the team with the most goals against them when a match against Kuwait resulted in a score of twenty-nil.

Bhutan's team captain Karma Shedrup Tshering is quoted as saying 'Everyone was talking about us being at the bottom but we didn't feel any pressure because you can only go one way from there and that's upwards.'

The word 'Bhutan' roughly translates as 'land of the thunder dragon', originating from the storms and landslides that are typical there. This small kingdom, a little bigger than Taiwan or Belgium, is situated in the eastern part of the Himalayas. The capital city Thimphu is a giddy-making 2,648 metres above sea level and this may be one reason why the team has never lost a football game at home.

Western and modern influences have been allowed into the country only slowly and in a controlled manner. Although Bhutan is a popular trekking destination, tourism is permitted exclusively through authorized package tours. Television and the Internet were not available there until 1999. Bhutan is the only country to measure happiness at a country level. 'Gross National Happiness' (GNH), a term coined by former king, Jigme Dorji Wangchuk, in 1972, aims to help people strike a balance between material and spiritual concerns.

Archery is the national sport but football has slowly grown in popularity, arriving with foreign teachers recruited into schools in the 1950s. In the early 80s, there was a strong national team but no players to succeed them once they had retired and, although the government supported football, there were other priorities to invest in, like health and education. Bhutan became a member of FIFA in 2000 and now receives some funding.

The team is ever optimistic despite the infamous game with Kuwait. The current national coach, Chokey Nima, was a player in that match and everyone there knows that nothing motivates quite like a beating like that. In March 2015, the team won two games against Sri Lanka in the qualifiers for the 2018 World Cup. The win moved them swiftly up the FIFA table to number 159. 'We kept our calm and let our football talk for us,' said Captain Karma Shedrup Tshering about the game.

3 Complete the sentences. Read the article again to check.

1 Playing football for fame and glory is an _____ motivator.

2 Thimphu is situated at a high altitude and can make people feel _____ .

3 The former king of Bhutan was the first to use the term Gross National Happiness – he _____ it.

4 _____ , Bhutan's national sport, involves firing arrows towards a target to score points.

5 The game against Kuwait has become _____ – well-known for being so bad.

4 🎧 2 15 Listen and circle the correct answers.

1 The bottom *eight / twelve* teams battle it out to qualify.

2 FIFA made *$30,000 / $300,000* available.

3 Thailand offered the use of their *football stadium / training camp*.

4 The team needed to get used to the *humidity / altitude*.

5 Tickets for the home game were *cheap / free*.

6 The winning goal was scored in the *nineteenth / ninetieth* minute.

VOCABULARY Teams and teamwork

5 Match the verbs (1–8) with the phrases (a–h).

1	to be	5 **a**	as a group
2	to do your	7 **b**	a team player
3	to go	1 **c**	part of things
4	to pull	6 **d**	a sense of belonging
5	to bond	3 **e**	the extra mile
6	to feel a	4 **f**	your weight
7	to have	8 **g**	the load
8	to share	2 **h**	fair share

6 Complete the sentences with the correct form of the expressions from Exercise 5.

1 To _____ you have to be good at working with others and work towards the same goals.

2 If any new players join, it's important to _____ as early as possible, and build good relationships both on and off the pitch.

3 Once new players have settled in and have _____ , the real training can begin.

4 Each member has to _____ but they also have to understand that players' roles may require that they contribute differently to the team effort.

5 To players, _____ may seem like different amounts for different people, but a skilful coach will smooth out any differences.

6 _____ means that individuals do what they can do best to reach the overall goal for the team. They contribute different skills.

7 The more the players are united and feel _____ , the better they can work together.

8 A team that is highly motivated will be willing to _____ and keep achieving greater things.

WORDBUILDING Noun formation

7 Rewrite each sentence replacing the word(s) in italics with a noun to make it sound more formal. You may have to add or change words to keep the sentence grammatical.

1 The department manager didn't *seem able* to motivate the team and needed support.
   The department manager *lacked the **ability** to motivate the team and needed support.*

2 The enjoyment of the game itself *motivated* the team to play well.
   The enjoyment of the game itself provided _____ .

3 When we *awarded* extra holiday as an incentive, it proved more effective than overtime payments.
   The_____ .

4 He *knew* a great deal about the background of the match.
   He had extensive background _____ .

5 The crowd enjoyed the *exciting* game and festive atmosphere.
   The crowd _____ .

6 Thimphu is an *inconvenient* city to travel to because of the mountains.
   The_____ .

7 The Thai team was *generous* about training, making competing possible.
   The Thai team's _____ .

8 The team was highly *committed* to winning throughout the game.
   The team's _____ .

WORD FOCUS *work*

8 Complete the phrasal verbs with these prepositions.

at	around	in	off	on	towards

1 The best way for me to work _____ stress is to go for a run.

2 We need to try and work _in___ a holiday theme for the next newsletter as it will be coming out in December.

3 It's not easy to work around his absence. It's a real setback at this stage.

4 I've worked _____ my French over the years but I still sound like a British man speaking schoolboy French.

5 At the moment the team is working _____ cutting costs in the department to present at the next management meeting.

6 We should both start working _____ an early retirement by saving more of our salaries each month.

9 Match the meanings a–f with the phrasal verbs (1–6) from Exercise 8.

a	include	☐	**d** accommodate ☐
b	practise	☐	**e** prepare for ☐
c	find ways to	☐	**f** get rid of ☐

8.4 If you'll just let me finish …

TAKING PART IN A MEETING

1 Put the words in the correct order to make phrases and decide if they are interrupting (I) or stopping interruption (S).

1 I / just / here / something / can / say? ☐ ☐
_____

2 just / saying / finish / what / could / I / I / was? ☐ ☐
_____

3 finish / me / if / 'll / let / you / … ☐ ☐
_____

4 interrupt, / hate / but / I / to / … ☐ ☐
_____

5 jump / dying / I / you're / know / to / but / in, / … ☐ ☐
I know you're dying to jump in, but.

6 but / sorry / interrupting, / for / … ☐ ☐
_____

7 just / you / say / before / can / continue, / I / … ☐ ☐
Before you continue, can I just …

8 if / finish / you'll / me / allow / to / … ☐ ☐

2 🎧2 **16** Listen to a meeting about a job rotation programme. Tick (✓) the phrases in Exercise 1 that you hear.

3 🎧2 **16** Listen again and write the phrase used to open the discussion and the one used to invite participation.

1 Opening a discussion _____
2 Inviting participation _____

4 🎧2 **17** Complete the sentences for wrapping up a meeting and inviting participation. Use these words. Then listen and check your answers.

| finish | thoughts | everything | take | continue |

1 What's your _____ on the benefits of changing departments?
2 Any _____ on the expanded programme?
3 Before you _____, can I just say thank you for all your help with this?
4 I think that's nearly _____ .
5 I think we can _____ there for today.

PRONUNCIATION Emphasizing the main focus in the sentence

5 🎧2 **18** Underline the main stress in each sentence depending on the meaning in brackets. Then listen and check your answers.

1 I'd like to start the discussion by asking if everyone's read the information sent around. (This is how we'll begin the meeting.)
2 It'll probably make a difference to the discussion. (There will be more to talk about if people have done the preparation.)
3 There will be a chance for everyone to have their say. (No one will be left out)
4 You mean with hindsight it was more useful than when you were actually doing it? (After the event it took on more meaning.)
5 It could be a great retention tool, as well as promoting innovation. (A way to keep employees in the company.)
6 I would like us all to suggest one or two employees to put forward and answer the questions. (It's something I think is important.)

WRITING Debriefing questionnaire

6 Put the topics for a debriefing questionnaire in the correct order.

a The biggest challenge ☐
b Suggested changes for next project ☐
c Project summary ☐
d Successes and reasons for these ☐
e The biggest learning outcome ☐

7 Read the linking devices. Tick (✓) the ones that are used to express result.

1 as a result of ☐
2 also ☐
3 however ☐
4 overall ☐
5 because ☐
6 as a consequence ☐
7 thanks to ☐

8 Complete the debriefing questionnaire with the linking devices from Exercise 7. More than one option is sometimes possible.

> **Briefly summarize your rotation assignment.**
> I went to the London office for four weeks from Madrid, for a project and to improve links between the two offices. I was able to contribute to processes and write documents in Spanish and in English. I was
> 1 _____ able to improve my English.
>
> **What contributed to the assignment's success?**
> 2 _____ the fact that the organization was so good, I didn't have to spend time finding accommodation or finding my feet. This was partly
> 3 _____ the 'buddy scheme' that was set up beforehand – I had contact with my buddy before I arrived and was looked after by them during my visit.
>
> **What was the biggest challenge?**
> Certainly the cultural differences were the biggest challenge. 4 _____, they made the assignment very interesting.
>
> **What was most valuable for your own development and why?**
> I had thought that, apart from language, European countries were very similar. I actually found there were a lot of differences in the way our two countries approach things. 5 _____ of these differences, I'll probably take a different approach in future.
> 6 _____, I'm going to pass on what I've learned to my colleagues.
>
> **What could be improved about the programme and why?**
> 7 _____, I'm grateful to have taken part in the programme. I would say that more employees should be encouraged to participate; it shouldn't just be for young people like myself.

9 Complete the debriefing questionnaire using the model from Exercise 8, the notes below and suitable linking devices.

1 Briefly summarize your rotation assignment.

a I went to Berlin for six weeks / only colleague available
I went to Berlin for six weeks because I was the only colleague available.

b short notice / urgent IT project

_____

c not well prepared / fix the problem

_____

2 What contributed to the assignment's success?

a IT systems identical / 'speak' common language

_____

b built good relationships

_____

3 What was the biggest challenge?

a counterparts not speak good English / I not speak good German

_____

b understanding German / confusing experiences

_____

c improved / understanding European colleagues

_____

4 What was most valuable for your own development and why?

a learning / simplify message / avoid misunderstandings

_____

5 What could be improved about the programme and why?

a recommend / basic language course

_____

The informal email you will read in Exercise 2 is in answer to the following exam question.

From: roman@crgs.com

To: marta@mailbox.cz

Subject: Your conference

Hi Marta,

It was great to hear from you.

How did the conference go in the end? I know you were really looking forward to it. Do you feel like you learned anything new? Was it worth it?

Let me know how it went,

Roman

Write your informal email in **220–260 words** in an appropriate style.

IDEAS

1 Tick (✓) the things you would expect to see in the informal email.

a advice for how to organize a conference ☐
b an informal greeting ☐
c information about Marta's job ☐
d a reference to Roman's previous email ☐
e a sign-off message, encouraging the reader to reply ☐
f a general statement about how the conference went ☐
g descriptions of specific events from the conference ☐

MODEL

2 Read the informal email. Match the five sections with a description (a–g) from Exercise 1.

1 ☐ 2 ☐ 3 ☐ 4 ☐ 5 ☐

3 Read the email again. Are these statements true (T) or false (F)?

1 The conference lived up to Marta's expectations. ☐
2 The first part of the day taught Marta a lot about the other conference attendees. ☐
3 The person organizing the conference didn't realize when things weren't going to plan. ☐
4 Marta felt her presentation went smoothly. ☐
5 Marta and the other attendees didn't feel comfortable doing the final activity. ☐

| TO: | roman@crgs.com | FROM: | marta@mailbox.cz |
| SUBJECT: | Conference | | |

¹Hi Roman,

²Thanks for your message.

³The conference was a total disaster from start to finish. My colleagues and I figured it would be a great break from the day to day of the office, as it had been in previous years, but we ended up being disappointed.

⁴It started off with a 'getting to know you' activity, but we've been going to these one-day conferences for five years already and the same people are there every time! The new facilitator, the woman who was running the whole thing this time round, didn't notice that we already knew each other – she was very unobservant.

Another thing I had to do was present one of the projects we've been working on in our office. It was meant to be inspiring and motivating, but it was just before lunch and everyone clearly wanted to have a break. I was feeling nervous too, so I tried to finish as fast as possible. I couldn't wait to get it over with!

To finish the day off, we had to reflect on everything we'd learned from the conference and comment on the best and worst sessions we'd seen during the day. Nobody wanted to say anything bad about the sessions, because we all know each other. It turned out to be a complete waste of time.

All in all, I'd say we'd have been better off just staying in the office!

⁵I'd be interested to hear if you've ever been to a conference this bad. I hope they're not that common!

Marta

USEFUL LANGUAGE

4 Replace part of each sentence from the negative email with one of these positive phrases, so that it means the opposite.

do it all again   a huge success   pleasantly surprised
it was worth every penny   the best way we could have
spent our day

1 It was *a total disaster* from start to finish. *a huge success*
2 We ended up being really disappointed. _____
3 We couldn't wait to get it over with. _____
4 It turned out to be a complete waste of time.

_____

5 All in all, I'd say we'd have been better off saving our money. _____

5 Match the phrases (a–o) with the categories (1–5).

1 Referring to the reader
2 Summarizing the experience
3 Describing how the experience started
4 Describing later parts of the experience
5 Encouraging the reader to reply

a a very memorable experience ☐
b First up, ☐
c How's everything with you? ☐
d I'd love to hear from you. ☐
e It was great to get your message! ☐
f It was very interesting at first ☐
g Let me know what you think. ☐
h Looking forward to hearing from you soon. ☐
i one of the worst days of my life ☐
j so it was a pleasant surprise when ☐
k The first thing I want to tell you about is ☐
l the holiday of a lifetime ☐
m Then it was on to ☐
n We ended up ☐
o What's up with you? ☐

6 Rewrite the more formal phrases from an email with ones from Exercise 5.

1 I'm very grateful that you sent me an email to tell me your news.

_____

2 I've just had a particularly good holiday in Thailand.

_____

3 I would like to begin by describing the hotels we stayed in.

_____

4 We were satisfied when we found out that all our food and drink was included in the price – great value for money!

_____

5 Afterwards we went to Bangkok for a week.

_____

6 I'd love to take you to Thailand one day. Could you tell me if that would interest you?

_____

7 Complete the collocations (1–6) with these adjectives. Are they positive (P) or negative (N) descriptions?

breathtaking (the) ideal	dreadful (a) rewarding	(with) disastrous welcoming

1 _____ views ☐   4 _____ results ☐
2 _____ people ☐   5 _____ weather ☐
3 _____ place ☐   6 _____ experience ☐

PLANNING

You will answer the following question.

TO:	FROM:

SUBJECT: Great photos!

Hi there,

I've just seen your photos. Have you been away? Where did you go? What did you do? Did you have a good time? Tell me all about it!

Sally

8 Plan your informal email. Write notes to answer these questions. Don't write full sentences yet.

1 Where will you write about? What adjectives/adverbs can you use to describe it?
2 What specific event(s) will you describe? What adjectives/adverbs can you use to describe it/them?
3 How will you summarize the experience?

WRITING

9 Write an informal email to reply to the message in Exercise 8. In your email you should:

• open and close the email in a friendly way
• summarize the experience briefly so the reader knows what to expect
• write more specifically about the place you went to and the things you did
• use vivid, descriptive language to make it clear whether you enjoyed it or not

Write **220–260 words** in an appropriate style.

ANALYSIS

10 Check your informal email. Answer the questions.

• **Content:** Does the informal email describe the place you went to and the things you did? Is it 220 to 260 words long?
• **Communicative achievement:** Is it written in an informal, friendly style? Is the text sufficiently descriptive? Is it clear to the reader whether you enjoyed the experience or not?
• **Organization:** Is the email logically organized? Are the ideas connected?
• **Language:** Does it use correct grammar and vocabulary? Is a good range of structures used?

9 Stress and relaxation

9.1 All it takes is 10 mindful minutes

TEDTALKS

ANDY PUDDICOMBE was born in 1972, raised in Bristol, England, and first discovered meditation and what it could do for his mind aged eleven. Later, he lost several close friends in a freak accident and the stress related to this led him to leave university and embrace meditation full time. From 1994 to 2004, he travelled to retreats and monasteries in Asia, Russia and Australia, studying first as a lay person, and later, after he was ordained, as a Tibetan Buddhist monk. He was a dedicated teacher and, once he'd mastered techniques himself – through up to eighteen hours of meditation a day over ten years — he worked 'to demystify meditation for a secular audience'.

After he decided to leave monastic life in 2004, he used his interest in juggling to study for a degree in circus arts in London. He also became a mindfulness consultant and set up a meditation practice. One of the people he introduced to meditation later became his business partner. This was Rich Pierson, a marketing and brand expert with whom he created and launched *Headspace* in 2010. 'We both thought, how could we present meditation in a way that our friends would genuinely give it a try?' says Puddicombe. The mission is to help create a happier, healthier world through mindfulness by teaching the skills of meditation. The *Headspace* book was published in 2011 and the app in 2012. Puddicombe has also written for and appeared in the media. Today the *Headspace* business is worth an estimated £25 million and has one million registered users. Every paid subscription triggers a donation so, rather like karma, when you get some headspace yourself, you also give some to someone else in need of headspace.

Andy Puddicombe

CAREER PATHWAYS

1 Read the text. Answer the questions.

1. Why did Andy Puddicombe drop out of university?
2. What qualifications has he gained in life?
3. What skills from each partner contribute to the business success of *Headspace*?
4. What key question helped the pair develop the concept of the business?
5. What do they aim to achieve with *Headspace*?

TED PLAYLIST

2 Other TED speakers are interested in topics similar to Andy Puddicombe's TED Talk. Read the descriptions of four TED Talks at the top of page 85. In your opinion, which is the best title for this playlist, a, b or c?

a. Finding happiness through seeking pleasure
b. Finding happiness through increasing mindfulness
c. Finding happiness through confidence building

3 Complete the six-word summary (1–4) that corresponds to each talk in the TED playlist. Use these words.

curing	happy	living	valuable

1. From hectic _living_ to finding peace.
2. Every moment is a _valuable_ opportunity.
3. _Curing_ crime's distorted mind with meditation.
4. Wandering minds don't make us _happy_.

4 Match the verbs (1–5) with their collocates (a–e). Check your answers in the playlist descriptions.

1 to gain	2 a advantage of
2 to take	5 b on the present
3 to transform	4 c one of the toughest prisons
4 to track	3 d people's state of mind
5 to focus	1 e incredible insights and pleasure

5 Which talk would you most like to see? Why? Watch the talk at TED.com.

▶ **Pico Iyer: The art of stillness**

Pico Iyer is a prolific traveller and travel writer. In his calm and lyrical talk he goes on a more inward journey away from the hustle and bustle of everyday life. He tells us with quiet confidence of the incredible insights and pleasure we can gain from being still and how this emptiness enables us to escape the demands of the modern world and process our thoughts.

▶ **David Steindl-Rast: Want to be happy? Be grateful**

Brother David Steindl-Rast, a monk and interfaith scholar, has a recipe for being happy which involves stopping, appreciating and being grateful. In this way, he counsels, we can ensure we fully contemplate and take advantage of the chances we're presented with in life, before they pass us by. In his contemplative talk he also reminds us that while we all seek happiness outside ourselves, it is we who ultimately create it through our own gratitude.

▶ **Kiran Bedi: A police chief with a difference**

Kiran Bedi is a trailblazer who became India's first and highest-ranking female police officer. Before that she ran and transformed one of the country's toughest prisons into a centre for learning and meditation. In her straight-talking and down-to-earth presentation, she shares her philosophy of '90:10' with us: 90 per cent of what happens to us is our own creation and it's only the remaining ten per cent that is down to fate or nature.

▶ **Matt Killingsworth: Want to be happier? Stay in the moment**

Matt Killingsworth is a researcher who gathers data on when we are happy or unhappy, using an app he built to track people's state of mind. In his talk full of data revelations, he shows us that we are happiest when we are focused on the present – but that our minds stray off topic nearly half of all our waking hours.

AUTHENTIC LISTENING SKILLS
Understanding mid-sentence changes in direction

6 **⌒2 19** You are going to hear a podcast in which a member of the *Keynote* team talks about Matt Killingsworth's TED Talk, *Want to be happier? Stay in the moment*. Listen and complete the sentences.

1 This talk was of interest to – _____ _____ because I try to practise mindfulness in my daily life.
2 His main subject is happiness, _____ _____.
3 That is the paradox of happiness, what looked like it should bring – _____ – doesn't always.

LISTENING

7 **⌒2 20** Listen to the full podcast. Answer the questions.

1 Why was Helen drawn to the talk by Matt Killingsworth?
2 According to the podcaster, what does Killingsworth mean by the paradox of happiness?
3 What was Helen's specific question?
4 Which data might help Helen answer her question?

8 **⌒2 20** Listen again. Are these statements true (T) or false (F)?

1 Matt Killingsworth collected the data using an app. ☐
2 He analyzed 15,000 reports from 650 people. ☐
3 Mind wandering during unpopular tasks improves happiness levels. ☐
4 The podcaster finds driving makes her prone to mind wandering. ☐
5 Helen feels that her happiness can't impact on other people. ☐

VOCABULARY IN CONTEXT

9 Read the extracts from the podcast. Choose the correct meaning of the words in bold.

1 His presentation style and way of talking **emanated** a distinct scientific feel ...
   a gave ☑
   b tried to contain ☐
   c hid ☐
2 What interested me particularly about the talk was what he said about staying in the moment and **wandering** minds.
   a uninteresting ☐
   b unfocused ☑
   c walking ☐
3 His research with the tracking app 'Trackyourhappiness .org' has revealed that mind wandering is **ubiquitous**.
   a rare ☐
   b dangerous ☐
   c widespread ☑
4 Matt Killingsworth analyzed data from 650,000 real-time reports from 15,000 people **hailing from** 80 countries ...
   a working in ☐
   b coming from ☑
   c describing ☐
5 Driving is an activity where I am most **distracted**, so I'm going to be very conscious of staying present.
   a unable to concentrate ☑
   b busy ☐
   c focused ☐

9.2 Even holidays are stressful

GRAMMAR Intensifying adverbs

1 Choose the correct options to complete the text.

The Black-hole Château

The château is ¹*utterly / exquisitely / totally* located in ² *beautifully / fully / totally* kept gardens and extensive wooded grounds. The spacious rooms are ³ *well / magnificently / extremely* comfortable, ⁴ *tastefully / absolutely / utterly* furnished and most ⁵ *fully / importantly / well* are ⁶ *tastefully / completely / well* quiet. The entire complex is ⁷ *extremely / fully / exquisitely* accessible for wheelchair users and all staff speak French, German and English.

At the Black-hole Château we believe that holiday breaks are to be savoured and should be ⁸ *completely / beautifully / tastefully* stress free. Your holiday is ⁹ *well / beautifully / utterly* earned and we aim to allow you every opportunity to unwind and recharge your batteries. Black-hole Château is ¹⁰ *totally / beautifully / importantly* cut off from the outside world. There are no televisions, computers or other screens on the premises and our slogan is 'slow food, slow stay and slow down'.

2 Answer the questions. Use the prompts and at least two adverbs in each answer.

absolutely (x2)	beautifully (x2)	completely
exquisitely	totally (x2)	

1 What's the hotel's unique selling point (USP)? (device free / peaceful)

_____

2 What activities can be enjoyed at the château? (walking or riding in traffic free / quiet surroundings)

quite surrounding.

_____

3 Where else can guests relax? (modern spa and pool complex / comfortable sofas and seats inside and outside)

_____

4 How should holidays be according to the brochure? (relaxing / perfect)

_____

3 Complete the sentences about the hotel with the correct adverb.

1 Our stay was *extremely / such* relaxing in every way. ✓

2 We felt *completely / beautifully* rejuvenated when we returned. ✓

3 Throughout our stay we *barely / always* saw or spoke to any of the other guests. ✓

4 Every meal was *freshly / incredibly* cooked to order. ✓

5 A substantial amount of produce is *locally / so* sourced. ✓

6 *Utterly, / Amazingly,* I didn't miss the technology I thought I couldn't live without. ✓

7 *Intelligently / Expertly* trained riding and golfing coaches made learning fun. ✓

8 All amenities were also *completely / very* wheelchair accessible, I was happy to find. ✓

4 Match the adverbs (1–5) with the adjectives (a–e) to make common combinations.

1 absolutely   3 **a** sociable
2 blissfully   4 **b** growing
3 naturally   5 **c** busy
4 rapidly   1 **d** clear
5 horribly   2 **e** happy

5 Use the adverb-adjective combinations from Exercise 4 to complete the sentences.

1 After a wonderful week we reluctantly said goodbye and returned to our *horribly busy* lives.

2 We don't want any more misunderstandings. Is that *absolutely clear*?

3 Being *naturally sociable* makes her the perfect choice to work with customers.

4 Our *rapidly growing* international reputation is down to word-of-mouth.

5 We notice how people arrive very stressed and leave *blissfully happy*.

PRONUNCIATION Stress with intensifying adverbs

6 🎧 **2 21** Underline the words you think will be stressed. Then listen and check your answers.

1 Although he was nervous, he delivered the presentation incredibly calmly.

2 After the sales team had used it for a year, it was utterly ruined.

3 He learned the skills fantastically quickly.

4 The spare parts are readily available in most electronics stores.

5 We discovered this place accidentally on the way back last year.

GRAMMAR EXTRA! Time expressions

7 Complete the sentences with these time expressions. Use the context to help.

already	finally	just	last	now
recently	tomorrow	yesterday	when	while

1 I've only _____ met him.

2 I saw him _____ I was waiting for the train.

3 I haven't spoken to him _____. The last time was nearly three weeks ago.

4 I phoned him _____ but he wasn't at home.

5 I'm meeting him for coffee _____.

6 I'm looking at him _____. He's sitting in the corner.

7 _____ I see him, I'll tell him you're looking for him.

8 I _____ saw him a month ago.

9 After spending nearly an hour looking for him, I _____ found him waiting at reception.

10 I've _____ seen him twice today.

DICTATION

8 🎧 **2 22** Listen and complete the paragraph.

_____ – both medical doctors – who travel every year to a different destination. _____, but take a busman's holiday where they offer their medical expertise in remote places to people in need. Before leaving _____ remove any evidence of wealth and privilege. They travel with an organization and, _____ the victims of natural disasters. _____ and arrive back eager to explain how much they have gained from the whole experience and the kindness of strangers.

READING

1 Look at the title of the article. Then complete these phrases about humour with the correct preposition/particle.

    1 It's important to be able to laugh _____ yourself.

    2 At the time it wasn't funny, but afterwards we had a good laugh _____ it.

    3 Often I chat and joke _____ colleagues about our work.

    4 It's such a funny book. It made me laugh _____ loud.

2 Read the article and answer the questions.

    1 Who is the advice in the article aimed at?

    2 Is there a solid scientific basis for the advice?

    3 What does the writer suggest we should joke about?

3 Read the article again. Would the author definitely (D), probably (P) or almost certainly not (N) agree with these statements?

    1 Laughing is a suitable response to any kind of stress.

    2 Laughing is a natural way to relieve stress.

    3 Stress makes us pessimistic.

    4 Laughing makes people feel good about themselves.

    5 Employers don't mean work to be fun.

    6 Looking at non-work related websites at work is OK.

    7 Never take yourself too seriously.

    8 Don't worry about offending others when you make a joke.

Laugh in the face of stress

Now, don't get the wrong idea from the title of this article. I don't want to belittle your problems or to suggest there are times when stress isn't justified: times of financial worries or health concerns, times of loss or heartache. I just want to offer help with the type of stress that most of us live with daily, and which, joking aside, is the cause of more heart-related conditions in the USA than anything else: and that's work-related stress. Because most work is just organized stress. Deadlines, targets and critical meetings weigh heavily on us, increasing the pressure until it becomes overwhelming. Yet we all possess an in-built coping mechanism, a valve that allows us to release that pressure and rebalance ourselves. It's called the ability to laugh and if you're not exercising it, you're missing an important trick.

The physiological benefits of laughter are well-documented. The muscles stop tensing, blood pressure drops, the blood gets more oxygen, and the brain releases endorphins, the body's natural pain killers. Psychologically, our mood improves and we break out of the cycle of negative thoughts. We start to think more positively about things, including ourselves – several studies have shown that laughter boosts self-esteem. They have also shown that after a good laugh, people begin to think more clearly and more open-mindedly. So how do you build humour into your working day?

Look for the ridiculous in seemingly difficult situations. Of course you're going to take your work seriously, but don't take it too seriously. At a board meeting our chairman announced that it was nothing to get too worried about, but some big cuts were going to have to be made in the company. Everyone looked at each other, all thinking the same thing – 'Is it going to be my department?'. Then one colleague broke the tension by pointing to a sign on the fire exit door that said 'This door is alarmed' and said, 'I don't know about the rest of you, but the door's certainly worried'.

Allow yourself light-hearted breaks from work in the day to chat and joke with colleagues. Take time out to read a funny article or watch a YouTube clip. Something that just makes you smile is as good as something that makes you laugh out loud.

Laugh at yourself at least as often as you make jokes about anything else. Someone I work with, who is often criticized for changing his mind, used this Groucho Marx quote when someone disagreed with him 'Well, those are my principles and if you don't like them ... I've got others'.

Try to defuse tense situations for others. For example, when a colleague says, 'I'm going to lose my job if I don't make my targets this month', ask them if you can have their desk by the window when they're gone.

Too many of us wait, weeks or months at times, for stress to pass before we allow ourselves to look back at a situation with humour. But that doesn't actually cure the stress. You need to lighten up now. Try it – it will do wonders for your blood pressure.

4 Read the words and phrases (1–8). Find a phrase in the article that means the same.

1 Don't misunderstand me (para 1)
Don't get the wrong idea

2 seriously (para 1) _____

3 you're not taking advantage of a useful solution (para 1)
_____

4 written about a lot (para 2) _____

5 stop doing the same thing again and again (para 2)
_____

6 don't worry about it too much (para 3) _____

7 Have a break and … (para 4) _____

8 don't be so serious (para 7) _____

VOCABULARY Idioms related to the body

5 Match the body idioms (1–8) with the meanings (a–h).

1 to be up to your eyeballs   **a** to anger you
2 to keep your chin up   **b** to enjoy yourself without inhibitions
3 to make your blood boil   **c** to tell someone how you feel
4 to get cold feet   **d** to have a lot to do
5 to let your hair down   **e** to be an annoyance
6 to get something off your chest   **f** to be a relief
7 to be a pain in the neck   **g** to stay positive
8 to be a weight off your shoulders   **h** to lose courage at the last moment

6 Use the correct form of the body idioms (1–8) from Exercise 5 to complete the sentences.

1 He had prepared the talk very well, but on the day of the presentation he *got cold feet*

2 When I think about how hard you've worked and how badly they've treated you it *makes my blood boil.*

3 Sorry I can't help you this week. I'm *up to my eyeballs* with work.

4 I'm trying to *keep my chin up* but that's the fourth rejection I've had in a row.

5 I'm sorry you have to rewrite the article or at least cut it down. It's *a pain in the neck* I know, but the magazine insists that it can't be over 300 words.

6 Sorry to bore you about my troubles at work. I just had to *something off my chest*

7 At the end of a long year's training and participating in competitions, she can now finally go out and *let her hair down.*

8 Paying the final instalment on the car last week *was a weight off your shoulders.* I'll actually have a bit of spare cash now.

WORDBUILDING -ing adjectives

7 Look at the examples of -ing adjectives then match the -ing adjectives (1–7) with the effects (a–g).

1 empowering ☐   3 devastating ☐
2 thrilling ☐   4 reassuring ☐

5 off-putting ☐   7 puzzling ☐
6 touching ☐

a makes you feel very excited
b helps you to feel everything is OK
c makes you feel sad or sentimental
d makes you feel everything is ruined and hopeless
e makes you feel confused
f makes you feel you can succeed at something by yourself
g stops you wanting to do something

8 Choose the correct intensifying adverb to go with each adjective.

1 The government's decision to go ahead with the building of the dam was *very / quite* devastating for the local community.

2 I find it *utterly / very* puzzling that they should want to move house when they have everything they want here.

3 Watching him eat the whole crab with his hands was *awkwardly / acutely* off-putting.

4 Having an experienced guide in the mountains was *extremely / exceptionally* reassuring.

5 I cried almost all the way through the film. It was *deeply / relatively* moving.

6 It's a(n) *very / overly* empowering training course. I'd strongly recommend it.

7 The amount of work I have to do at the moment is *totally / carefully* overwhelming.

8 The zip-wire ride is *absolutely / nicely* thrilling. You reach speeds of up to 100 kph.

WORD FOCUS live

9 Look at the phrasal verb with *live* in the article (para 1). Then match the phrasal verbs with *live* (1–6) with the phrases (a–f) that they collocate with.

1 to live on   **a** everyone's expectations
2 to live through   **b** the shame of coming last
3 to live for   **c** just a few dollars a day
4 to live with   **d** difficult times
5 to live down   **e** the weekend
6 to live up to   **f** my decision

10 Complete the sentences with the phrasal verbs (1–6) from Exercise 9. Use the correct form.

1 In the war they _____ a great deal of hardship.

2 I don't think I will ever _____ the embarrassment of having to sing in front of 200 people.

3 She feels a lot of pressure to _____ the achievements of her elder sister.

4 She _____ her work. It's the thing that she enjoys above everything else.

5 We weren't good enough and we're just going to have to _____ that fact.

6 After we've paid all the bills, we have hardly anything left to _____ .

9.4 Have you got a minute?

DEALING WITH AWKWARD SITUATIONS

1 🎧 **2** **23** Complete the conversation. Then listen and check your answers.

Y: Hedvig. Have ¹ _____ ?
H: Yes, OK, let me just finish this sentence ... Yep. What can ² _____ ?
Y: There's something ³ _____ .
H: OK. What is it, Yassin?
Y: Well, ⁴ _____ , I think I've opened an email with a virus or something. I'm not sure what to do.
H: Oh, dear. That's a ⁵ _____ . Well, we'll have to alert IT straightaway.
Y: You ⁶ _____ contact them for me, could you? I feel so stupid.
H: I ⁷ _____ , but I'm afraid I can't. You'll have to deal with it as they'll have questions about the email, etc. I'll put you through ...

2 🎧 **2** **24** Complete the conversation with phrases a–g so that it means the same as the conversation in Exercise 1. Then listen and check your answers.

a Unfortunately
b Could I have a word
c I've got a confession to make
d I don't suppose
e What's on your mind
f there's a slight problem with
g That's a bit of a pain

Y: Hedvig.¹ _____ ?
H: Yes, OK, let me just finish this sentence ... Yep.
  ² _____ ?
Y: ³ _____ .
H: OK. What is it, Yassin?
Y: Well, ⁴ _____ an email I've opened with a virus or something. I'm not sure what to do.
H: Oh, dear. ⁵ _____ . We'll have to alert IT.
Y: ⁶ _____ you could contact them for me, could you? I feel so stupid.
H: ⁷ _____ , I can't. You'll have to deal with it as they'll have questions about the email, etc. I'll put you through ...

3 Complete the phrases or questions for each function (1–4). Use the prompts to help you.

1 Starting a conversation:
  a (sorry / if / have / moment)
  _____

2 Raising an awkward topic:
  a (have / apologize)
  _____

3 Asking a favour:
  a (there / any)
  _____

  b (have / favour / ask)
  _____

4 Responses:
  a (shame / understand)
  _____

  b (worry / matter)
  _____

PRONUNCIATION Polite and assertive intonation

4 🎧 **2 25** Listen to two versions of each sentence. Decide which version (a or b) is polite (P) and which is assertive (A).

		a	b
1	Could I have a word?	☐	☐
2	What's on your mind?	☐	☐
3	I have a favour to ask.	☐	☐
4	Is there any way … ?	☐	☐
5	Actually, that's a bit awkward.	☐	☐
6	Don't worry. It's not important.	☐	☐

WRITING SKILL Reporting verbs

5 Match the reporting verbs (1–8) with a more informal equivalent (a–h).

1	admitted	**a**	accepted
2	denied	**b**	encouraged
3	acknowledged	**c**	said … wasn't true
4	proposed	**d**	claimed
5	urged	**e**	said no to
6	alleged	**f**	said yes to
7	agreed to	**g**	agreed … was true
8	refused	**h**	suggested

6 Correct one mistake in each sentence of the report.

1 This report details the oversight the store claiming to be the reason for not executing policy.

2 It was allegedly that the purchasing department hadn't ordered sufficient tablets.

3 But the purchasing department denied make a mistake.

4 The error was admitted for the store manager and traced to a mistake in an email that had been hastily written.

5 He acknowledged that the mistake and apologized.

6 It has since been propose that tablets will be bought locally.

7 The board has agreed of the higher costs.

8 All managers urge to check substantial orders carefully.

7 Choose the correct reporting verbs to complete the minutes of the meeting.

Present: James (C), Angie, Mia, Xavier
Apologies: Betty and Alastair

A meeting regarding recent problems with a key client was called. The team [1]*acknowledged / claimed* the need to discuss sensitive issues openly to avoid repeating any mistakes in the future. Xavier [2]*accepted / admitted* to having forgotten to add an update to the existing order prior to his holiday. Angie [3]*accused / urged* Xavier of being careless and reminded him of a similar situation the previous year. Xavier [4]*denied / insisted* being careless but apologized for causing problems and [5]*suggested / alleged* using checklists in future to increase the accuracy of information being gathered. Mia [6]*refused / insisted* that there were enough steps in the process without adding more and concluded that working closer together was the only solution. James collected concrete ideas as to how this was to be done and [7]*agreed / urged* to book a training session to improve communication.

8 Complete the minutes of a meeting about how email is used in an office. Use the prompts.

1 The team (acknowledge / not / always / answer emails / quickly enough)

2 They (discuss / briefly / acceptable / agree / reply customers / within twenty-four hours)

3 It (claim / emails / more time / information gathering)

4 It (propose / short email / update / contact concerned)

5 Two members (allege / see / no system / who to copy in)

6 They (urge / look / today's emails / as examples)

7 Several members (admit / copying in / too many)

8 All (ask / monitor / reduce recipients / if possible)

YOUR IDEA

1 Read the paragraphs about developing skills in different ways. Match the paragraphs with the summaries (a, b, c).

1 Since I started working here, I've learned a lot of things. I've had to work out how to use specialist software, like image-editing programs and presentation packages. I've had the chance to develop my public-speaking skills through delivering staff training sessions. I work in quite a large department, so it's common for us to be grouped into teams for particular projects. That means having to work as part of a team, negotiating your role within the group, organizing tasks as necessary – dealing with different personalities can be a hard thing to do. It's quite a skill to have to be able to get on with people in a work setting, if you ask me. ☐

2 Lots of people don't realize the skills they use every day. I mean, for example, you might think that you don't know very much or there isn't very much you can do. I'd get people to think about what they do every week or even every day. Do you do the shopping? That means you have to know how to manage money and you might be good at budgeting. Do you ever cook from a recipe book? That means you can follow simple instructions and know how to measure quantity and time. There are lots of skills we can develop all the time, if we only recognize them. ☐

3 Joining a football team is one of the most challenging things I have ever done. I've had to manage my time to make sure I don't miss training sessions. There is quite a lot of kit and equipment that I need, so I have to make sure it's all ready for each game. It's quite a challenge to be organized enough, but I manage to do it. Team games like football also require you to work as part of a team – you have to be able to communicate otherwise there's no way you'll be successful. ☐

a Skills I've learned from my hobbies.
b Skills I've learned from my job.
c Skills you can learn from your home life.

2 Write notes about things that you have done and the skills you might have developed. Think about your work, studies, home life and any hobbies you have.

_____

_____

_____

_____

3 Look at your notes and identify the different skills you have developed. Place them into categories like these.

Organizational skills _____

_____

Interpersonal skills _____

_____

Financial management skills _____

_____

Time management skills _____

_____

4 Practise talking about your skills out loud. Try to consider your audience:

- What do they already know about the topic?
- What might get them excited and interested in the talk?

ORGANIZING YOUR PRESENTATION

5 Match the four steps of a presentation with two examples of useful language (a–h).

1 Starting the presentation ☐ ☐
2 Introducing the area of your life you're going to talk about ☐ ☐
3 Explaining what skills you have developed ☐ ☐
4 Finishing the talk ☐ ☐

a This relates to my day job and the tasks I have to complete in this role.
b That's the end of my talk. Do you have any questions for me?
c Through doing this I have been able to …
d Today, I'd like to talk about how I have developed some important skills.
e You might wonder what I gained from this. Actually, I …
f So, that's all about what I've managed to do. Do we have any questions from the audience?
g In this talk I'm going to tell you about how I developed some useful skills from different areas of my life.
h I've gained a lot of experience and learned how to do things just from my home life.

YOUR PRESENTATION

6 Read the useful language on the left and make notes for your presentation.

1 Start the presentation Today, I'd like to talk about … This talk is going to be about … Today, I'd like to explain …	
2 Introduce the area of your life you're going to talk about This relates to … I've learned this from … From … I've managed to develop some skills.	
3 Explain what skills you have been able to develop Through doing this I have … From this I've been able to … What I have learned is …	
4 Finish the talk and encourage the audience to recognize their own skills That's it about my skills. Have you got any … ?	

7 Film yourself giving your presentation or practise in front of a mirror.
Give yourself marks out of ten for …

- considering the audience ☐ /10
- following the four steps in Exercise 6. ☐ /10
- using correct grammar. ☐ /10

10 Risk

10.1 Protecting Twitter users (sometimes from themselves)

TEDTALKS

DEL HARVEY's TED profile describes her as a security *maven* – meaning expert or connoisseur. She's worked for Twitter since 2008 and, according to her LinkedIn profile, rose steadily and impressively from being the only member of the safety department to becoming Vice President of Trust and Safety in September 2014. This promotion reflects her success in keeping people safe and encouraging others to report abuse. She and her team work closely with every department at Twitter so the 288 million active users per month can be protected from abuse and remain as spam- and troll*-free as possible. Harvey passionately believes in making the Internet a safer place.

Del Harvey is her professional name – on- and off-line – not her real name, presumably to allow her to have a private as well as a public life. She uses her Twitter handle @delbius to respond to pleas for help from users and as a PR tool for events and groups she supports in her very public position. Before working for Twitter she worked for PJFI – a group fighting child exploitation. Working there and bringing criminals to justice must have made her particularly mindful of the need for identity protection and also informed her current job. Despite the unpleasantness she is probably privy to, she's optimistic enough to have had the heart emoticon symbolizing hope tattooed on her wrist.

troll (n) someone who posts deliberately controversial, offensive or abusive comments on the Internet

Del Harvey

CAREER PATHWAYS

1 Read the text. Answer the questions.

1 How has Del Harvey been promoted?
2 Why might she give herself a different name to her legal one?
3 What previous experience taught her the importance of protecting identities?
4 What example is given of her optimistic attitude?

TED PLAYLIST

2 Other TED speakers are interested in topics similar to Del Harvey's TED Talk. Read the descriptions of four TED Talks at the top of page 95. In your opinion, which is the best title for this playlist, a, b or c?

a Connectedness in a fast-changing modern world
b The slowdown of progress in technology
c Privacy and control in the modern world

3 Complete the six-word summary (1–4) that corresponds to each talk in the TED playlist. Use these words.

need	others	preferences	risks

1 _____ reveal more than we think.
2 The effect of connecting with _____ .
3 The _____ of posting information online.
4 The _____ for a Plan B.

4 Match the verbs (1–5) with their collocates (a–e). Check them in the playlist descriptions.

1 to educate   a privacy
2 to spread   b users
3 to reveal   c information
4 to preserve   d people of the need
5 to warn   e through social networks

5 Which talk would you most like to see? Why? Watch the talk at TED.com.

▶ **Jennifer Golbeck: The curly fry conundrum: Why social media 'likes' say more than you might think**

Jennifer Golbeck is a computer scientist with our best interests at heart. She studies how people use social media and thinks about ways users can be aware of their interactions. In her eye-opening talk she tells us about what can be accurately deduced from social media 'likes' because of the sheer volume of data involved. With half the planet using Facebook she thinks it's time to educate and inform users on being more cautious with and taking control of the data they share.

▶ **Nicholas Christakis: The hidden influence of social networks**

Nicholas Christakis is a physician and social scientist. He explores how social networks influence our lives and how characteristics like obesity, altruism, political preferences, emotions and more can be spread through them. In his talk, he uses animated statistics to explain how social networks change and grow almost like living things. He's now investigating the genetic and evolutionary beginnings for the social networks that humans form. What, according to Christakis is at the root of them? Goodness.

▶ **Alessandro Acquisti: What will a future without secrets look like?**

Alessandro Acquisti studies the behavioural economics of privacy in social media networks. His talk is both thought-provoking and chilling as he describes how easily we reveal information about ourselves, our preferences and our identities. His research focuses on how, by not preserving our privacy, we potentially put ourselves at risk and enable others to access this information.

▶ **Danny Hillis: The Internet could crash. We need a Plan B**

Internet pioneer Danny Hillis is an inventor, scientist and engineer. In his TED Talk, he describes the world when the Internet had just begun and only a handful of people had email addresses. Nowadays, it's hard to imagine a life without the Internet – something that we use for almost everything. He urges us to remember that the Internet was never expected to become so big and warns us of the need for a back-up plan in the event of the Internet breaking down.

AUTHENTIC LISTENING SKILLS Listening for key information

6 🎧 **2 26** You are going to hear a podcast in which a member of the *Keynote* team talks about Nicholas Christakis's TED Talk *The hidden influence of social networks*. Listen to the introduction to the podcast and complete the sentences to convey the main information.

1 The podcaster's name is _____ .
2 He is the senior consultant for _____ .
3 He has _____ around the world.
4 Before he was a rep he was a _____ .
5 Every _____ means the beginning of a new network.

LISTENING

7 🎧 **2 27** Listen to the full podcast. Answer the questions.

1 What increased the podcaster's social network?
2 What does he particularly value in his network?
3 What did the talk make him think about?
4 What feels like a 'big responsibility' to him?

8 🎧 **2 27** Are the statements (T) true or (F) false? Listen again to check your answers.

1 The podcaster used to live in a small town in northern England. ☐
2 Christakis's research into obesity changed his view of the world and the course of his research. ☐
3 The risk of suffering from obesity is higher the closer your relationship is to someone else with it. ☐
4 Christakis includes the saying about 'training with lions' to remind us that we should try to be brave and strong. ☐
5 Michael recommends the talk to encourage people to appreciate the positive influence networks can have. ☐

VOCABULARY IN CONTEXT

9 Read the extracts from the podcast. Choose the correct meaning of the words in bold.

1 ... I was living in a small **quaint** town in the North of England ...
   a attractive and old-fashioned ☐
   b ugly and old-fashioned ☐
   c odd and old-fashioned ☐
2 I love the **notion** that social networks are fundamentally something related to goodness, ...
   a knowledge ☐ b idea ☐ c fact ☐
3 This talk left me **pondering** a number of things.
   a believing ☐ b suggesting ☐
   c wondering about ☐
4 After doing research into widowhood, he found that when someone is widowed, its effects aren't limited to the **spouses** ...
   a children ☐ b family ☐ c partners ☐
5 He later studied other topics like happiness and **altruism** ...
   a thinking of others ☐ b noticing others ☐
   c rewarding others ☐

GRAMMAR Passive reporting verbs

1 Complete the text with the correct form of the words in brackets.

The history of insurance

Early forms of household insurance in the seventeenth century ¹Were___ (mostly / consider) to be necessary for protection against fire. In the Great Fire of London 13,000 houses ²were reported (report) to have been lost. Nowadays it ³is widely believed (widely / believe) that you can buy insurance for just about everything. But why do people need insurance? Since the early twentieth century it ⁴has been (generally / consider) to be too risky for expensive items like property and cars not to have insurance cover – the potential loss ⁵was thought (think) to be too high and it has become illegal

not to insure our properties and vehicles. Additionally, in recent years, private individuals ⁶have been (sometimes / know) to buy insurance for very specialized items. Indeed, a pianist or surgeon insuring their hands or a ballet dancer their legs is not unusual as these are key to their profession. It ⁷_____ (expect) that user connectivity will change insurance products, particularly for motoring and health. Usage based insurance (UBI) – where actual client behaviour can be monitored using tracking technology – ⁸_____ (estimate) to become more widespread in the future.

2 Match the two parts of the sentences.

1 The UK insurance industry is reported   `e`
2 It is thought that life insurance   `d`
3 It's estimated that over 100,000   `a`
4 It's been revealed that about a third of people   `b`
5 An Italian bride is understood   `c`

a people work in the insurance industry in the UK.
b underestimate the value of their possessions.
c to have made a claim for her dress after it caught fire during her wedding.
d was invented in 1693 by Edmund Halley, who is more famous for his discoveries about comets.
e to be the biggest in Europe.

3 Complete the sentences with the correct form of the verb in brackets.

1 At the time, the Titanic _was said_ (say) to be the most luxurious ocean liner ever built.
2 It _was reported_ (report) in the press that, despite the high claim of a million pounds, the insurers paid out the sum for the Titanic within thirty days.
3 It _is feared_ (fear) that insurance premiums will rise as a result of climate change.
4 Since the floods it _has been agreed_ (agree) that a fund to repair extensive damage in the area will be set up.
5 It _was decided_ (decide) at a recent meeting that claims under a certain value would be paid immediately.
6 It _has been estimated_ (estimate) that the damage amounts to at least €250,000.

7 After investigation it <u>was alleged</u> (allege) that the transaction was fraudulent.

8 It <u>was not expected</u> (not expect) that insurance company profits will report reduced revenues this year.

4 Rewrite the sentences using type 1 passive reporting verbs in brackets (subject + *be* + past participle of reporting verb + *to* infinitive). You may need to change some of the other verbs.

1 News of the sinking of the Titanic caused shock worldwide. (report)
News of the sinking of the Titanic was reported to have caused shock worldwide.

2 Captain Edward John Smith must have drowned though his body was never found. (presume)
C E J S was presumed to have drown because his body was never found

3 1,500 passengers and crew didn't survive. (know)
It is known that . . . . .

4 A technical failure wasn't the cause in the surveyors' reports. (show)
A technical failure wasn't shown to be cause . . . . .

5 The Titanic is the most famous shipwreck. (say)
It is said that the Titanic is the most famous shipwreck

6 The Titanic was unsinkable when it was built. (believe)
The Titanic was believed to be unsinkable . . . . .

7 The Titanic was a low marine risk according to Lloyd's. (consider)
The Titanic was considered to be a low marine . . . .

5 Rewrite the sentences from Exercise 4 with type 2 passive reporting verbs (*It* + *be* + past participle of reporting verb + (*that*) + clause). Keep the meaning the same.

1 It *was reported that the sinking of the Titanic caused shock worldwide.*

2 It _____

3 It _____

4 It _____

5 It _____

6 It _____

7 It _____

DICTATION

6 🎧 2 28 Listen to someone talking about Lloyd's of London. Complete the paragraph.

Lloyd's of London _____

Technically, _____
_____ but a corporate body of 94 syndicates or 'Names', as they are called. It was founded in a City coffee house in 1688 where merchants bought insurance for their ships. The Lutine Bell _____
_____, as has been done for all other ships lost or missing since 1799.
_____
_____ and in fact incurred gigantic losses due to asbestos claims flooding the market. _____
_____, where the insurance market is much less developed than Britain.

10.3 Follow your gut instinct

READING

1 You are going to look at a questionnaire about attitude to risk. Decide which of these areas (a–f) you would expect to see in a questionnaire about risk.
   a making financial decisions
   b work
   c social life
   d sports or activities
   e trust of others (strangers and friends)
   f driving

2 Read the questionnaire. Which items don't fall into any of the categories above?

General attitude to risk questionnaire

Circle the answer that best describes you.

1 When undertaking a new project, you ...
   A first look at all the things that could possibly go wrong.
   B weigh up the pros and cons and then seek the guidance of someone experienced.
   C are generally confident that if anything goes wrong, you can extricate yourself.

2 In your professional life you ...
   A tend to avoid conflict and competition.
   B take competition into account and look for fair ways to further your own interests.
   C like to compete and win.

3 When driving a car, you ...
   A always obey traffic laws and avoid dangerous situations.
   B are ready to break the laws if you think you won't be caught.
   C often exceed the speed limit and overtake other cars when you can.

4 If the opinion of the majority of people differs from your own ...
   A you adopt it, accepting it must be a more valid view.
   B it irritates you but you go along with it.
   C you stick firmly to your own opinion and try to persuade others to change to it.

5 You like the company of people who ...
   A are trustworthy and competent.
   B are determined and energetic.
   C are adventurous and courageous.

6 In social situations you ...
   A don't like to be the centre of attention, but join in with what's going on.
   B seek out the company of the people who interest you most.
   C like to be the leader of the group and actively dictate the agenda.

7 When it comes to clothes ...
   A you like to be elegant and smart, but not in a showy way.
   B your main consideration is just to feel comfortable.
   C you like to wear something eye-catching and different.

8 When faced with a difficult decision, you ...
   A put off making it in the hope that some new evidence will come to light.
   B trust to luck rather than any reasoned approach.
   C trust in your own rightness and banish any thoughts of later regret.

9 If a friend offered you a chance to invest in their business you ...
   A would decline the offer, not wanting to mix business and friendship.
   B would see what guarantees they could give you that the investment was safe.
   C would look for the quickest and most substantial return.

10 Your main concern in life is ...
   A to have financial security.
   B to be professionally competent and well-respected.
   C to keep seeking out new challenges and experiences.

3 Choose the correct meaning for each of these phrases.

1 'extricate yourself' (question 1)
 a start the project again
 b get out of a difficult situation ✓
2 'further your own interests' (question 2)
 a help your career progress ✓
 b explore new areas
3 'go along with it' (question 4)
 a accept it ✓
 b change your view
4 'dictate the agenda' (question 6)
 a decide what everyone should do ✓
 b organize social events for everyone
5 'banish any thoughts of' (question 8)
 a postpone thinking about
 b stop thinking about ✓
6 'the most substantial return' (question 9)
 a the easiest way to get your money back
 b the largest amount of profit ✓

4 🎧 **2 29** Listen to an expert talking about this questionnaire. Answer the questions.

1 What doesn't he like about questionnaires in general?
2 What doesn't he like about this questionnaire?
3 What does he like about this questionnaire?

VOCABULARY Risk and probability

5 Complete the sentences with the missing word. The first letter has been given.

1 I'm sorry I have to go now, I don't want to
 r _un_ the risk of missing the flight.
2 The virus only **p** _osses_ a threat if you try to open the attachment in the email. So just delete the email.
3 Taking vitamin C and zinc tablets doesn't prevent you from getting a cold. It just **r** _educes_ the chances of your getting one.
4 What is the **l** _ikelihood_ of it raining tomorrow? We're planning to take a boat out on the river.
5 The **o** _dds_ of being struck by lightning in your lifetime are about 12,000 to one.
6 I'd love you to come and stay, but the chances are **h** _igh_ that we'll be out of the country in July.
7 Even if there's only a one **i** _n_ a million chance of the cable breaking, it's not a risk I want to take.

WORDBUILDING Suffix -ity

6 Complete the second sentence so that it means the same as the first, replacing the adjective with a noun ending in -ity.

1 My main concern in life is to be financially secure.
 My main concern in life is to have financial _security._
2 Can you check if the Kingston Suite is still available?
 Can you check the _availability_ of the Kingston Suite?

3 The people in Tunisia were so generous, I was overwhelmed.
 I was overwhelmed by the _generousity_ of the people in Tunisia.
4 Just so that it is clear, could you write the details down for me?
 For the sake of _clearity_ , could you write the details down for me?
5 We respect that our clients have the right to remain anonymous.
 We respect our clients' right to _anonymity_.
6 Thank you for being so hospitable.
 Thank you for all your _hospitality_.
7 They sent the Picasso drawing to an art gallery to confirm it was authentic.
 They sent the Picasso drawing to an art gallery to confirm its _authenicity_.
8 It's not necessary to reserve a seat. We still have plenty.
 There's no _neccessity_ to reserve a seat. We still have plenty.
9 I really love how simple the painting is. There's a childlike quality to it.
 I really love the _simplicity_ of the painting. There's a childlike quality to it.

WORD FOCUS face

7 Choose the correct options to complete the idiomatic phrases with face.

1 We need to **face _facts_ / information** here. No one is going to spend $100 on a toothbrush.
2 To write such a horrible article about us when he was so complimentary on the phone is completely **one-faced / _two-faced_**.
3 I know it's disappointing to lose, but we need to **put a brave face in it / _on it_** and move on.
4 Just go and tell her that you messed up. You're going to have to **face the _music_ / song** sooner or later.
5 To find out they were going on holiday without me after all the research I did for them was a real **touch / _slap_ in the face**.
6 I don't think things are going very well for her, because when I asked her, she just **pulled a short / _long_ face**.

8 Match the definitions (a–f) with the idioms 1–6 from Exercise 7.

a an insult _a slap in the face_
b show you're not affected by a setback
 put a brave face on it
c be realistic
 face facts
d be hypocritical
 two-faced
e accept punishment or criticism
 face the music
f make a sad expression
 pulled a long face

10.4 All things considered …

ASSESSING RISK

1 Match the business risks (1–4) to the risk areas (a–d).

1	data security	**a**	market / environmental risks
2	fraud	**b**	theft
3	fire	**c**	industry regulations
4	burglary	**d**	financial risks

2 🎧 **2 30** Listen and decide what risk from Exercise 1 is being talked about. _____

3 🎧 **2 30** Choose the correct options in these phrases to discuss alternatives. Listen to the conversation again and check your answers.

1 *They were / There are* some pretty interesting options to choose from.

2 *Possibly / Probably* the most obvious one is …

3 A *drawback / hurdle* of the camera is that …

4 *Additionally / According to* the brochure, a combination lock is another option to consider.

5 On the plus side, we *wouldn't / don't* need keys any more.

6 … but the *downside / downsize* is we're only strengthening the door.

7 An alarm system protects doors and windows, which makes it a very *attractive / alternative* possibility.

8 Hmm, yes but considering the price, I'm not *secure / sure* it's the best option.

4 🎧 **2 31** Listen to the continuation of the conversation and complete the sentences.

1 In _____ the increase in criminal activity in the area, I think we should invest in an alarm and a safe.

2 A _____ that might do the job is a dog.

3 Ultimately, _____ does seem to be the alarm system.

4 OK. _____ , it makes sense to go with an alarm …

5 Write the phrases from Exercises 3 and 4 under the correct heading.

Presenting options

_____

_____

_____

_____

Discussing pros and cons

_____

_____

_____

_____

Considering options

_____

_____

_____

_____

PRONUNCIATION Saying lists

6 🎧 **2 32** Say the following lists as closed lists, and then as open lists. Listen and check. Use *and* only for the closed lists.

1 In the burglary they took two computers, a printer, €450 in cash (and) a mobile phone.

2 I've heard about it happening to the bookstore, the sandwich shop on the corner (and) the DIY store.

3 What did she lose from her handbag? A phone, her wallet including credit cards, her car keys (and) some jewellery.

WRITING SKILL Using qualifiers

7 Look at the examples (a–g). Then write the correct qualifier in bold next to the descriptions (1–5) below.

a It was a **pretty** easy solution in the end to install a video camera.
b It is a **fairly** straightforward procedure to follow.
c The instructions were **a bit** unclear.
d He was **quite** pleased that he'd invested in the security system.
e It was **rather** more than he had expected to pay for it.
f The cost of this one seems **a little** high in comparison.
g We would have to pay **slightly** more for that model.

1 _____ modifies adverbs and adjectives. It means 'to a limited degree'.
2 _____ modifies adverbs, adjectives, nouns and verbs to a higher degree than item 1.
3 _____ modifies adverbs and adjectives to an even higher degree (informally) than items 1 and 2. It can also mean 'more than usual'.
4 _____ , _____ and _____ soften adverbs, adjectives and verbs, making criticism less direct.
5 _____ softens adverbs, adjectives, nouns and verbs, making criticism less direct. Also used to show disappointment, criticism or surprise.

8 Read these sentences about the qualifiers in Exercise 7. Are they (T) true or (F) false?

1 All of them can soften adjectives. ☐
2 Only two of them soften nouns. ☐
3 Three of them soften adjectives, adverbs, nouns and verbs. ☐
4 Four of them can be used to make criticism less direct. ☐

9 Rewrite the sentences more diplomatically. Use the qualifiers in brackets.

1 It was a waste of money. (rather)

2 They were poorer quality than we'd expected. (slightly)

3 The XJ7 model is more complicated to install. (a bit)

4 He was impatient and unfriendly when he explained it. (quite, a little)

5 I found it uninspiring and old-fashioned. (rather, pretty)

6 The company is disorganized. (fairly)

7 That's a worrying state of affairs. (rather)

8 The model they chose was easy to use. (reasonably)

10 Choose the correct qualifiers to make three-, two- and one-star reviews.

★ ★ ★ We bought this system on a friend's recommendation. We were ¹ *quite / rather* satisfied with the service and the pricing was ² *a bit / fairly* competitive.

★ ★ We had a ³ *bit / rather* lengthy wait for the system modifications we'd requested. We paid ⁴ *quite / slightly* more for it than we were quoted.

★ The order took ⁵ *quite / fairly* ⁶ *rather / a bit* longer than we were promised. It was ⁷ *rather / fairly* disappointing.

11 Write a short review for a new door intercom with a camera using the notes.

- low price attractive
- product arrived promptly
- faulty
- better maintenance service than expected
- overall package
- reasonable

101

The letter of thanks you will read in Exercise 2 is in answer to the following exam question.

> A training company recently ran a health and safety course at your company's office. Afterwards, you received this email from your manager:
>
> Hi,
>
> Can you put together a thank you letter for HSAW for running the training day on Tuesday? It went really well in the end, despite the initial problems. Please mention the excellent job their trainer did, and how clear everything was. Feel free to offer them a 10% discount next time they need something from us. I'll sign it when you're done.
>
> Thanks,
>
> DW
>
> Write your letter of thanks in **220–260 words** in an appropriate style.

IDEAS

1 Tick (✓) the things you would expect to see in the letter of thanks.

a a formal greeting ☐
b descriptions of the products the company sells ☐
c compliments for the HSAW staff and their communication skills ☐
d advice for how to organize a health and safety course ☐
e the reason the letter has been written ☐
f details of a reward for HSAW's good service ☐
g a description of a problem ☐

MODEL

2 Read the letter of thanks. Match the five sections with a description (a–g) from Exercise 1.

1 ☐   2 ☐   3 ☐   4 ☐   5 ☐

3 Read the letter of thanks again. Are these statements true (T) or false (F)?

1 The course was originally planned for the 18th September. ☐
2 The HSAW staff dealt well with problems when they occurred. ☐
3 The staff at the company were expecting to learn a lot from the course. ☐
4 Information supplied during the course will still be used in the office at a later date. ☐
5 Della would like to work with HSAW again soon. ☐

---

[1]To whom it may concern:

[2]We are writing to thank you for the informative and useful health and safety course which Emma from HSAW ran at our office on Tuesday 18th September.

[3]We were initially worried when we had to cancel the original day set for the training due to unforeseen circumstances. [4]However, your team took it in their stride and new arrangements were made with the minimum of fuss. The whole day ran smoothly and this reflects very well on the professionalism of your staff, who organized everything thoroughly beforehand and communicated regularly with us throughout the whole process.

On behalf of our whole team, please convey our thanks to Emma for the excellent job she did at explaining health and safety requirements to a group of office workers who thought the course would all be common sense and would not challenge us. I am pleased to say that this was not true and we all came away from the course feeling as if we had learned something new.

Finally, I'd like to mention the resources given to us by HSAW which are all very clear and are now being used around the office. I am sure we will continue to refer to them for a long time to come.

[5]In token of our gratitude, we would like to offer all HSAW staff a 10% discount on any products from our catalogue. We look forward to doing business with you again in the near future.

Yours sincerely,

Della Walters

USEFUL LANGUAGE

4 Match the two parts of the sentences to make letter beginnings.

1 We are so grateful ☐
2 I wanted to let you know how much ☐
3 Thank you ☐
4 I would just like to express ☐
5 Let me take this opportunity ☐
6 We would like to thank you for ☐
7 I cannot thank you ☐
8 I would like to ☐

a my gratitude for …
b the excellent service we received at …
c enough for …
d for the assistance we received on …
e compliment you on …
f so much for your help with …
g we appreciate …
h to thank you for …

5 Complete the sentences used to pay compliments in a letter of thanks. Use these words.

dedication	knowledgeable	professionally
prompt	remarkably	wealth

1 Your staff are very _____ and polite.
2 The responses we received were always _____ .
3 The brochure contained a _____ of useful information.
4 Everyone has been _____ patient and helpful.
5 They handled any problems very _____ .
6 Their _____ to their careers is to be commended.

6 Complete the letter of thanks. Use these words and phrases.

a time	fortunate	impressed	not only
once again	regret	stood out	

Dear Miss Sanchez,

I would like to say a huge thank you for the meditation course which I attended last week at the yoga centre.

The course was a gift from my sister when she realized that I was starting to get ill from work-related stress. I was not sure if I would enjoy it as I have never been interested in yoga or meditation, but in the end I did not ¹ _____ going for one moment. I can't remember ² _____ when I have ever felt as calm as I have in the past week. ³ _____ did you help me to relax on the evening, but you also taught me useful exercises which I can use whenever I feel the stress coming on.

I would like to mention how ⁴ _____ the yoga centre is to have such a caring, committed instructor on their team. One thing that particularly ⁵ _____ was the time you spent on each of the course participants' individual needs. I was particularly ⁶ _____ by this, given that the group was much larger than you expected due to your colleague being absent.

⁷ _____ , I would like to express my thanks and to say that I will certainly return to the centre for further courses.

Yours sincerely,

Amy Jefferson

7 Put the words into the correct order to create recommendations.

1 recommend / to / we / not / customers / will / hesitate / you / our / to
2 recommend / restaurant / my / I / friends / will / all / your / to
3 hotel / I / certainly / again / use / your / will
4 we / forward / to / soon / with / you / again / look / doing / business
5 continuing / look / we / forward / business / our / relationship / to
6 to / we / others / recommended / company / have / your …
7 … will / to / and / continue / so / do

PLANNING

You will answer the following question.

> You have just been on holiday where you stayed in a hotel. Write a letter of thanks. In your letter, mention the staff, the restaurant and one idea of your own.

8 Plan your letter of thanks. Write notes to answer these questions. Don't write full sentences yet.

1 Where did you go on holiday?
2 What will you write about the staff?
3 What will you mention about the restaurant?
4 What other aspect of your stay will you write about?

WRITING

9 Write a letter of thanks based on the situation in Exercise 8. In your letter you should:

- give your reason for writing
- mention the hotel staff and the restaurant
- write about one more idea of your own
- state what you will do as a result of your stay at the hotel (e.g. recommend it?)

Write your letter in **220–260 words** in an appropriate style.

ANALYSIS

10 Check your letter of thanks. Then answer the questions.

- **Content:** Does the letter mention the staff, the restaurant and one other idea? Is it 220 to 260 words long?
- **Communicative achievement:** Is it written in a neutral or formal style? Is it clear to the reader why you are thanking them?
- **Organization:** Is the letter logically organized? Are the ideas connected?
- **Language:** Does it use correct grammar and vocabulary? Is a good range of structures used?

11 Vision

11.1 How to build with clay and community

TEDTALKS

DIÉBÉDO FRANCIS KÉRÉ was born in 1965 in Gando, Burkina Faso, the eldest son of the chief of the village. His father hoped that his son would learn to read and write but Kéré learned a great deal more. First, he completed an apprenticeship in carpentry in the country's capital Ouagadougou and then he studied to become a teacher. In 1990, he won a scholarship to Berlin and moved there to finish his schooling. He went on to train to be an architect, completing his degree in 2004 at the Technical University of Berlin where he has since lectured.

In 1998, he founded the company 'Bricks for Gando School' through which he raised funds for his first building project, the construction of Gando primary school. When he came back he did so with skills, funds and a government grant to train people in the village to build with local materials in order to give them marketable skills.

He won an award with his first building, the primary school he built with others in his village. Other awards followed, six by 2015. He started his own architecture business in 2005 and has designed buildings in Africa, India, the USA and Europe. His designs have been exhibited in DAM, the Architecture museum in Frankfurt, and in MoMA in New York, and he's a fellow at both the British and American Institutes of Architects. When he left to study in Germany all those years ago, the village women gave him pennies to ensure his return. Not only did he return, but what he brought back with him has allowed him to improve and empower his community.

Diébédo Francis Kéré

CAREER PATHWAYS

1 Read the text. Answer the questions.

1 What did his father hope for Diébédo Francis Kéré?
2 What did Kéré study?
3 How did he finance the first school in Gando?
4 How much recognition has his work received?

TED PLAYLIST

2 Other TED speakers are interested in topics similar to Diébédo Francis Kéré's TED Talk. Read the descriptions of four TED Talks at the top of page 105. In your opinion, which is the best title for this playlist, a, b or c?

a Community matters matter
b Training communities to build ✓
c Sustainable housing solutions

3 Complete the six-word summary (1–4) that corresponds to each talk in the TED playlist. Use these words.

| design | space | surprising | sustainable |

1 A neglected _space_ becomes an attraction.
2 Promoting _sustainable_ development for minority communities.
3 Building clever homes in _surprising_ places.
4 Collaborative _design_ solves local problems creatively.

4 Match the verbs (1–5) with their collocates (a–e). Check your answers in the playlist descriptions.

1 to bring   4 a the world
2 to suffer   3 b for equality
3 to campaign   2 c injustice
4 to travel   5 d with issues of scale
5 to deal   1 e people together

5 Which talk would you most like to see? Why? Watch the talk at TED.com.

▶ **Candy Chang: Before I die I want to …**

Candy Chang is an artist, urban planner and TED Fellow. In her New Orleans neighbourhood she turned an abandoned building into a massive community chalkboard with the incomplete statement that is also the title of her TED Talk. Her moving talk describes how similar community art projects have brought people together and begun important conversations in over 1,000 cities in 70 countries.

▶ **Majora Carter: Greening the ghetto**

Majora Carter is an activist and winner of the MacArthur 'Genius' Award. She talks emotionally and with conviction about the environmental injustice suffered by the residents of high-poverty and high-minority neighbourhoods. In her own neighbourhood of the South Bronx in New York City, she successfully campaigned for more environmental equality and brought a waterfront park and additional funds for green development to the community.

▶ **Iwan Baan: Ingenious homes in unexpected places**

Iwan Baan is an urban documentary photographer who's interested in built environments, particularly makeshift _put together_ ones. He travels the world, exploring and photographing communities and their individual solutions to the problem of adequate, affordable housing. His talk is a lively illustrated account of communities living in resourceful ways in unusual places in Nigeria, Venezuela, Egypt and China.

▶ **Alejandro Aravena: My architectural philosophy? Bring the community into the process**

Alejandro Aravena is an urban architect used to solving difficult problems in unusual ways. He routinely deals with issues of scale, speed and scarcity of means. In his engaging talk he takes us through the problem-solving steps he used in some of his projects, and highlights how his work was improved when he invited community members to help come up with some of the solutions.

AUTHENTIC LISTENING SKILLS Dealing with accents: different stress patterns

6 🎧 **2 33** You are going to hear a podcast in which a member of the *Keynote* team talks about Iwan Baan's TED Talk, *Ingenious homes in unexpected places*. Listen to each sentence being read first by the Greek podcaster and then an English native speaker. Underline the part of the word or compound in bold which is stressed in each version.

1 a My job involves **extensive** travelling …
  b My job involves **extensive** travelling …
2 a … I've seen many 'weird-looking' homes around the world.
  b … I've seen many 'weird-looking' homes around the world.
3 a Originally, the title made me think that it was going to be one more of those demonstrations of funny, posh or extravagant houses some **techno-geek** or multi-millionaire has built.
  b Originally, the title made me think that it was going to be one more of those demonstrations of funny, posh or extravagant houses some **techno-geek** or multi-millionaire has built.

LISTENING

7 🎧 **2 34** Listen to the full podcast. Are these statements true (T) or false (F)?

1 Baan showed photographs of homes in Greece. ☐
2 The podcaster describes refugees in Greece wanting to build somewhere to cook, to sleep and to pray. ☐
3 The speaker explains why people find themselves in these difficult situations. ☐

8 🎧 **2 34** Listen again. Answer the questions.

1 What did the podcaster fear the talk would show?
2 What does he say people like to do with their homes?
3 Why did the talk resonate with the podcaster?
4 What made Baan a good TED speaker?
5 Who will Eftychis recommend the talk to?

VOCABULARY IN CONTEXT

9 Read the extracts from the podcast. Choose the correct meaning of the words in bold.

1 One of my favourite TED Talks is Iwan Baan's '**Ingenious** homes in unexpected places'.
  a strange ☑   b clever ☐   c remote ☐

2 Originally, the title made me think that it was going to be one more of those demonstrations of funny, **posh** or extravagant houses …
  a expensive-looking ☑   b old-fashioned ☐
  c humble ☐

3 He showed people living … in **dwellings** on and in the rubbish heaps.
  a sheds ☐   b homes ☐   c tents ☐

4 Generally people are unhappy with '**cookie-cutter**' solutions; they like to personalize their environments.
  a instant ☐   b childish ☑   c standardized ☐

5 … what cities can look like away from the **tourist spots** and off the beaten track.
  a motorways ☐   b top destinations ☐
  c historic sites ☑

11.2 A vision for saving the world

GRAMMAR Subordinate clauses

1 Complete the text with these words.

although	by the time	given that	in case
in spite of the fact	once	provided that
when	whereas

Making banana bread, not wasting bananas!

The German business studies students Lars Peters and Tim Gudelj were travelling in Australia in 2012 ¹_____ they tried banana bread for the first time. It was love at first bite. ²_____ it's called 'bread' as it's baked in a loaf form, it is actually like cake. ³_____ that it's sold in fast-food chains, it's not fast food per se; it's more of a health food and has just seven basic ingredients. ⁴_____ Peters and Gudelj got back to Germany, they'd made a plan. Their parents consented to lend them the seed capital for their business ⁵_____ the students agreed to complete their master's degrees. They founded their company, Bebananas, in 2013, selling their bread in bakeries, local cafés and online. The entrepreneurial pair are food sharers which – ⁶_____ you don't know – involves picking up food legally from shops, markets or restaurants ⁷_____ it's been thrown away. Ripe bananas can't be sold in supermarkets ⁸_____ they are exactly what's required for banana bread. ⁹_____ their product is made of fifty per cent bananas, this provides a cheap and sustainable way to make delicious banana bread.

2 Use the prompts and the conjunctions to write sentences.

1 food fads / go / banana bread / healthy / as / made / fifty per cent / bananas (as far as)
As far as food fads go, banana bread is a healthy one, as it's made of fifty per cent bananas.

2 I / eat / banana bread / when / live / Australia (the last time)
The last time I ate bb, was when I was living in Australia.

3 I / late / save me / piece of cake (in case)
In case I'm late, save me a piece of cake.

4 not waste / food / banana bread / excellent idea (as far as)
As far as not wasting food, bb is an excellent idea.

5 it / taste / very sweet / no sugar (considering)
Considering that it has no sugar it taste very sweet.

6 he / smell / the dish / reminds / home (whenever)
_____
_____

7 she / not like / bananas / chose / carrot cake instead (in view of the fact that)
_____
_____

considering: although, even though.

3 Choose the correct options to complete the sentences so that they all have a similar meaning

1 *As long as / If* they don't finish their studies, they won't receive the loan.

2 They won't receive the loan *unless / provided that* they finish their studies.

3 *Supposing / As long as* they finish their studies, they'll receive the loan from their parents.

4 *As long as / Supposing* they don't finish their studies, they will have to pay back the entire loan.

5 *Provided that / Unless* they continue studying and finish their course, they'll receive the loan.

GRAMMAR EXTRA! Other conjunctions

4 Choose the correct options to complete the recipe.

1 Take four bananas. They are ready to use *as soon as / while* they are ripe. Mash them well.

2 Cream half a cup of sugar and half a cup of butter *by the time / until* they are fluffy.

3 Mix two eggs into the butter mixture. *Until / Once* it is blended together well, add the bananas.

4 *Once / After* mixing in the dry ingredients – two cups of flour, a quarter of a teaspoon of salt and a teaspoon of baking powder – pour into a loaf tin.

5 *Until / By the time* it's been in an oven at 175 degrees C for about an hour, it will be cooked. Enjoy!

5 Put the words in the correct order to make good housekeeping and dietary advice.

1 fruit and vegetables / as / buy / far / in season / when / are / concerned, / them / as / they / are

_____

_____ .

2 recipes / new / necessary, / find / use / leftovers / if / to / up

_____

_____ .

3 doubt, / when / sell-by date / don't / past / in / food / that's / eat / its

_____

_____ .

4 eat / told / unless / your / foods / of / a / otherwise / by / different / doctor, / variety

_____

_____ .

5 learned / once / you'll / meals / you've / to / cook / fresh food, / it / prefer / processed / to

_____

_____ .

DICTATION

6 🎧 **2** **35** Listen to someone talking about food sharing. Complete the paragraph.

The amount of food waste increases _____

_____

Ninety million tons of food are thrown away each year by Europeans. Food sharing _____

_____

colossal waste. Valentin Thurn's documentary film *Taste the Waste* raised awareness and, _____

_____ .

The www.foodsharing.de website connects people who have food to give to people who need it and, _____

_____

at strategic points, too. Food sharing is happening in 240 cities in Germany _____

_____ .

It's not only individuals, but also businesses that benefit from this practice, _____

_____ .

Finally, health and safety laws ensure that no one shares anything unfit for consumption.

11.3 A personal calling

READING

1 Match the four types of writing (1–4) with the definitions (a–d).

1 a feature article

2 an editorial

3 an advertisement

4 an advertorial

a a notice or display designed to sell something

b a piece that deals with a topic or person in depth

c a piece that looks like a regular article but is actually designed to sell something

d an article that expresses the opinion of the publisher

2 Read the text. Decide which of the four writing types in Exercise 1 it is.

3 Read the text again. Are these statements true (T) or false (F)?

1 The company's products are aimed at all types of businesses.

2 Small business owners are generally not enthusiastic enough about what they do.

3 Small businesses mainly get new customers from personal recommendations.

4 Most business cards do their job adequately, but not excitingly.

5 A B-Creative Cards business card is something you will be proud of owning.

6 All the examples of B-Creative Cards in the article give you extra useful information beyond just someone's contact details.

7 The gardener's business card is the only one not made of paper or card.

8 The main benefit of the cards is that they help people to share your enthusiasm for your work.

How a business card can transform your sales

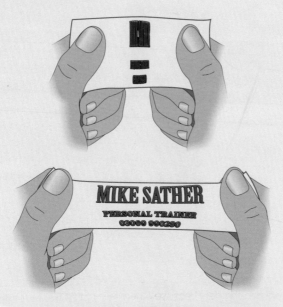

This is one for all you small business owners out there – whether you be a sole-trading painter and decorator or a team of IT consultants, a yoga studio or a garage owner. You care passionately about what you do; it's what you do all day and often think about at night. But you haven't managed to transmit that passion to enough potential customers. Because you're only small, your advertising budget is limited. Yes, you've got a website and from time to time you place advertisements in the local newspaper. You hand out business cards to interested parties whenever you get the opportunity, but mainly you're just relying on word-of-mouth. You want to take your business to another level, but it just isn't happening. Well, here's an idea that could be a shortcut to more business and help transform your fortunes.

B-Creative Cards specialize in making business cards that really stand out. Let's face it – most business cards end up at the back of our wallets or collecting dust on a shelf somewhere and never get looked at again. They only fulfil one function – to have a written record of a contact – and most don't even do that very well if they get put to one side and forgotten. What B-Creative Cards do is to produce cards that become objects of desire in themselves – cards that are so fun and original that you want to show them off to other people. Here are some examples:

- a rubber card for a personal fitness trainer that you have to stretch out with both hands before the name and contact details of the trainer become visible

- a gardener's calling card that is actually a little envelope with a few free flower seeds inside

- a first aid trainer's card that opens out into a leaflet with some key first aid tips inside

- an Italian restaurant's business card in the shape of an aubergine with a recipe for Aubergine Parmigiana on the back

The clever thing about these calling cards is a) you actually want to keep them and b) they bring a smile to your face. They're also great for handing out at trade fairs or roadshows. They may cost more than a standard business card, but what you end up with is a personal calling card that truly reflects your personal calling.

4 ⋒ 2 36 Listen to the owner of a yoga studio who used B-Creative Cards to make a business card. Write down the adjectives used to describe these things.

1 their advertising budget _____
2 the first B-Creative design (straw) _____
3 the cost of the straw _____
4 the second design (card) _____
5 what customers think of the card _____

5 Match the meanings a–e with the adjectives (1–5) from Exercise 4.

a impressive ☐   d tiny ☐
b fashionable ☐   e expensive ☐
c original and attractive ☐

VOCABULARY Expressions with *look* and *see*

6 Match the expressions with *look* and *see* (1–6) with the definitions (a–f).

1 to look into
2 to see eye to eye (on)
3 to be on the lookout for
4 to see about
5 to look up to
6 to oversee

2 a to agree (on)
6 b to supervise
4 c attend to / deal with
1 d to investigate
3 e to be waiting to find/do/get
5 f to admire

7 Use the correct form of the expressions from Exercise 6 to complete the sentences.

1 We agreed about the main points but we didn't _see eye to eye_ some details.
2 I felt very honoured to be put in charge of _overseeing_ the whole project.
3 We _are on the lookout_ experienced people, but they're not easy to find.
4 If you can sort out the publicity, I'll _see about_ hiring a venue.
5 I've always really _looked up to_ my older brother and listened to his advice.
6 I'll _look into_ how we can get tickets, but I can't promise anything.

WORDBUILDING Compound nouns

8 Look at these compound nouns from the text. What type(s) of word is each noun composed of?

website	newspaper	shortcut	roadshow

9 Complete the compound nouns 1–8 with these words.

cross	data	dead	note
self-	share	short	work

1 _dead_ line
2 _work_ space
3 _short_ list
4 _cross_ roads
5 _note_ book
6 _self_ esteem
7 _share_ holder
8 _data_ base

10 Match the two parts of the sentences.

1 The deadline for applications is written   d
2 I feel I'm at a crossroads   f
3 We drew up a shortlist   a
4 A list of the principal shareholders is kept   e
5 Not getting the associate director job was a blow   b
6 I have a small workspace   c

a of potential candidates.
b to my self-esteem.
c at home.
d in my notebook.
e on our database.
f in my life.

WORD FOCUS *time*

11 Complete the idioms using these words.

behind	dead	hard	high
kill	make	move	pushed

1 Numbers for students wanting to do psychology at university is **at an all-time** _high_ .
2 Your phone doesn't have the Internet? You're a bit _behind_ **the times**, aren't you?
3 Sorry I can't speak now. I'm rather _pushed_ **for time**.
4 It's very good of you to _make_ **time** to see me. I know how busy you are.
5 The plane was delayed for two hours so we just had to _kill_ **time** at the airport.
6 You may not like using social media, but everyone else is using it. You've got to _move_ **with the times**.
7 Swiss trains are incredibly reliable. They always arrive and leave _dead_ **on time**.
8 Please don't **give her a** _hard_ **time**. She was only doing what she thought was right.

12 Complete the sentences with the idioms from Exercise 11.

1 There's Jack now – _dead on time_. I told you he wouldn't be late.
2 I always _make time_ to do some exercise during the day, because otherwise I'm just sitting down in front of my computer all day long.
3 She _gave me a hard time_ about missing the meeting. But actually I didn't even know about it until ten minutes before.
4 Temperatures this winter were _____ . It was exceptionally mild.
5 We just _____ chatting and playing cards during the journey. We were there before we knew it!

11.4 A dream come true

TALKING ABOUT A VISION OF THE FUTURE

1 Match the skills (1–4) to the jobs (a–d).

1 Communication   **a** journalist, artist, designer, chef
2 Being creative   **b** doctor, nurse, teacher, receptionist
3 Helping people   **c** IT specialist, mechanic, consultant
4 Problem solving   **d** sales rep, manager, blogger

2 🎧 **2 37** Match the two parts of the sentences. Listen to a coaching session to check your answers.

1 We've always fancied
2 I can envisage
3 If money were no object,
4 To be perfectly honest I'd like to
5 I could see myself cooking
6 But I can't see

a a quieter life, having a smaller B&B place somewhere nice.
b do something different.
c setting up our own business.
d myself at the front desk any more. I need a bit more of a challenge.
e I'd buy my own hotel somewhere.
f in a restaurant or café.

3 Put the words in the correct order to make phrases.

a wouldn't / great / be / it / to
b see / I / myself / can
c money / no / could / were / if / object, / we
d fancied / always / I've
e love / to / I'd
f envisage / can't / I

4 🎧 **2 38** Complete the conversation with the phrases from Exercise 3. Listen and check.

Dan: It was interesting what we found out in the session. Turned out a little different to what I was expecting. ¹_____ exactly what we might do yet though.

Maja: Yeah, I know what you mean. I've got so many ideas going round my head now. But ²_____ combine the things we love doing with a small business?

Dan: ³_____ buy somewhere nice and have lots of bikes and rent them out to tourists, but I don't think we could afford it.

Maja: And ⁴_____ bake tasty cakes for all those hungry cyclists and serve them tea in a café … Yes, ⁵_____ doing that.

Dan: I can see it too actually. If it was a biggish place we could have a couple of rooms for B&B, but not too many. We can have a look around here and in a couple of the tourist spots down south.

Maja: ⁶_____ living somewhere pretty, by the sea or in the hills. We've always lived in cities. It's time for a change, don't you think?

PRONUNCIATION Sure and unsure tones

5 🎧 **2** **39** Listen. Decide which version (a or b) of the sentence is sure (S) and which is unsure (U).

		a	b
1	Can you envisage us buying a new place?	☐	☐
2	But wouldn't it be great to combine the things we love doing with a small business?	☐	☐
3	If money were no object, I'd buy somewhere pretty.	☐	☐
4	Yes, I can see myself doing that.	☐	☐
5	I've always fancied living somewhere by the sea or in the hills.	☐	☐

WRITING An endorsement

6 Read the comments endorsing people. Tick (✓) the two most positive adjectives / adverbs.

1 We were … with his programming skills.
a highly impressed ☐
b pleased ☐
c satisfied ☐

2 She … helping us achieve our aims.
a was good at ☐
b excelled at ☐
c was extremely good at ☐

3 His … communication style was an asset to the team.
a confident ☐
b natural ☐
c reserved ☐

4 She has … sense of responsibility.
a an admirable ☐
b a strong ☐
c quite a strong ☐

5 He was … proactive in completing the tasks set.
a generally ☐
b completely ☐
c consistently ☐

6 Working with her was a real …
a privilege ☐
b honour ☐
c support ☐

7 Choose the best adjectives / adverbs to complete the endorsements.

Dan worked [1]*consistently / completely* hard to integrate new members into the team seamlessly. He demonstrates [2]*a reserved / an admirable* sense of personal and professional responsibility and his sense of humour meant he was a pleasure to work for.

Maja was [3]*a pretty / an extremely* hard-working and proactive member of the team. She was often chosen to represent the staff at management meetings because of her [4]*reserved / confident* communication style and sociable nature.

Maja was [5]*not bad / a pleasure* to work with and a great example for the rest of us. She was always focused and hard-working and [6]*pleased / quick* to solve problems or ease dissatisfaction with customers proactively.

Dan was an asset to the organization, his ambition to [7]*generally / consistently* improve performance paid off with real results. He inspired others with his vision and his ability to get the [8]*best / strong* out of and support staff at the same time.

8 Match the verbs (1–8) with their collocates (a–h), then read the endorsements to check.

1 to integrate ☐
2 to demonstrate ☐
3 to represent ☐
4 to be quick ☐
5 to ease ☐
6 to improve ☐
7 to inspire ☐
8 to get the best ☐

a with the vision
b to solve problems
c customer dissatisfaction
d performance
e new members into the team
f out of staff
g staff at a meeting
h a sense of professional responsibility

9 Complete an endorsement for Carolyn, written by Dan and Maja. Use the collocations from Exercise 8 and complete the sentences. Add any additional words which will contribute to the overall positive impression.

1 Carolyn / demonstrate / strong
Carolyn demonstrated a consistently strong sense of professional responsibility.

2 She / quick / proactively / creatively

3 The coaching / improve / decision making

4 We / inspire / help / form

5 The life coaching session / help / best / new situation

YOUR IDEA

1 Look at the three images. Match the images with the paragraphs about improvements in the local area (a, b, c).

1 ☐

2 ☐

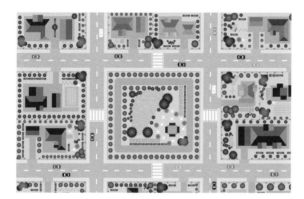

3 ☐

a Do you want to meet new people in the neighbourhood? Do you like to read and discuss literature? If so, this new book club may be the perfect thing for you. Come along – sessions last for two hours and are held every fortnight at the local library. It's free of charge and refreshments are provided.

b A group of young people have decided to work together to do something about the terrible state of their local park. Recently the park has become something of a dumping ground – often at the end of the day it's covered in rubbish. But these youths have decided to try to make a difference.

c The estate's new development will provide a green space between the housing blocks where residents can walk, relax and meet up together. This will be somewhere for families to come to get away from their busy home lives, making this a more peaceful place to live.

2 Write notes about an improvement you have made in your local area or one that you would like to see happen. Think about places in your local area, clubs that people could join and neighbourhood schemes that could be implemented.

_____

_____

_____

_____

3 Match the two parts of the sentences to describe the possible effects of improvements in your area.

1 This development would make ☐
2 Investment in this area would create ☐
3 Setting up a youth club would give ☐
4 A park would give ☐
5 This club would improve ☐

a young people something to do.
b job opportunities.
c people happier.
d people's lives greatly.
e people somewhere to relax.

4 Practise talking about an improvement in your area. Remember to …
- speak clearly and don't rush through your points – this will help you relax and your audience will be able to follow your talk more easily.
- use examples or short stories to illustrate your points.
- pause to emphasize the main points and essential information in your talk – but don't overdo it.

ORGANIZING YOUR PRESENTATION

5 Match the six steps of the presentation with the examples of useful language (a–f).

1 Start the presentation ☐
2 Tell a brief personal story ☐
3 Introduce the improvement to the area ☐
4 Explain how this improvement can be made ☐
5 Say what this improvement means to you ☐
6 Conclude ☐

a Growing up in my area …
b A big thank you for listening.
c It's good to see everyone. Let me get started.
d We could do this by …
e I feel this is so important because …
f What we need where I live is …

YOUR PRESENTATION

6 Read the useful language on the left and make notes for your presentation.

1 Start the presentation Hello and welcome. It's good to see everyone. Let me get started.	
2 Tell a brief personal story Where I live … Growing up in my area … I have a good friend who …	
3 Introduce the improvement to the area What we need here is … An improvement for this area is …	
4 Explain how this improvement can be made We could do this by … To do this …	
5 Say what this improvement means to you I feel this is particularly important because … If this improvement was made I …	
6 Conclude Thanks so much for … A huge thank you for … Does anyone have any questions?	

7 Film yourself giving your presentation or practise in front of a mirror.
Give yourself marks out of ten for …

- speaking clearly. ☐ /10
- using the pace of your talk for emphasis. ☐ /10
- following the six steps in Exercise 6. ☐ /10
- using correct grammar. ☐ /10

12 The future

12.1 Image recognition that triggers augmented reality

TEDTALKS

When they wowed the TED audience with their talk in 2012, **MATT MILLS** and **TAMARA ROUKAERTS** did so as a team – he was Global Head of *Aurasma* and she was Head of Marketing. *Aurasma* is the world's leading augmented-reality app and online platform which launched in 2011 and now has customers in 100 different countries. Since its launch, the app has received several awards, including the Mobile Excellence Award two years in a row. They describe augmented reality as 'the next step on from simply browsing the Internet' because it allows the 'digital content we discover, create and share' to be integrated with what we see around us.

Tamara Roukaerts and Matt Mills

Tamara Roukaerts started her career in advertising at Saatchi & Saatchi before working on Light Blue Optics – a joint venture between Cambridge University and Massachusetts Institute of Technology (MIT). She is now a founding Director of TRM&C, a company that supports high-tech companies with strategic marketing advice.

Matt Mills is a technologist. Before starting at *Aurasma*, he worked first for Autonomy, the company that developed *Aurasma*, managing European sales. Since 2013, Mills has been Commercial Director at Featurespace – a cutting-edge tech company that develops applications to manage and prevent fraud.

CAREER PATHWAYS

1 Read the text. Answer the questions.

  1 What roles did Matt Mills and Tamara Roukaerts have at *Aurasma* at the time of giving the talk?
  2 What professional background did Roukaerts bring?
  3 How has she moved on from *Aurasma*?
  4 What area did Mills start working in after 2013?

TED PLAYLIST

2 Other TED speakers are interested in topics similar to Matt Mills's and Tamara Roukaerts's TED Talk. Read the descriptions of four TED Talks at the top of page 115. In your opinion, which is the best title for the playlist, a, b or c?

  a Future ways to experience the world's wonders safely
  b Interfaces between technology, mind and matter
  c Using Google for education and new inventions

3 Complete the six-word summary (1–4) that corresponds to each talk in the TED playlist. Use these words.

eye	greater	minds	redefining

  1 _____ online maps with 3D capabilities.
  2 _____ experiences from technology in sports.
  3 Making _____ contact with the world.
  4 Using our _____ to control reality.

4 Match the verbs (1–5) with their collocates (a–e). Check your answers in the playlist descriptions.

  1 to showcase   a the idea
  2 to pitch   b somebody's brainwaves
  3 to engage with   c the world
  4 to read   d virtual and physical objects
  5 to control   e capabilities

5 Which talk would you most like to see? Why? Watch the talk at TED.com.

▶ **Blaise Aguera y Arcas: Augmented-reality maps**

Blaise Aguera y Arcas now works on machine learning at Google. Earlier in his career he was the co-creator of Photosynth, a technology that assembles digital photos into 3D environments. In his hands-on talk, he uses futuristic technology, Google Maps and his friends strategically placed at a market to showcase the capabilities of these jaw-dropping augmented-reality maps.

▶ **Chris Kluwe: How augmented reality will change sports ... and build empathy**

Chris Kluwe is a former professional American football player. He pitches the idea of using augmented-reality technology on the sports field in order to more accurately convey the pace and excitement the players experience. Beyond the sports arena, he also suggests that this technology could help people appreciate real global issues and ultimately become more empathetic.

▶ **Sergey Brin: Why Google Glass?**

Sergey Brin is one half of the team who founded Google and leads the development of special projects like Google Glass. Brin explains the philosophy behind this amazing new technology: the desire to engage with the physical and digital worlds simultaneously head on, rather than hunched over our mobile devices.

▶ **Tan Le: A headset that reads your brainwaves**

Tan Le is a technologist and founder and CEO of Emotiv, a bioinformatics company. In her talk she demonstrates an incredible innovation: a headset that reads the wearers' brainwaves and enables them to control virtual and physical objects with only their mind. As she herself says, the demonstration only scratches the surface of what we may ultimately be able to do with technology like this.

AUTHENTIC LISTENING SKILLS Listening for grammatical chunks

6 🎧 **2 40** You are going to hear a podcast in which a member of the *Keynote* team talks about Tan Le's TED Talk, *A headset that reads your brainwaves*. Listen to the sentences and underline the stressed words. Then listen again and circle the grammatical chunks (that are often unstressed).

1 One of my favourite TED Talks is the one from Tan Le called *A headset that reads your brainwaves*.
2 Tan Le starts her talk with her vision to expand human and computer interaction.
3 She reminds us that interpersonal communication is more complex than mere commands.
4 The headset will cost only a few hundred dollars, not thousands.

LISTENING

7 🎧 **2 41** Listen to the full podcast. Answer the questions.

1 According to the podcaster, in what ways is the new technology accessible?
2 What does Rosane mention enjoying about Tan Le's presentation style?
3 What real-life applications are mentioned for the headset?
4 Why will Rosane recommend the talk?

8 🎧 **2 41** Complete the missing words about the talk and the demonstration. Listen again and check your answers.

1 It is explained clearly in three sections: _____ , _____ and _____ .

2 For the demonstration, Evan Grant _____ on stage, _____ the headset and _____ out two tasks.
3 First he tried a simple _____ – he chose 'pull' – and second he tried the much more _____ command, 'disappear'.
4 When the second task didn't quite work he _____ a second neural signal which made the cube disappear.
5 The wheelchair user uses blinks and _____ to tell his chair which way to move.

VOCABULARY IN CONTEXT

9 Read the extracts from the podcast. Choose the correct meaning of the words in bold.

1 Tan Le starts her talk with her vision to expand human and computer **interaction** to include facial expressions and emotions ...
  a science ☐   **b** communication ☐
  c programmes ☐

2 Tan Le manages the whole presentation in such a calm, clear and collected **fashion** that it seems effortless.
  a way ☐   **b** sense ☐   **c** mannerism ☐

3 Mr Grant was a willing **guinea pig** and performed the first task perfectly.
  a display ☐   **b** robot ☐   **c** volunteer ☐

4 If Ms Tan had called someone randomly it could have given even more **credibility** to it.
  a estimation ☐   **b** admiration ☐   **c** value ☐

5 Some people, like this young woman, are **dedicating** their time to developing systems that can help ... people.
  a engaging ☐   **b** giving ☐   **c** doing ☐

12.2 They saw it coming

GRAMMAR Future in the past

1 Choose the best options to complete the text.

The massive impact of a tiny invention

Texas Instruments made the first transistor radio in May 1954 and a few months afterwards [1]*were about to / were to* produce the first ones to sell to the mass market. At about this time the company also employed engineer Jack Kilby, who [2]*was about to / was bound to* invent the integrated circuit for which he received a Nobel Prize. The portable transistor radio [3]*would / was likely to* dramatically change people's listening habits and lifestyles. It [4]*was bound to / were bound to* be a hit with the younger generation, but it also became a hugely popular mobile communications device and billions were manufactured. However, if it hadn't been for another research group's earlier invention, the transistor component by Bell laboratories in 1947, the small size of the transistor [5]*wasn't / wouldn't have been* possible at all. When the small team of three inventors made their discovery, they didn't know how it [6]*was going to be / were going to be* used just a few years later. When they presented it at a conference it was considered [7]*likely to be / unlikely to be* useful and rather odd. Had they known then what it's used for now, it [8]*would have been / would be* a sensation. Walter Brattain, John Bardeen and William Shockley were awarded the Nobel Prize in Physics in 1956 for inventing the small component that [9]*was to be / was bound to be* essential for telecommunications, audio and video recording and aviation systems in years to come.

2 Complete the sentences with these words.

> bound   going   likely   was   were   would

1 If you were _going_ to listen to the radio in 1955 it was probably on a TR19 transistor.

2 The invention of the transistor _was_ to have a huge impact on electronic products being produced in the fifties and sixties.

3 The pocket-sized transistor radio launched in October 1954 was _bound_ to attract large sales as it allowed people to listen to the radio anywhere.

4 When Brattain, Bardeen and Shockley were working on their invention they didn't know they _were_ to be later awarded the Nobel Prize for physics.

5 Other companies were _likely_ to have been planning similar devices but Texas Instruments were the first to corner the market for transistor radios.

6 The invention of the transistor _would_ transform people's listening experience for ever.

3 Match the two parts of the sentences.

1 Until he lived in France he believed the language wouldn't ☐
2 She was bound to get nervous ☐
3 They were about to close the gate ☐
4 The new recruit was unlikely to need help ☐
5 It looked likely to rain ☐
6 We were going to fly ☐

a so she put an umbrella in her bag.
b before the presentation; she always did.
c but the train was much cheaper.
d interest him.
e when he appeared and managed to board the plane.
f from anyone as he was extremely self-sufficient.

4 Choose the best expressions describing the future in the past.

1 A Spanish woman, Juliana Morrell, *was to become / was becoming* the first woman to obtain a university degree in 1608.

2 For many years women *were going to be / were about to be* in the minority in further education.

3 It was *bound to be / unlikely to be* straightforward for women to get the same educational rights as men.

4 Women *would not teach / were to teach* at university until Laura Bassi, an Italian, became the first to teach at a European university in 1732.

5 In 1850 Lucy Sessions *will / would* earn a degree in the USA, becoming the first black woman to do so.

6 The Edinburgh Seven, a group of female students who began studies in medicine in 1869, could not finish their studies but *were / would* to gain publicity for the rights of women to study at university.

7 Legislation was going *to pass / to be passed* in 1877 to allow women to attend university.

GRAMMAR EXTRA! Tentative use of the past when talking about the future

5 🎧 **2 42** Listen to the conversation. When do they make an appointment for?

6 🎧 **2 42** Try to complete the conversation with the correct form of the verb in brackets. Then listen and check. Which verb isn't a tentative use of the past to talk about the future?

I: Hi, Frank. How's it going? Actually, I
¹ _____ (wonder) if we could squeeze in a meeting before I go away.

F: OK. Let's see. When ² _____ (have) in mind?

I: Well, I was going to go to Frankfurt for two days, but that's been cancelled. So I ³ _____ (think) of Wednesday the twelfth or Thursday the thirteenth.

F: Well, I ⁴ _____ (be) down to be in a teleconference on Wednesday afternoon ….

I: It's just that I ⁵ _____ (hope) to hand over the project before I go away. How about Thursday morning?

F: OK. What time ⁶ _____ (want) to meet? Any time after ten is fine with me.

I: Let's say ten-thirty then. Thank you. That's great. It wouldn't have been possible if the Frankfurt trip
⁷ _____ (cancel).

PRONUNCIATION Sentence stress in explaining outcomes

7 🎧 **2 43** Underline the word(s) that will be stressed in order to convey the meaning expressed in brackets. Then listen and check your answers.

1 The project team was going to meet again before my holiday. (not after)

2 They were going to cancel the launch meeting. (not rearrange)

3 I was thinking of Thursday morning. (not Tuesday)

4 I thought Ricardo was going to call. (not you)

DICTATION

8 🎧 **2 44** Listen to someone talking about a fair. Complete the paragraph.

In 1964, _____
of the future than we have today? Ryan Ritchey thinks so and explores the topic in his documentary, *After the Fair*, about the World's Fair in 1964 in New York. This fair _____
and other technological and cultural trends face to face for the first time. It _____
made it in the two six-month seasons it was open. It was a vision of the future, _____
_____ colonies on the moon and cities underwater. On the other hand, many visitors _____
_____ and getting an answer, something many of us do regularly now. There were also picture phones that _____
because outward appearances were less important then than they are nowadays.

12.3 Half full or half empty?

READING

1 ∩ 2 45 Match the generations (1–5) with the dates (a–e). Then listen and check.

1 Generation Y / Millennials ☐
2 Generation Z ☐
3 Baby Boomers ☐
4 Mature Silents ☐
5 Generation X ☐

a 1927–1945
b 1946–1964
c 1965–1980
d 1981–2000
e 2001 onwards

2 Complete the article (a–e) with the generation headings from Exercise 1 (1–5).

What about the future?

I've been thinking about the future: do generations see it differently? I contacted people I know belonging to each demographic and asked: 'What changes do you think the next five years will bring?'

a_____ is the most ethnically diverse and it's the 'Kids Growing Older Younger' generation or KGOY. This generation aren't children for long and are making their own choices earlier than any previous generation. They embrace computers, digital content and learning and say:

'People will spend more time using their mobile phones but actually communicate less.' Lily

'Cities will be even more crowded, there will be more plastic waste. I think more people will be vegetarians.' Mia

b_____ is the 'latchkey' generation where both parents worked and whose world view is based on change. Most had computers at high school and are comfortable with technology. They are entrepreneurial with little commitment to one career or company. They say:

'The biggest changes will come from quantum leaps in technology as the Internet of things finally arrives.' Nick

'I hope 2020 brings scientific developments in medical advancement to reduce suffering due to disease.' Dy

c_____ is a disciplined and cautious generation. It was the first to have television and rock and roll. Men tended to be the breadwinners and were loyal to one company while women stayed at home to look after the children. They say:

'I just want my grandchildren to inherit a clean and safe world.' Sonia

'The drive to automate jobs; for example: self-service check-outs, driverless vehicles, online services, means there is a real threat, perhaps even more than global warming. There's a real risk that many people will have no work.' Mike

d_____ are concerned with both family and friends and the world beyond their own neighbourhoods – the local and global community. The first digital natives, they are very comfortable with the latest technologies. They don't expect a job for life and prefer more relaxed work environments. They say:

'Consumerism will increase but the education system will improve. It will be easier for kids with special needs to attend the same school as their peers.' Adrian

'I think that in five years' time, it will be even more important for people to speak up and start working actively towards change.' Janis

e_____ have two subsets: the 'hippies' concerned with harmony and happiness, and 'yuppies' who climbed the career ladder and earn and live very well. Women started to work and children became independent quickly. They were the first physically fit and wealthy generation and have grown up with television but are digital immigrants. They say:

'I guess, unfortunately, that the social gap between people doing well and those doing less well will increase significantly.' Tina

'Mainstream consumer goods like music, clothes and digital content will cost almost nothing once you are a member of an accepted social community. But anything special will cost much more.' Sam

Overall, interestingly, the comments showed more similarity than difference in their hopes for a better world.

3 Read the article. Are these statements true (T) or false (F)?

1 The youngest generation is the most ethnically diverse. ☐

2 The opinions in the final section (e) include those of both yuppies and hippies. ☐

3 The oldest generation are the most comfortable with change. ☐

4 Baby Boomers expected to have a lifetime career with the same company. ☐

5 At least two generations are described as being good at making their own way in the world. ☐

6 Generation X is the first generation to live with fewer diseases. ☐

4 ∩ 2 46 Listen and choose the correct options to complete the notes about predictions for the next five years.

1 Generation Z: *more / less* laziness; *more / less* understanding

2 Generation Y: *everything / some things* worse; hope for *less / more* support for each other

3 Generation X: *very little / a great deal of* change; *fewer / more* phones

4 Baby Boomers: should be *more / less* concerned with technological changes; should *appreciate / try to improve* what we have

5 Mature Silents: should *return to / move away from* old family traditions; this is *likely / unlikely* to happen

VOCABULARY Optimism and pessimism

5 Complete the sentences. Use these words and phrases.

bad things	bright side	cloud	dark cloud
half empty	half full	hope	tunnel

1 She's ever the optimist isn't she? She always finds a way to look on the _____ .

2 It's time we faced up to it. There really is no _____ in sight for our team. They'll certainly go down a division next season.

3 The way I see it is that he's a glass _____ type of person; he tends to think that the outlook is bleak.

4 The project is nearly finished; we can finally see a light at the end of the _____ .

5 'If _____ can happen, they certainly will' is almost a self-fulfilling prophecy. I prefer positive thinking; then good things are more likely to happen.

6 Our colleagues from Marketing are paid to see the glass as _____ . They say we can focus our efforts on maximizing the strengths of the brand.

7 I can't help seeing a _____ on the horizon; the last meeting made it clear they don't want to work with us on this. I think we are back to square one.

8 He wasn't selected for promotion but then he found a better job at another company. Every _____ has a silver lining.

WORDBUILDING Compound adjectives

6 Compound adjectives are made up of two adjectives or an adverb + adjective combination. Match the opposites (1–6) with the adjectives they collocate with (a–f) to make compound adjectives.

1 open- / narrow-   **a** populated
2 highly / poorly   **b** witted
3 quick- / slow-   **c** minded
4 densely / sparsely   **d** willed
5 well- / poorly-   **e** skilled
6 strong- / weak-   **f** educated

7 Complete the sentences with the correct compound adjectives from Exercise 6.

1 Along with Mongolia and Namibia, Australia is one of the most _____ countries in the world with just three people or fewer per square kilometre.

2 He's very _____ ; he's kept to the strict diet the doctor put him on for the last six months.

3 The company philosophy is an _____ one, embracing all forms of diversity.

4 Massive Open Online Courses (MOOCs), widely available since 2012, allow less _____ people with access to the Internet to get a university-level education.

5 She's such a _____ young woman. She comes up with great ideas and she picks things up very quickly.

6 Rather than exploit _____ people in areas of high unemployment, companies could offer training to improve their skills.

WORD FOCUS Partitive expressions

8 Partitive expressions are used to describe a part of or an example of something. Match the partitives (1–6) with the nouns they are used with (a–f).

1 a glimmer   **a** of luck
2 a drop   **b** of inspiration
3 a bundle   **c** of information
4 a flash   **d** of hope
5 a stroke   **e** of rain
6 a mine   **f** of laughs

9 Complete the sentences with the partitive expressions from Exercise 8.

1 She was lost for ideas but suddenly had a _____ for her presentation opening and used a short film clip.

2 The weekend meeting wasn't a _____ as you can imagine. Think yourself lucky you didn't have to go.

3 When I was an intern, my colleagues were such a _____ . I learned so much from them.

4 Thanks to a worldwide campaign there is now a _____ for this endangered species.

5 Despite what the weather forecast predicted there wasn't a _____ at the wedding.

6 That was a _____ ! I was late but my train was even later.

12.4 Is Friday good for you?

MAKING ARRANGEMENTS

1 Match the verbs (1–6) with the correct words (a–f).

1 to arrange to	**a** work
2 to make the	**b** something in
3 to make something	**c** someone
4 to organize / cancel	**d** meeting
5 to pencil	**e** a meeting
6 to confirm with	**f** meet

2 🎧 2 47 Listen to a conversation. What is the meeting about? Tick (✓) the expressions from Exercise 1 as you hear them.

1 I want to arrange to meet about ☐
2 you could make the meeting ☐
3 like to cancel our meeting ☐
4 make something work ☐
5 Let's pencil it in ☐
6 can confirm with everyone else ☐

3 🎧 2 47 Complete the phrases for making arrangements under each heading. Then listen again and check your answers.

Asking about availability

1 _____, if you could make the meeting next week.

2 _____ Tuesday morning?

3 _____ that work for you?

Saying yes

4 _____ be good.

5 If I can participate by phone _____ .

Saying no

6 It's not ideal timewise, _____ .

7 Wednesday and Thursday are _____ , I'm afraid.

8 Tuesday morning? I'm _____ .

Agreeing

9 _____ pencil it in.

10 _____ great.

4 Complete the emails. Use these words.

any good	can reschedule	confirmed then
postpone to	supposed to	was meant

a

Thanks Sam. Yes. I can make it by phone. My train's ¹ _____ leave at 18.15 so I can join the meeting then. Hope Bert and Liz can make it. Looking forward to it. Felix.

b

Hi all,
I ² _____ to be in Bert's team meeting on Tuesday as well, so I can make it.
Have a good day.
Liz

c

Hi all,
Thanks everyone. That's ³ _____ . Tuesday at six thirty. The board is forwarding us some information about what they'd like so we can think things over beforehand.
Best wishes
Sam

d

Hi all,
Hope you had a good holiday, Felix. Anyway, yes, the meeting. I was going to have a team meeting at that time, but I ⁴ _____ it easily. So, yeah, I'm around. Any time after six is fine.
Bert

e

Hi all,
About meeting next week to discuss our 25-year anniversary event: is Tuesday after six ⁵ _____ for you? Please accept or decline as soon as possible.
Best wishes, Sam

f

Hi all,
Good you can all make it. I'm supposed to be in another meeting until half past but I can attend, if we ⁶ _____ six thirty.
Or if everyone's ready early, start without me.
All the best, Norma

5 Put the emails to and from the team (a–f) in the order in which they were likely to have been sent (1–6).

1 ☐ **2** ☐ **3** ☐ **4** ☐ **5** ☐ **6** ☐

PRONUNCIATION Sentence stress in making arrangements

6 🎧 **2 48** Listen to the conversation. Underline the words that are most strongly stressed in each question or statement.

1 a Is Thursday afternoon any good for you?
  b Any time after two is fine.
2 a Would Friday at nine work for you?
  b I'm supposed to be meeting Jake but I may be able to postpone it.
3 a It's not ideal, to be honest, but if we make it ten instead of nine I can manage it.
  b Sure, yeah, I'm around.
4 a How about Monday morning?
  b Monday's out for me but Tuesday would work.

WRITING SKILL Impersonal language

7 Complete the email from the management team to the planning committee about the event. Use these phrases.

another suggestion	been planned	one proposal
the objection	various suggestions	was agreed
was discussed	was suggested	

Dear Sam and the rest of the team,

We met last week to discuss plans for our anniversary event. ¹_____ were made about the form it should take. ²_____ was to invite retired employees to attend as well as staff and their families and our customers. It ³_____ that this would be a good idea.

An overall theme for the event ⁴_____ , but not everyone could agree on it. ⁵_____ for activities was to have a light-hearted quiz with prizes but ⁶_____ to this was that it's difficult to hold 200 people's attention. Catering ⁷_____ and we agreed on a budget. We also decided to use a local catering firm so that our canteen staff can attend the event. A short programme of speeches, announcements and a short film has ⁸_____ . We would like you to suggest two other activities, an overall theme and a final highlight.

We look forward to hearing your ideas.

Best regards

Mary, Ben & Donald, The management board

8 Complete the notes recording what has been agreed so far.

1 Participants _____
2 Overall theme _____
3 Activity 1 _____
4 Activity 2 _____
5 Food and drinks _____
6 Official programme _____
7 Highlight _____

9 Rewrite the ideas from the meeting in impersonal language.

1 Bert proposed a local catering company who have vintage BBQ carts and cater for summer parties.
(food and drink) One proposal *was to use a local catering company, who cater for summer parties with vintage BBQ carts.*
2 Felix suggested a Western theme – inspired by our latest product range.
The suggestion _____ .
3 Sam suggested fireworks as a highlight, but Norma didn't think it was a good idea.
Not everyone _____ .
4 Sam, Norma, Bert, Felix and Liz said a barn dance would match the theme and be fun.
It _____ .
5 Liz suggested a rodeo bull-riding machine as an activity that's fun to do and watch.
The suggestion _____ .

10 Complete the email to the board with the suggestions from the meeting. Use impersonal language and the information from Exercise 9 and the notes below.

Dear Mary, Ben and Donald,
1 Opening: We / pleased / present ideas / anniversary event / from / recent meeting
_____
2 Overall theme: / most appropriate
_____
3 Food and drinks: / fits theme
_____
4 Activity 1: / after discussion
_____
5 Activity 2: / unusual
_____
6 Highlight: / in the end / activities are enough
_____

Best regards

The planning committee

The essay you will read in Exercise 2 is in answer to the following exam question.

> You have recently attended a seminar about how tourism can be made more environmentally friendly. You made the following notes while at the seminar:
>
> **Ways to make tourism more environmentally friendly**
>
> Supporting conservation projects
> Limiting the number of visitors to some sites
> Using vehicles run on renewable energy
>
> Some opinions expressed in the discussion:
> 'That's a great way to learn about the place you're visiting.'
> 'I'd hate to arrive somewhere and find I couldn't get in!'
> 'Who is going to pay for the new vehicles?'
>
> Write an **essay** discussing **two** of the ways tourism could be made more environmentally friendly. You should **explain which you think will be more effective, giving reasons** to support your opinion.
> You may, if you wish, make use of the opinions expressed in the discussion, but you should use your own words as far as possible.
> Write your essay in **220–260 words** in an appropriate style.

IDEAS

1 Tick (✓) the things you would expect to see in the essay.

a one or two sentences summarizing the aim of the essay ☐

b a conclusion, summarizing the writer's opinion ☐

c a description of one way tourism could be made more environmentally friendly ☐

d a second way tourism could be improved, with reasons ☐

e a third paragraph describing another way tourism could be made more sustainable ☐

f a description of an ideal tourist destination ☐

3 Read the essay again. Are these statements true (T) or false (F)?

1 The impact travel has on the environment has increased. ☐

2 Discovering the local culture may encourage tourists to change their habits. ☐

3 You can visit Machu Picchu at any time. ☐

4 Limiting visitor numbers means important sites will be accessible in the future. ☐

5 The writer believes that there should be restrictions on visitor numbers to important sites. ☐

MODEL

2 Read the essay. Match the four paragraphs with a description (a–f) from Exercise 1.

1 ☐   **2** ☐   **3** ☐   **4** ☐

---

¹Human society is having an increasing effect on our environment, particularly through our desire to travel to other places. It is important to consider the consequences of this, and how to reduce the negative effects tourism can have.

²A good way of encouraging tourists to find out about the culture of the places they're visiting would be to help them participate in local conservation projects.

If they understand the impact their actions have on the environment, visitors may be more likely to look after it, for example, by recycling more or not leaving rubbish behind. Tourists may also reduce their carbon footprint by choosing to holiday closer to home or travelling by bus or train rather than by plane.

³One area where tourism has a particularly big impact is the amount of people who visit sensitive sites like Machu Picchu in Peru. The authorities introduced a licence system to limit the number of people walking the Inca Trail each day and give the area time to recover. Although it can be disappointing for tourists who have not planned ahead, it is an important method of controlling our impact on these important places and preserving them for future generations. It may also encourage tourists to find out more about their destination before they travel.

⁴Taking all of these points into consideration, I feel the best way to make tourism more sustainable, and reduce our impact, would be to limit the number of visitors who can go to each place. This will show them that we cannot travel without considering the consequences.

USEFUL LANGUAGE

4 Match the two parts of the introductory sentences.

1 The question of whether volunteers or paid workers are better ☐
2 The way a charity's money should be divided is often ☐
3 More and more companies ☐
4 Over the past twenty years or so, ☐
5 With the large number of charities that now exist, ☐
6 Undoubtedly, it is important to volunteer, ☐

a the number of charities has increased considerably.
b are giving their employees time to volunteer.
c always causes debate.
d how can you decide which one to volunteer for?
e a contentious issue.
f but the question is how can we encourage people to do it.

5 Find and correct the mistake in each sentence. It may be a grammar, vocabulary or punctuation mistake.

1 To begin, by visiting a nature park people can experience the natural world first hand.
2 It would be therefore easier for them to watch programmes on their own television.
3 Besides companies are much more likely to listen to the government than their customers.
4 It is well-known fact that travelling on the underground is faster than using buses.
5 On the other side, a rapid bus system would be much cheaper to develop than a new underground system.
6 Instead of create a large area of solar panels, we could put them on individual buildings.

6 Complete the summarizing sentences. Use these words.

balance	bearing	compared	favour
former	outweigh	rather	sum

1 On _____ , while both visits to nature parks and programmes about the natural world are important, I am in _____ of the latter as the best way to teach people about the environment.
2 _____ all that in mind, I believe that the government should focus on reducing the amount of plastic used in packaging _____ than on trying to make us recycle it.
3 To _____ up, while both types of public transport have their advantages and disadvantages, in my opinion, the benefits of a rapid bus system _____ those of a new underground system.
4 In conclusion, if the advantages of solar power are _____ to those of building new wind turbines, the _____ is clearly more useful to the community.

PLANNING

You will answer the following question.

> Your company has recently been discussing whether they should start a volunteering scheme. As part of the discussion, the following notes were made about possible ways to organize it:
>
> **Structuring the volunteer scheme**
> Each employee chooses their own project
> One project per team
> A company-wide project
>
> Some opinions expressed in the discussion:
> 'We can all choose something that speaks to us.'
> 'We'll work together so much better after that.'
> 'What if you're not interested in the chosen project?'
>
> Write an **essay** discussing **two** of the ways the scheme could be organized. You should **explain which you think will be more effective, giving reasons** to support your opinion.
>
> If you use some of the opinions expressed in the discussion, use your own words as far as possible.

7 Plan your essay. Write notes to answer these questions. Don't write full sentences yet.

1 Which two structures will you write about?
2 Which do you think is more effective?
3 What reasons will you give to support your choice?

WRITING

8 Write an essay to answer the question in Exercise 7. In your essay you should:

- introduce the topic so the reader knows what to expect
- discuss two of the possible structures for the volunteer scheme, saying which you think will be more effective
- give reasons to support your opinion
- write a conclusion which summarizes the essay

Write **220–260 words**.

ANALYSIS

9 Check your essay. Then answer the questions.

- **Content:** Does the essay cover two of the possible structures for the scheme? Does it give supporting reasons? Is it 220 to 260 words long?
- **Communicative achievement:** Is it written in a neutral or formal style? Is it clear?
- **Organization:** Is the essay logically organized? Are the ideas connected?
- **Language:** Does it use correct grammar and a good range of structures and all your own words?

Answer key

UNIT 1

1.1 Less stuff, more happiness

1

1 Currently two. (He's started four (SiteWerks, TreeHugger, Lifeedited and ExceptionLab) and sold the first two.)
2 Webber, designer, environmentalist, entrepreneur and author.
3 Before he travelled the world and lived with less he had large properties and a personal shopper, but then he started simplifying his life and possessions.
4 The ability to edit – our lives and possessions.

2

b Raising awareness about sustainability

3

1 matter   2 rubbish   3 statistics   4 outfit

4

1 c   2 d   3 a   4 e   5 b

6

1 kind of   2 should have   3 want to
4 have to

7

1 T
2 F – He is very passionate about the materials he uses.
3 F – 70–80 per cent of the building materials are recycled.
4 T
5 T

8

1 He got it for $20, including the delivery.
2 By smashing up toilets and using the bits for tiles, in order to recreate the look of froth in a bathroom with a beer theme.
3 What one person doesn't value and throws away can be something wonderful for someone else.
4 Time (to see the potential in things) and the right mindset or way of looking at things.
5 It might inspire us to rethink our quest for perfection and instead to embrace the diverse and the different. (Also to question what is valuable and why.)

9

1 c   2 c   3 a   4 c   5 b

1.2 Luxury or necessity?

2

1 've never had
2 has integrated
3 has almost attained
4 have tended
5 has become
6 had already gained
7 had reached
8 have been drinking
9 will even have found

3

a have you been working   b worked
c perfected   d have you made   e found

4

1 've worked / 've been working
2 'd worked / 'd been working
3 've had
4 'd watched
5 've spent
6 have bought
7 have heated
8 has made
9 will have made
10 'll have inherited
11 've started

5

1 been   2 been   3 gone   4 been   5 been
6 gone

6

1 gone to seed   2 long gone   3 been there, done that   4 has-been   5 been and gone

7

The Grand Café in Oxford was started in 1650 on the site of the oldest coffee house in England. However, the Queen's Lane Coffee House, which has been selling coffee since 1654, is the longest established coffee house in England. Twenty-five years after the first place opened, another 3,000 had been established in Britain. Over the years, they have acted as social centres and places where business has been done. If you have had the chance to drink in a historic café, you will have experienced the special atmosphere. Even before your first sip you will have been transported to another era.

1.3 I'm wide awake

1

1 b   2 a   3 f   4 c   5 e   6 d

2

1 G   2 D   3 C   4 H   5 F   6 A   7 B   8 E

3

1 f   2 e   3 b   4 a   5 c   6 d

4

1 over   2 under   3 under   4 over   5 under

5

1 dissatisfied   2 uncomfortable   3 impolite
4 non-existent   5 inefficient   6 misunderstood
7 illegible   8 decentralized

a 3   b 5   c 7   d 8   e 1   f 4   g 6   h 2

6

1 decentralized   2 dissatisfied
3 uncomfortable   4 impolite   5 inefficient
6 misunderstood   7 illegible   8 non-existent

7

1 sleep on   2 sleep off   3 sleep through
4 sleep over   5 sleep in

8

1 sleep through   2 sleeping on   3 sleep over
4 slept in   5 sleep it off

1.4 Keep it to the bare minimum

1

1 It would help him decide exactly what to study so he doesn't waste money studying the wrong course.
2 It would be a chance to broaden his horizons and gain life experience.
3 It's seen favourably by universities and employers.

2

1 c   2 d   3 b   4 e   5 a

3

a I don't know about you, but
b You might possibly
c It might not be a bad idea to
d It seems to me
e Maybe you're right
f it's reasonable to assume that
g I'm no expert, but

4

1 it's reasonable to assume that
2 it might not be a bad idea to
3 It seems to me
4 I'm no expert, but
5 maybe you're right
6 I don't know about you but
7 you might possibly

5

1 Y   2 Y   3 R   4 W   5 R   6 W

6

a shouldn't necessarily be
b it's worth considering
c can probably conclude
d in all likelihood
e it could be said to be
f There seems to be a widely held view that
g it would appear
h it's often thought that

7

1 f   2 h   3 d   4 c   5 b   6 a   7 e   8 g

8

1 or 2 are most likely as the others don't benefit the planet and the community and au pairing doesn't involve a team.

9

1 F – Most people
2 T
3 F – The person doing it reaps the most benefit.
4 T
5 T

10

1 suggesting suggests   2 to consider considering   3 in every likelihood in all likelihood
4 certain certainly   5 will would   6 say said

11 (Example answer)

Dear Martin

Thank you for your interest in our organization. I'm pleased to provide some more details of the programmes you mention.

It is often thought that conservation projects require hard physical work. This may not be entirely true – the work is challenging and volunteers need to be physically fit – but we use machines too.

It's arguably more important that volunteers aren't afraid to be outdoors and get dirty than that they are strong.

The projects start four times a year with a short orientation in Auckland. There will almost certainly be places free, should you be interested in joining us this September.

There will probably be projects involving erosion management, as well as tree planting, looking for willing young people like yourself to join them.

We look forward to receiving your application.

Best regards

Jake

PRESENTATION 1

1

a Aiko **b** Vanessa **c** Jan **d** Vanessa
e Aiko **f** Jan

3 (Example answers)

1 My lifestyle is about changing my habits and eating more healthily.
2 Cookery books are some of the most important things in making my lifestyle possible. I get so much inspiration from them, as well as taking advice on new recipes from friends and family.
3 I had to buy quite a lot of equipment – cooking utensils and some electric appliances – in order to be able to prepare the food I wanted to cook.
4 Kitchen and cooking utensils

5

1 d 2 a 3 b 4 c

6 (Example answers)

1 My name's (name) and today I'm going to talk to you about my lifestyle.
2 Staying mentally active is an important part of my lifestyle. I try to exercise my brain and imagination whenever I can. I think it can help prevent a lot of problems relating to mental health.
3 The most important thing for me is making sure that my brain is fully engaged and tested every day. I can do this in small ways, like doing crosswords and Sudoku puzzles, but this doesn't always give me the mental workout I need. So I try more challenging things like learning new languages or attending workshops and seminars.
4 That's it from me. Does anyone have any questions?

UNIT 2

2.1 Who am I? Think again

1

1 British, Indian, and Chinese / Taiwanese.
2 75 exhibitions internationally, alone and in groups.
3 Getting him to help with transforming a car into a work of art. Performing with him in a dance which explores the issue of nature vs. nurture.
4 It explores how Patel's identity was shaped by both his Indian origin and the influences of popular culture.

2

b Discovering and exploring identity

3

1 rhyming 2 tales 3 constant 4 soul

4

1 d 2 a 3 b 4 e 5 c

6

1 Pico Iyer's talk resonated deeply with me on a personal level.
2 I was born in the south of England, but I've lived abroad much longer than I've lived in Britain.
3 This last statement seems to ring true for him, and it certainly does for me.
4 Pico Iyer is such a crisp, clear and calm presenter.

7

1 something you feel inside of you
2 paints with his words
3 his house being burned down
4 loved the quiet it offered

8

1 She has lived abroad a lot and calls a country other than her own home.
2 People who live in countries that aren't where they grew up or where they originate from.
3 That you can lose everything and still have a home. Home is not four walls.
4 He developed a strong liking for silence and stillness, was able to make decisions and did some of his most important work.
5 Noticing things that have been taken for granted, being more aware of your surroundings.

9

1 b 2 a 3 a 4 a 5 c

2.2 Cyber crime

1

1 defrauding 2 impersonating 3 obtaining
4 using 5 revealing

2

1 g 2 a 3 f 4 d 5 b 6 c 7 e

3

1 The vast majority of
2 A sizeable portion of
3 About half of targets
4 a little less than a quarter
5 A little over a third
6 a small number
7 About twice as many

4

1 plural 2 singular 3 singular 4 singular and plural 5 plural

5

1 deal of, is
2 twice as many
3 small minority of, are
4 does, a handful
5 vast majority of, don't
6 fifty per cent

6

1 A large amount of
2 double the number of
3 a handful of
4 a tiny number
5 A considerable number of

7

1 Yes, 12, 14, 16 of March and 19 and 20 of March – all in the same week. (all weak)
2 If you didn't make those payments yourself, you may well have been a victim of a phishing scam. (not weak)
3 Unfortunately, only a very small minority of criminals are caught, but the credit card company does cover the losses in all but a handful of cases. (all weak)

8

The vast majority of software companies say the key to preventing phishing scams is awareness, caution and using up-to-date security. However, a considerable number of insurance companies offer policies to protect us from identity theft too. Apparently, it's the fastest growing form of insurance according to the Insurance Information Institute. A great deal of policies are available for a little less than $30. But, as only a small minority of banks and credit card providers don't reimburse people suffering a loss, is it really necessary? Statistics show that under fifty per cent of people suffering losses due to ID theft had to pay more than $1,000 themselves. Insurers cover up to five times this amount with their service and offer peace of mind.

2.3 You are what you wear

1

1 b 2 c 3 a

2

1 T
2 F — less formal
3 F — It merged with an IT company.
4 T
5 F — it excludes clothing usually worn at the gym

3

1 summarize **2** similarly **3** displayed
4 consolidate **5** appropriate for **6** adapted
7 usually **8** started

4

1 dark and smart
2 hoodies and scruffy
3 shirts and blouses
4 suits and ties
5 pullovers
6 sportswear and slogan

5

1 d **2** c **3** a **4** h **5** b **6** e **7** f **8** g

6

1 looks trendy, unconventional
2 tasteful suit
3 scruffy jeans
4 glamorous clothes, imaginative look
5 clashing clothes, classic style

7

1 d **2** f **3** b **4** c **5** e **6** a **7** h **8** g

8

1 roll our sleeves up
2 dressing up
3 take your hat off to her
4 fits him like a glove
5 pull up his socks / pull his socks up
6 under her belt
7 given the boot
8 to be in your/his/her/their shoes

2.4 I need to work on my image

1

1 starting your own business
2 ask for some professional advice
3 reading a self-help book
4 Doing a course to get started
5 rewriting your CV

2

1 Have you considered that
2 Remember
3 Don't lose heart
4 You mustn't
5 I would seriously consider

3

1 d **2** a **3** f **4** b **5** e **6** c

4

1 ↑↑ **2** ↑↓ **3** – **4** ↓↓ **5** ↓↑ **6** ↑↑
Sentences 3 and 5

5

Dear Erik,
Thank you for your hard work on the course.
I can really see that you've made progress, particularly with your shyness.
I appreciated your positive contributions in group discussions.
I was impressed by the way you worked on your body language and eye contact,
in particular when you were talking about your last job in the second interview recording. I can really see an improvement.
You also improved how you answered the questions. You were more focused and that made a better impression.
However, as we said on the course, *your general appearance needs to be a little smarter and a visit to the hairdresser could make a difference.*

If I were you, I'd keep trying to find a job in the hotel sector as you seemed to really enjoy the last job you had. *Don't give up* and *don't forget that it wasn't the quality of your work that was the reason for the redundancy.*

We will keep in contact over the next few weeks. Please keep me informed of your interview experience and *let me know if I can support you further.*

I wish you the very best of luck with your continuing job search.

Best regards

Amanda

6

1 it
2 ~~impressive~~ impressed
3 ~~the more~~ the most
4 ~~took on~~ take on
5 ~~to work~~ working
6 ~~a haircut have~~ have a haircut
7 ~~interested~~ interesting
8 ~~be~~ being

7 (Possible answers)

1 (a little) more confident **2** more computer literate **3** a little smarter **4** with real experience in marketing / with marketing skills **5** with better communication skills **6** who can speak some French

8

1 considering how nervous you were at the start
2 your use of humour to relax the group
3 the way you took feedback on board
4 you managed your papers
5 your appearance with your hair tied back
6 you still need practice
7 I would rewrite your CV
8 taking an IT course

WRITING 1

1 a, c, d, f

2 **1** a **2** c **3** d **4** f

3 **1** T **2** F – It would be fairly cheap **3** T
 4 F – our urban office environment **5** T

4

1 The purpose | of this proposal | is to recommend | a destination for | a weekend away | and to give reasons | for my choice.
2 This proposal | has been written | to evaluate | suggestions for | a weekend away | and to decide | which is best.
3 The aim | of this proposal | is to outline | possible destinations for | a weekend away | and to select | the best option | for the company to book.
4 This proposal | is intended | to summarize | the outcomes of Thursday's meeting | and to suggest | a destination | for the company weekend away.

5

1 The whole team would **definitely** benefit much more from spending time outside.
2 We could do a tour of the castle, in addition **to** visiting the cathedral.
3 **Another** major benefit of visiting an activity centre would be the choice of sporting activities available.
4 Spending time in the city **should offer** something for everyone.
5 **Not only** does a national park offer beautiful views, but it also gives you the chance to learn more about nature.

6

1 experience **2** highlight **3** mentioned
4 importance **5** doubt **6** reason

7

1 a **2** d **3** c **4** e **5** b

9 (Example answer)

I recently realized that tourists' exposure to Paraguayan culture is not as wide-ranging as it could be when they visit our country. I have therefore decided to propose a cultural tour of Paraguay to improve this situation.

Guarani

Guarani is the most widely spoken language in Paraguay, more so than Spanish. If you hire a Guarani teacher to lead short classes on the first day of the tour, they could teach basic polite phrases, numbers and food. Organizing these classes in the capital city, Asunción, would also give people time to get used to the heat in the country when they first arrive.

Handicrafts

Visits to see traditional arts and crafts being produced would be a key part of any cultural tour of Paraguay. To build their awareness of the range of traditional art produced in our country, you could offer visitors various options as part of their tour, for instance, seeing traditional embroidery called 'ao po'i' or 'fine textile' in Guaira, 'ñanduti' lace making in Asunción or leather work in Ypacarai.

Caacupé

Finally, a key part of Paraguayan life is the Catholic religion, so it should certainly be included in a cultural tour of the country. The most important site is a town called Caacupé, outside Asunción, where visitors would be able to learn about the pilgrimage which takes place there on 8th December every year.

I am confident that if a tour focusing on these aspects of Paraguayan life were to be put together, tourists would leave our country with a much more complete view of our culture.

UNIT 3

3.1 Making peace is a marathon

1

1 Local children, because they were curious.
2 Vision and determination.
3 Local and international, elite and non-elite runners, and wheelchair users.
4 Peace

2

c Working towards mutual understanding

3

1 foreign 2 poster 3 persuasion 4 world

4

1 c 2 d 3 a 4 e 5 b

6

1 d 2 b 3 c 4 e 5 a

7

1 b 2 d 3 a 4 c

8

1 They are very candid (honest) and show ordinary people from both sides, distinguishable only by their flags.
2 Because it has the feel-good optimism we associate with a film.
3 Both online and real face-to-face friendships.
4 It made her think about her brother's humanitarian work in the Middle East (and of all the pictures she has seen and stories she's heard about the intelligence and humanity of the people he's met.)
5 When she reads about a nation in conflict, she will have very different images in her head as a result of the pictures Edry has shown us of kind committed people.

9

1 a 2 b 3 b 4 c 5 a

3.2 What's the magic number?

1

Cleft sentences: 3, 5, 7, 8

2

1 It's working on my own that I've had enough of.
2 It's been twenty years since I've had (any) colleagues.
3 I thought it was the freedom and independence that you liked.
4 What I don't want to give up is my freedom.

5 What I've been thinking is that I'd really like to go into partnership with someone else.
6 The person I need is someone with good social media skills.
7 The thing I miss is having someone to share ideas with.
8 The way you/to solve problems is by talking about them with someone.

3

1 who it is that I have in mind
2 would work well is that we would both benefit from
3 you're lacking is social media skills
4 it's your project that gave me the idea

4

1 It's great communication skills that can make or break a career in PR.
2 It's working on my own that I've had enough of.
3 I thought it was the freedom and independence that you liked.
4 Actually, it's your project that gave me the idea.
5 What I don't want is to give up my freedom.

5

1 c 2 d 3 b 4 a

6

1 attending the PR course did was change
2 happened was the co-founders started to disagree about everything
3 thing the marketing manager is interested in is
4 I'll / I will do is make sure the trade fair dates are
5 the reporter focused on was the
6 until I changed companies that I realized how competitive

7

Public relations, or PR, is what businesses do to improve and maintain their reputations and increase brand awareness in the eyes of the public. What's key to PR is how the message is spread and to whom. Nowadays, it's not just the press release that counts; it's the combined effect of press, media and social media channels. And it's not only positive stories that create good public responses according to a 2011 survey. The surprising thing the survey found was that about a third of reviewers react positively after a negative review is dealt with appropriately by the company in question.

3.3 Dare to be different

1

b An economist's unusual take on everyday problems packaged in a readable way.

2

1 When Dubner was asked to interview Levitt for an article.
2 Radio shows, podcasts, blogs, (five) books, a film.
3 Levitt has a quirky way of looking at the world; Dubner brings the ideas across to a lay audience, making them more accessible.

4 Insatiable curiosity, quick wit and enthusiasm for trying things out.

3

1 creatively
2 daring to
3 not to do
4 more effective
5 different to
6 possibly went unnoticed by

4

1 e 2 c 3 f 4 a 5 b 6 d

5

1 in 2 in 3 out

6

1 playing it safe
2 fitted in
3 blend in, to go with the flow
4 rocked the boat
5 stick his neck out

7

1 e 2 b 3 f 4 d 5 c 6 a

8

1 wind and wind 2 content and content
3 minute and minute 4 close and close
5 bow and bow 6 present and present

9

1 playing with fire d 2 play it by ear c
3 playing games a 4 play your cards right b
5 playing for time e 6 play along with f

3.4 Which one gets your vote?

1

1 d 2 c 3 b 4 a

2

1 views 2 don't 3 proposal 4 Right
5 your take 6 condition, agree 7 view
8 suggest

3

2 I don't know about you, but I think it's better to share out what we give.
3 Do we really want to be restricted in the future?
4 I may be wrong, but I think it's more complicated with a money transfer.
5 We could look at this from a different perspective: what are our core values? OR We could look at this from a different perspective and think about our core values.
6 Can you seriously picture the whole company agreeing to support the environment?

4

1 I don't know about you, but I think it's better to share it out.
2 Do we really want to be restricted?
3 Why don't we choose the special needs school?

4 I may be <u>wrong</u>, but I think it's <u>more complicated</u>.

5 We could look at this from a <u>different perspective</u>.

6 Hmmm, I'm not so sure I <u>agree</u>.

7 I'll <u>agree</u> to the proposal so long as we choose something else <u>next year</u>.

8 Can we resolve this by agreeing that we invite Childtrust to <u>meet</u> with us?

5

1 I'd like to thank   **2** I'm afraid I may not
3 had second thoughts   **4** As you know
5 may not be   **6** let me know

6

1 To reach a consensus.
2 Some participants had second thoughts.
3 To meet both charities and make a more informed choice, spending more time, if necessary.

7

1 I'm afraid   **2** wonder if   **3** possibly find
4 may not be   **5** If we can

8

1 wonder if we could   **2** 've had second thoughts about   **3** Could we possibly
4 If we can have

9 (Example answer)

Dear Ant

I'm afraid I may not have explained myself very clearly in the meeting yesterday. I've had second thoughts about what we discussed. I did say I'd accept the local idea if we all agreed but I wonder if we could discuss it more as I think we should choose a more worthy cause. I'm afraid I don't think we thought things through enough. Could we discuss it again?

Thanks

Best wishes

Helen

PRESENTATION 2

1

1 c   **2** a   **3** b

5

1 d   **2** e   **3** a   **4** b   **5** c

6 (Example answers)

1 My name's (name). Today's presentation is about where I come from.
2 My home is in a town in the north of France and the place where I live is quiet and quite traditional. My family have been here for the past 60 or so years.
3 My family first came here because my grandparents were looking for work. They used to live on a farm in a nearby village, but over time it became tougher and tougher to make a living. They came when my father was a baby.

4 My grandfather says the pace of life is a lot faster here. On the farm, what happened every day depended on the time of year and working with animals or crops was a lot more peaceful compared to the urban environment we live in now. However, a faster lifestyle can have some benefits – like being able to go to the shops and get things that can't be easily found in the countryside.
5 It's been great to share this with you today. I hope you understand a little bit more about where I come from. Does anyone have any questions?

UNIT 4

4.1 How I beat stage fright

1

1 He's a musician and graphic designer, takes photos and is good at various crafts.
2 He agreed to give the TED Talk and then found a way (using his own stage fright as the topic) to help him with his fear.
3 He practised about a hundred times and had coaching.
4 It was a TED Talk of the week, it has attracted over one million views and has probably led to more publicity for his other songs and albums.

2

a Changing our perceptions

3

1 potential   **2** fear   **3** future   **4** stress

4

1 c   **2** a   **3** e   **4** d   **5** b

6 (Possible answers)

1 1,000 people were asked about their perceived stress levels. Study 2
2 30,000 people were asked about their perceived stress levels. Study 1
3 Five years – duration of Study 2 when 1,000 adults were studied. Study 2
4 30% increased chance of dying if people suffer stressful life experience. Study 2
5 43% higher chance of dying if adults believed stress was bad for them. Study 1

7

1 F – She used to. Now she sees it as something that can be managed.
2 T
3 F – It reduces the harmful effects of stress.

8

1 Stress can be useful as long as you think positively about it. It's getting stressed about stress that can make us sick.
2 Social contact makes our body more resilient to stress.
3 The science is accessible through simple explanations, pictures and examples.
4 It makes us focus too much on our present, our problems and ourselves.

5 She'll recommend it to several friends who have always considered stress as a risk, danger or threat.

9

1 c   **2** c   **3** a   **4** a   **5** b

4.2 Information overload

1

1 approximately   **2** as many as   **3** roughly
4 as much as   **5** about   **6** just over
7 around   **8** nearly   **9** more or less
10 some

2

1 T
2 T
3 T
4 T
5 F – as many as fifty
6 F – about two days

3

1 a   **2** c   **3** b   **4** c   **5** a   **6** c

4

1 f   **2** g   **3** e   **4** c   **5** b   **6** h   **7** d   **8** a

5

1 tallish   **2** newish   **3** thirtyish   **4** latish
5 childish   **6** longish

6

1 odd   **2** a kind of   **3** something like   **4** stuff
5 other things   **6** sort of

7

Stress usually on the content words of the sentence which may sometimes be the approximation.
1 Yes, sometimes as many as <u>a hundred</u>.
2 No, it cost about a <u>fiver</u> but it's really good.
3 It did! It's just over <u>350 a minute</u> at the moment.
4 <u>More or less</u> all morning most days.
5 Oh, by as much as <u>fifteen per cent</u> they say.
6 Yes, and it took me <u>approximately</u> two hours to read.
7 <u>Nearly 25</u>. A few extra joined at the last minute.
8 Roughly <u>one and a half</u>, but it depends on the week.

8

The brain is the most complex organ in the body. <u>It has a surface area of approximately 150–200</u> cm². That is kind of like a double page of a newspaper. The human brain <u>weighs about 1,300 grams and is roughly the size of</u> a small cauliflower. It makes up around 2% of what the body weighs but it uses <u>20% of the oxygen and 20% of the energy needed by</u> the body. It's made up of as many as 100 billion neurons and the senses send the brain <u>up to 11 million bits of information per second for processing</u>. Most of the processing is automatic but <u>the brain consciously processes some 50 bits per</u>

second of information. Research shows that the brain can make new connections, grow and adapt even with increasing age.

4.3 Get the name right

1

1 b   2 a   3 d   4 c

2

1 N   2 E   3 N   4 DS   5 E   6 E

3

1 naming consultant   2 verbal identity
3 fun, excitement   4 something desirable   5 descriptive name   6 literal, metaphorical
7 short, catchy   8 imagination, Internet

4

1 c   2 f   3 h   4 g   5 a   6 d   7 e   8 b

5

1 got a cool reception
2 voiced our concerns
3 make a splash
4 came up against a brick wall
5 sold like hot cakes
6 met with opposition
7 is not an obstacle
8 address the issue

6

2 the problem is solvable   3 is changeable
4 Flats in London are unaffordable for most young people.   5 it's manageable   6 very approachable   7 The firework display we saw on the Rhine was unforgettable.

7

1 d   2 h   3 f   4 a   5 e   6 c   7 b   8 g

8

1 peace and quiet   2 wear and tear   3 heart and soul   4 pros and cons   5 safe and sound
6 black and white   7 bits and pieces   8 sick and tired

4.4 I thought it would be easy

1

b Explaining how to use a teleconferencing tool

2

1 b   2 d   3 e   4 a   5 c

3

1 with you, mind giving   2 Did you
3 Would you, missed that   4 just being

4

1 F   2 R   3 F   4 F   5 R   6 R

5

1 d   2 f   3 e   4 b   5 a   6 c

6

1 Don't let the cat sleep on the beds as/because he has his own bed.
2 Water the house plants if/when they need it.
3 Close the shutters at night for security reasons.
4 Let the neighbours use the lawnmower because/as we share tools.
5 Leave the key with the neighbours so the next guest can get in.

7

1 Beware of   2 I'd be grateful if you would
3 Bear in mind that   4 I've got one request
5 Just to be on the safe side   6 Be careful not to

8

1 Beware of shutting   2 Be sure to   3 Bear in mind   4 Just to be on the safe side   5 I'd be grateful

9 (Example answer)

Dear John

I hope you enjoy using the office when I'm away. There are a few things you should bear in mind:

Be sure to lock / unlock the phone with number 4546, so no one else uses it.

Just to be on the safe side, please check for viruses and updates on the computer so the system stays secure.

I'd be grateful if you watered my plant so it doesn't die.

Thanks in advance

Best wishes

Geraldine

WRITING 2

1 a, b, c, d, e

2 1 d   2 e   3 a   4 b   5 c

3 1 F   2 T   3 T   4 F   5 T

4

1 As a result of this
2 It is hoped that
3 It is my belief that
4 I would advise against
5 It would be to our advantage to
6 It would not be beneficial to

5

1 **The majority of people I spoke to** expressed a desire for fewer emails to be sent.
2 This report is written **in light of responses to a questionnaire** conducted last week.
3 We compiled this report **taking account of feedback received** over the previous quarter.
4 **According to the majority of respondents**, there is a need for managers to reduce the amount of messages they send.
5 This report aims to suggest ways to communicate more effectively **based on feedback collected from our staff.**

---

6 The recommendations in this report are **the result of a survey conducted among our colleagues** to find out their needs.

6 1 c   2 a   3 d   4 e   5 b

7

1 conduct   2 option   3 address   4 impact
5 measure   6 lead

9 (Example answer)

The aim of this report is to detail areas in which GTST Ltd currently has a high carbon footprint and to suggest methods to make the company greener.

Effects on the environment

There are three major areas to be investigated:
1 **Paper:** We currently use three boxes of paper every day, much of which is quickly thrown away.
2 **Travel:** At present, the majority of our employees drive to work.
3 **Energy:** Electricity consumption is much higher than it needs to be.

Suggested solutions

To reduce the amount of paper used, a box for old paper could be put on each desk. It will therefore be easier for staff to use paper which has already been printed on, instead of using fresh paper all the time.

There are two possible schemes which could change people's travel habits:

- Car-sharing, perhaps in conjunction with other businesses in the local area. As well as being more environmentally friendly, it will also save our staff a lot of money on fuel.

- Free travel passes: to encourage staff to use public transport.

In order to reduce the amount of energy used, employees should be encouraged to consider carefully when to leave devices on and when to switch them off, for instance at night. We could also investigate 'green' ways of producing our own energy, such as having solar panels or wind turbines installed on the roof of the offices.

In conclusion, I am confident that by implementing these initiatives GTST Ltd will be able to drastically reduce its carbon footprint.

UNIT 5

5.1 I'm not your inspiration, thank you very much

1

1 A strong, fierce, flawed adult woman
2 It was controversial because it would be unacceptable to use about someone else, so she challenged preconceptions by using it of herself.
3 She worked as a journalist writing columns, blogs and for radio. The teaching qualification may have helped her spread her message in a way that made people listen.

4 She collaborated with the Australian government, toured for the US government and spoke on the radio and TV to spread a different message about disability.

2

c Changing perspectives positively

3

1 If   **2** wheelchair   **3** overcoming   **4** Multiple

4

1 d   **2** a   **3** e   **4** c   **5** b

6

1 When I first watched Maysoon Zayid's TED Talk, …
2 She begins by forthrightly saying that she isn't drunk but has cerebral palsy …
3 By answering the unasked question in everyone's minds, she clears the way for what she has to say.
4 The main content of her talk covers how she grew up in New Jersey with three older sisters …
5 She went to the same schools as her siblings …

7

1 inspirational, vibrant and funny
2 Why do you shake like that?
3 She turned to comedy.
4 It has inspired her to take up something she's been too shy to do.

8

1 F – Her parents treated her exactly like their other offspring.
2 F – She laughed all the way through.
3 T
4 F – on social media
5 T

9

1 a   **2** b   **3** b   **4** a   **5** a

5.2 If only I'd studied harder …

1

1 wished   **2** had   **3** would   **4** worked
5 sooner

2

1 were   **2** studied   **3** didn't get   **4** would take   **5** were offered   **6** 'd talk   **7** 'd apply
8 do   **9** 'd do   **10** completed

3

1 Supposing you were dissatisfied at work, would you apply for a new job?
2 If he had a problem at work, he wouldn't talk to his boss.
3 If I wanted a job abroad, I would update my CV.
4 I wish my boss would offer me a transfer. If he did, I'd take it.
5 If I were / was looking for a new job, I'd post my CV online.

6 It's high time you had more responsibility, you should talk to your boss about promotion opportunities.

4

1 'd / had seen   **2** 'd / would have gone
3 'd / would rather work   **4** 'd / had trained
5 had   **6** not have

5

1 e   **2** a   **3** b   **4** c   **5** d

6

2 Had I realized he'd worked here before, I'd have offered him the position.
3 Were she to update her CV, she would have a better chance of success.
4 Were I to attend more often, I'd be able to follow the meetings more easily.
5 Had she not had that idea, she wouldn't have set up her own business.
6 Were he to accept the job abroad, he wouldn't go back to university.
7 Had I not failed that interview, I wouldn't have done the course that led to this job.
8 Were we to employ more women and some younger people, we'd have more diverse ideas.

7

1 Had I known
2 would take
3 Had
4 Were
5 would have taken
6 Were

8

Supposing I were offered early retirement, would I take it? That's a good question. Well, leaving the salary considerations for now, I do wish I had more time at home, so I probably would. However, I would miss doing something worthwhile and the contact with people, so I would look into volunteering work either abroad or locally. I'd always rather work with people in some way. Were I to volunteer, I'd work with people in need. Actually it's not a bad idea – it's high time I used my degree; after all I studied special needs education. It would be nice to return to it at the end of my career. I always wished I had worked in Asia, so maybe I can even combine the two.

5.3 I've got it!

1

1 c   **2** a   **3** b

2

1 B   **2** E   **3** C   **4** D   **5** A

3

1 Ideas don't always come on demand, sometimes the topic or company can make it difficult.
2 Advantages: everyone can use them, visual way to record and show connections;

disadvantage is that some people find them restrictive.
3 By giving simple instructions to change one element of the idea at a time, then evaluating afterwards.
4 It's a model for evaluating ideas – plus, minus and interesting.
5 Because they get bigger when they are shared; taking an idea, crediting it and then improving it is innovative.

4

1 The meeting wasn't successful in finding a new idea for packaging.
2 Bob had the idea for packaging using cards to focus their ideas.
3 The packaging was redesigned eliminated by the team in the meeting.
4 Having total freedom some constraints helps new ideas form.

5

1 e   **2** f   **3** a   **4** b   **5** d   **6** c

6

1 drew a blank
2 have the faintest idea
3 occurred to her
4 dawned on
5 come up with
6 stuck for ideas

7

1 took off / has taken off
2 give up
3 dress up
4 paid off
5 call off
6 add up
7 follow up
8 saved up

8

b, e

9

d, h

10

1 dreamed up / conjured up / contributed / gathered, brilliant / innovative / original / worthwhile / unique
2 contributes / gathers / dreams up / conjures up / visualizes, unique / worthwhile / brilliant / crazy / innovative / original

5.4 Anyone got a bright idea?

1

1 **a** Let's   **b** need to
2 **a** fancy   **b** objections
3 **a** would be   **b** along
4 **a** Any   **b** goes
5 **a** Anyone   **b** Which
6 **a** may not   **b** That's
7 **a** should   **b** Let's go

2

a 2   **b** 7   **c** 5   **d** 3   **e** 6   **f** 4   **g** 1

3

1 Outdoor events aren't quite as predictable as indoor ones.
2 The speaker didn't get such good/positive feedback, did he?
3 I heard the caterers weren't especially friendly.
4 The atmosphere wasn't particularly warm.
5 I thought the speaker wasn't that interesting, actually.
6 The room wasn't quite warm enough.

4

1 predictable   2 such   3 especially
4 particularly   5 that   6 warm

5 (Possible answers)

1 Let's have the event indoors.
2 Why don't we hire a really good speaker?
3 We should change the caterers.
4 Any thoughts on a warm-up activity?
5 Let's inform the speaker about the topics that we'd like this time.
6 I really fancy using a smaller room, it's better for the atmosphere too.

6

a 5   b 3   c 1   d 4   e 2

7

1 e   2 f   3 j   4 h   5 a   6 b   7 d   8 i
9 c   10 g

8

1 Lessons learned: smaller room, better caterers and speaker.
2 Aim to improve communication through technology skills – bring smartphones, etc. to make interactive.
3 Karaoke.

9

1 Aug.   2 Mgt, incl.   3 approx.   4 dept.
5 asap   6 etc.   7 e.g.   8 Re: 9 i.e.

10

(Example answer)

Dear everyone

Re: The successful event

Thank you for all your hard work over the last few weeks. It really paid off!

We can honestly say that the department aims were fully met.

Sensible choices of theme and speaker led to / meant we had great talks including lots of technical information.

In fact, I even heard that approximately ten people thanked the speaker personally.

Catering, the ice-breaker and the fun activity were (very successful and) well chosen.

The weather didn't disappoint either. In fact, it was so good that we were able to have lunch outside / lunch outside was possible.

All in all, it was a complete success – thanks to all involved.

Best wishes

Sam

PRESENTATION 3

1

1 b   2 a   3 c

3 (Example answers)

1 My challenge relates to my studies. I had to prepare for an English exam.
2 I find exams quite stressful and I'm not the best student, so I was quite nervous.
3 It was difficult, but how I got through the challenge was just by focusing on preparing as best I could. I came up with a revision schedule to make sure I covered all the topics that might have been included in my exam.
4 My friends and family were a great help to me. They kept me motivated and made sure that I didn't get distracted when I was revising.

5

1 c, i   2 a, g   3 e, j   4 b, h   5 d, f

6 (Example answers)

1 Hello everyone. A very warm welcome to you all.
2 I'm (name).
3 A few years ago, I found many social situations quite stressful experiences. Something that was very difficult for me was going to parties and speaking to new people. It might sound silly, but as a shy person I found this almost impossible.
4 It was tough but I had to work on my anxiety and develop strategies to deal with my nerves when I met new people. I got a lot of self-help books, but what helped me most was just putting myself into different situations where I had to meet and talk to new people – I signed up for an evening class, I joined a local book club, basically I put myself out and about rather than just staying at home.
5 A big thank you for listening to me today.

UNIT 6

6.1 How to make filthy water drinkable

1

1 It took eighteen months of trial and error.
2 Over a hundred.
3 The 18.5-litre jerry can.
4 He earned it for services to innovation in recognition of his attempts to end global water poverty.

2

c   Saving lives simply, quickly and cheaply

3

1 affordable   2 Premature   3 public
4 lifesaving

4

1 e   2 c   3 a   4 b   5 d

6

1 I'd like to start by telling you about what particularly impressed me about this talk and why.

2 The first thing is Amy Smith is an engaging speaker, inspiring and passionate about using her resources, the resources available in a developed country, to make the world a better place.
3 Now that I've explained a little bit about her, I'll move on to describe what she said that was new for me: over two million people worldwide die annually from indoor cooking-fire fumes. Isn't that heart-breaking?
4 I'd like to tell you what the solutions are a little later.
5 OK, now for the work she tells us about in her talk: it really felt like people making a difference, a worthwhile investment.

7

1 F – The podcaster feels that she should do / would be good at it.
2 T
3 T
4 F – In India they had to use different waste as fuel.

8

1 Because the speaker was engaging, inspiring and passionate about making the world a better place (by dealing with indoor cooking-fire fumes).
2 Because he didn't realize that so many people die every year from cooking-fire fumes and he takes / we take for granted how easy it is for us to cook a meal for our families and ourselves.
3 That it's important not to stop farmers from becoming farmers, but to help them be successful farmers.
4 By giving people tools to make changes to improve their daily lives, their health and their economic situation.
5 The fact that there are dedicated, innovative individuals working towards a better world.

9

1 b   2 a   3 b   4 a   5 c

6.2 What a waste of time!

1

1 avoid   2 so as to   3 not in order to
4 for   5 so   6 so that

2

1 in order to   2 prevents   3 so as to
4 In order to   5 so that   6 avoid

3

2 … she goes to a different office **so that** she can meditate.
3 … turn it off **so** I'm not / I don't get interrupted.
4 … it's **in order to** be / stay more focused.
5 … it's **for** emergencies. It's a fire door.
6 … gets an earlier train **so as to** get / find a seat.
7 … went via Italy **so that** I could visit a client.
8 … he needs the computer **in order to** work at home tomorrow.

4

1 c 2 d 3 a 4 b 5 f 6 e

5

1 avoided/avoid/will avoid 2 prevented
3 avoids 4 prevented 5 avoid 6 avoided

6

1 c 2 e 3 b 4 a 5 f 6 h 7 d 8 g

7

1 with a view to 2 sense of purpose
3 at cross-purposes 4 For the sake of
5 as a means to an end 6 on purpose
7 accidentally on purpose 8 for the good of

8

Time management itself is a myth. <u>In order to</u>
<u>manage time you have to be master of it</u>, but
this is rarely possible. Everyone has the same
number of hours in the day. Fundamentally, it's
naïve of us to think that we can <u>use tricks so</u>
<u>as to obtain a small time advantage</u>. The best
way to manage time is to avoid doing things
<u>that prevent you from reaching the goals that</u>
<u>you've set</u>. In other words, dropping habits
and hobbies you don't like <u>frees your mind so</u>
<u>that it can focus</u> on the job in hand. Making a
'to-do' list <u>so that you can cross off the items</u>
<u>is a waste of time</u>, but making a note <u>so you</u>
<u>can remember</u> what personal goals you have
can be productive. Ultimately, it's not about
managing time itself; it's about managing what
you do with your time <u>so that you're spending it</u>
<u>doing something that</u> brings you closer to your
life goals.

6.3 Thinking outside the box

1

1 T
2 F – They're in Bonn.
3 T
4 F – It went public in 2000.

2

a 2 b 4 c 3 d 1

3

1 There was a strike so catalogues weren't
being delivered to the customers.
2 To deliver by taxi – yes, it was successful.
3 A new job in Dresden in the new world and
a new mindset.
4 Entrepreneurial thinking, new ideas because
the old ones didn't work. Thinking outside
the box.
5 They had to start from scratch with everything.

4

1 Russian soldiers were paid cash-in-hand to
sort parcels.
2 Unwanted machinery / equipment was sent
from West to East Germany.
3 Rental vehicles were brought over from the
west.
4 Delivery staff were recruited and trained.
6 Infrastructure was established.

5

1 backlog 2 mail-order 3 strike 4 eager
5 entrepreneurial 6 pioneer

6

1 h 2 f 3 a 4 g 5 c 6 b 7 e 8 d

7

1 did the trick 2 do it blindfolded 3 do me
a favour 4 does their bit 5 didn't do him
justice 6 do a double take 7 did her a good
turn 8 do you any harm

8

1 outside 2 leave 3 the off 4 take 5 fat
6 jump 7 stand a

9

1 fat chance
2 stood / stands a chance
3 leave it to chance
4 taking a chance on
5 jumped at the chance
6 on the off chance
7 outside chance

6.4 What are our options?

1

1 f 2 d 3 e 4 a 5 g 6 c 7 b

2

1 … for teambuilding, and trust us to get lost.
2 … till we recognize where we are.
3 … we could ring someone.
4 … stock.
5 … just took the wrong road.

3

1 a We could retrace our steps.
  b Why don't we try retracing our steps?
2 a It's worth a try.
  b What have we got to lose?
3 a I'm not (too) sure about that.
  b I'm not sure that'll work.
4 a Let's try it.
  b Let's give that/it a try.

4

1 It's <u>certainly</u> worth a <u>try</u>.
2 I'm not too <u>sure</u> about that.
3 I'd rather <u>keep looking</u>.
4 Let's <u>take stock</u>.
5 If we had <u>phones</u>, we could <u>ring</u>.
6 We could go <u>back</u> till we <u>recognize</u> it.

5

1 d 2 a 3 f 4 b 5 c 6 e

6

1 will probably 2 should consider 3 may /
might have 4 find it 5 the possibility
6 might / may find

7

1 Don't be afraid 2 Consider 3 Think about
4 may have to 5 the possibility 6 might like to

8

1 c 2 a 3 b

9 (Example answer)

Dear Jack

I was sorry to hear you are having trouble
keeping up with new technology. You might
consider asking your boss to provide training for
you and the department. You may have to be
prepared to attend and pay for a course privately
too but you might consider asking colleagues for
some support. If it appears to be a problem for
more colleagues, there's always the possibility of
talking about the issue in a department meeting
and establishing the extent of the problem so
that adequate training can be provided.

Hope that helps.

Best wishes

Amy

WRITING 3

1 a b d e f

2 1 d 2 e 3 f 4 b 5 a

3 1 T 2 F 3 T 4 T 5 F

4

1 On Saturday the New York Philharmonic |
were joined by | tenor Andrea Bocelli | for a
concert of | opera favourites | in Central Park.
2 I certainly wasn't alone | in my choice of
concert |– in fact, 60,000 people | saw
Coldplay | perform last night | at the BMW
Welt Auditorium in Munich.
3 To see Madonna perform | has long been |
one of my dreams, | and, in November last
year, | I achieved that dream | when I saw
her concert in Prague.
4 When I heard that | jazz pianist Herbie
Hancock | was playing at | the Barbican
Theatre in London, | I knew | I had to be
there.
5 As part of their farewell tour, | The Who
| were the final act | at the Glastonbury
Festival in 2015, | |and I was privileged
enough | to see them perform.

5

1 c 2 a 3 d 4 f 5 b 6 e

6

1 simply 2 huge 3 ultimate 4 severely
5 remarkably 6 wonderful

7

1 recommend 2 All in all 3 but also
4 Although 5 challenge

10 (Example answer)

Verdi's *Requiem* is a much-loved classical
piece, most recently performed by the
Liverpool Welsh Choral Union and the
Liverpool Philharmonic Orchestra at their
concert hall in the city.

It was my first experience of a classical concert, and I only went because my aunt is in the LWCU. I had no idea what to expect before I went in. The choir has over 100 members, and it seemed to take too long for them all to enter onto the stage. It felt like a long wait before the music began, starting with the quiet 'Kyrie' and building up to the dramatic and overpowering 'Dies Irae', the most famous piece from the *Requiem*. This had a huge effect on me because you could almost feel the music from the singers and the orchestra. It might sound strange to say that a piece of music originally written for a funeral could be so full of joy and life, but it really felt that way to me.

My only complaint was that I found the English translation of the Latin words, which was being projected above the stage, more distracting than useful. Other than that, seeing Verdi's *Requiem* live was one of the most memorable experiences of my life. I enjoyed it so much that I downloaded it immediately after the concert, because I would like to be able to listen to it many more times. I would definitely recommend the *Requiem* as a first classical concert experience to anyone, even those who think they don't really like classical music!

UNIT 7

7.1 Taking imagination seriously

1

1 She imagines her goals as a reality, then works backwards.
2 It is a 745-foot net sculpture which is partly powered by the public
3 She studied art and counselling psychology at university.
4 She tries to pay attention to her inner voice, she draws and writes using her less dominant hand.

2

c Stories and art that stretch the imagination

3

1 carpet **2** Pushing **3** everywhere
4 between

4

1 e **2** d **3** b **4** c **5** a

6

1 relevance **2** living **3** attention **4** belief
5 director

7

1 F – His narrative is so exciting that he doesn't need visuals to bring it to life – surprisingly for a film director, his presentation included no slides or film clips.
2 T
3 T
4 F – His dream was to see the Titanic wreck at the bottom of the ocean with his own eyes.

8

1 He was particularly interested in oceans and space.
2 He convinced the Hollywood studio it was necessary to film the ship's wreckage, the studio then funded the expedition, his movie became a success, delivering profit to the studio and entertainment to audiences.
3 CG animation, because he'd noticed that audiences were mesmerized by the magic of it.
4 That our ideal job will build from our personal interests and passions and that we shouldn't be afraid of exploring these for the benefit of both our work and personal life.

9

1 c **2** c **3** b **4** b **5** a

7.2 The power of daydreaming

1

1 B **2** C **3** A **4** E **5** D

2

1 were doing
2 controls
3 may not have known
4 will be doing
5 were working on
6 requires
7 are constantly changing
8 had never considered

3

1 Were you daydreaming
2 was thinking
3 Are you being
4 wasn't implying
5 was just wondering
6 've been daydreaming
7 was always getting caught
8 've been reading
9 'll probably be daydreaming

4

1 'd been working
2 're coming / 'll be coming / 're going to come
3 've been going
4 was working / 'd been working
5 hadn't been listening / wasn't listening
6 'll be exhibiting / 's going to be exhibiting / 's exhibiting
7 was dreaming / 'd been dreaming
8 's hoping

5

1 for the summer
2 last week
3 before last year
4 but there's a strike
5 she's moving this week
6 when they heard the news
7 before the end of the year
8 ever since I can remember

6

1 b **2** a **3** b **4** c **5** a

7

1 probably **2** definitely **3** probably
4 undoubtedly **5** certainly **6** definitely
7 most probably **8** surely

8

1 long, renting **2** staying **3** using **4** living
5 long, renting

9

Well, they say that daydreaming makes you more creative. I remember one time I had been trying to work out the details of a presentation. I'd got stuck trying to connect two distinct parts in the final section and needed a way of bringing them together. I'd been racking my brains for about a week and nothing had worked. Then I was travelling home by train and had started reading the paper but actually was just staring out of the window, daydreaming and sort of allowing my mind to freewheel. Suddenly there it was, the answer I had been looking for. It just popped into my head from nowhere. The perfect solution.

7.3 In my mind's eye

1

1 c **2** e **3** a **4** b **5** f **6** d

2

1 global cuisine
2 tailor-made service
3 Vermont Fresh Network
4 bold imagination
5 impeccable service

3

1 T
2 T
3 F – The chef and catering team tease out some details that are personal. When a clear idea has been established, Susanna starts to add her own ideas.
4 F – Mostly sourced locally.
5 T
6 F – Staff learn about the food to pass on relevant information to guests.

4

1 c **2** f **3** h **4** a **5** g **6** e **7** d **8** b

5

1 put my mind to it
2 bear in mind
3 in two minds
4 blow your mind
5 keep an open mind
6 ease my mind
7 see (the finish line) in your mind's eye
8 gave him peace of mind

6

1 hang	hanged b	hung a
2 go	been a	gone b
3 cost	costed a	cost b
4 lie	laid a	lied b
5 shine	shined b	shone a

7

1 laid 2 shined 3 gone 4 lied 5 costed
6 been 7 cost 8 hanged 9 hung
10 shone

8

1 f 2 d 3 a 4 b 5 c 6 e

9

1 keep an eye on
2 is / was, eye-catching
3 see, with the naked eye
4 up to their eyes in
5 do, with his eyes shut
6 opened my eyes to

7.4 That doesn't seem possible

1

1 I expect she's on holiday. ✓
2 I imagine she's on a training course.
3 She must be ill.
4 One of her children might be ill.
5 She's probably stuck in traffic. ✓
6 She may have overslept. ✓

2

1 Perhaps she's gone to the doctor.
2 Maybe there's been an accident that's delayed her.
3 She might have forgotten her phone

3

1 she can't have had her phone with her.
2 everyone must have left the building in time.
3 it's likely to have been a serious fire.
4 I guess she'll need a day off.
5 the children will probably be tired.
6 The firemen are bound to have found the cause of the fire by now.

4

1 've 2 've 3 've 4 've, 've 5 have
6 've

5

1 That can't be right.
2 I think you're onto something there.
3 I'm not entirely convinced.
4 It certainly looks that way.
5 That doesn't seem at all likely to me.
6 That seems a likely explanation.

6

1 reportedly 2 believe 3 claim
4 Apparently 5 said to 6 allegedly
7 speculation 8 by all accounts

7

1 Speculation 2 reportedly 3 is believed
4 by all accounts 5 said to 6 allegedly
7 claim 8 apparently

8

1 by ~~each~~ all accounts 2 claim~~inged~~
3 allegedly 4 ~~belief~~ believed 5 ~~say~~ said
6 ~~speculate~~ speculation

9 (Possible answers)

2 Allegedly, when employees are physically fitter it has a positive effect on the business too.
3 Top management is quoted as saying this is the reason they started the annual relay race five years ago.
4 By all accounts the race strengthens the company's corporate identity, provides year-long entertainment for staff and is fun.
5 Speculation about tactics builds throughout the year while departments bond through training regularly outside working hours.
6 It's said to be almost certain that the R&D department (will) win every time, as indeed they did this year too. But as ever there were some surprises in innovative tactics and the other positions.
7 Apparently a total of 250 employees, friends and family attended the race this year. The summer party was held afterwards in glorious weather with drinks and snacks provided by the company.
8 It's believed by many to be a highlight in the corporate year.

PRESENTATION 4

1

1 b 2 c 3 a

3 (Example answers)

1 When I was a child, I'd often go to the woods and pretend to be a courageous explorer.
2 I used to go there with my brother – we'd pretend to discover new imaginary lands together.
3 I remember that we felt so free when we were out in the woods – like nothing else mattered.

5

1 a, e 2 b, d 3 c, g 4 f, h

6 (Example answers)

1 Hello and thanks for joining me today. My name's (name).
2 I loved stories when I was younger. I would always be reading some fantasy or science fiction novel. I wouldn't just read, but I'd also write my own stories. Even though I don't think they were really that good, I think it helped me develop different ways of thinking.
3 It's so important for your day-to-day life really. If you can use your imagination, you can think of different solutions to problems and find unusual answers. Without imagination and creativity it's quite easy to become stuck.
4 Thank you so much for listening today.

UNIT 8

8.1 Build a tower, build a team

1

1 Because he's a visual thinker and communicator.
2 Although he now works in the fields of design and visual thinking, he originally studied Astronomy and Psychology at the University of Toronto.
3 Work at the museum designing interactive exhibits.
4 He attended his first TED conference in 1994. In addition to giving seven TED Talks, he's also been a visual artist and host at TED conferences, and he lists TED among his clients.
5 He's a fellow at Autodesk and is writing his fifth book.

2

b Collaboration drives innovation

3

1 origin 2 create 3 collaboration 4 complex

4

1 e 2 a 3 b 4 c 5 d

6

1 Gawande is able to take a step back from the detailed work of his job as a practising doctor to look at medicine as a whole.
2 He sets out to provide clarity to problems that show bewildering complexity.
3 … in 1970 the average hospital visit required care from two full-time clinicians. By the end of the twentieth century the number had risen to fifteen.
4 Gawande's message is an important one: medicine is broken but there are answers to its problems so it can be fixed.

7

1 Gawande steps back from his job and looks at the bigger picture of medicine as a whole.
2 The complexity comes from the increase in the number of people, procedures and drugs used in the health industry.
3 High-risk ones like aviation and high-rise construction.
4 His personal interest is his daughter's rare illness and the respect he's gained for the medical profession.

8

1 4,000, 6,000 2 40 per cent of, 60 per cent of, two million people 3 finding the failures, devising solutions, implementing the ideas
4 checklists 5 reduced complications, 47 per cent

9

1 a 2 c 3 a 4 b 5 a

8.2 Having an off day?

1

1 b 2 c 3 a

2

1 A recent audit resulted in the revelation that our small team of six don't work together as well as we could.

2 Taking part in a facilitated workshop was the consequence of the audit recommendations.

3 The boss's observations led to some proposals for change in some key areas.

4 Despite our initial scepticism, the workshop fostered rapport.

5 The feedback session contributed to us tightening our processes.

6 The workshop will bring about closer communication between us.

3

1 brought about
2 caused
3 gave rise to
4 stemmed from
5 resulted from
6 contributes to
7 fostered
8 resulted in

4

2 a The flights are so cheap that …
  b There are such cheap flights that …
3 a The order is so large that …
  b It is such a large order that …
4 a The presentation was so good that …
  b It was such a good presentation that …
5 a The workshop was so successful that …
  b The workshop was such a success that …
6 a Travelling in the rush hour was so time consuming that …
  b Travelling in the rush hour was such a time-consuming activity that …
7 a The setback caused by IT problems was so serious that …
  b There was such a serious setback caused by IT problems that …
8 a There were so many complaints that …
  b There were such a lot of complaints that …
9 a The product was so popular that …
  b It was such a popular product that …

5

1 worksh<u>op</u>   2 sh<u>ut</u>   3 la<u>ck</u>/la<u>g</u>   4 wor<u>k</u>

6

1 bad   2 Please   3 come   4 I.D.

7

When I have to achieve big goals, and <u>when this results in me having lots to deal with, I try to follow the</u> 'eating an elephant model'. Creighton Abrams, a US army general, came up with it and, <u>due to its bizarre nature, it's a memorable idea</u>. The fact that the originator was in the army <u>contributes to the notion of discipline and task completion.</u> Given the elephant's large size, the idea is that <u>breaking it down into smaller parts results in it being easier to deal with.</u> Otherwise, reaching a big goal might seem unobtainable <u>and kill motivation and jeopardize the work itself</u>. Last year, before moving premises, we agreed to throw away any unwanted papers and files. <u>The only way to achieve this</u> enormous task successfully was to deal with it bit by bit. <u>As a result, we threw away almost a ton of paper</u> and cleared the way for the move. As Abrams said: 'When eating an elephant, take one bite at a time'.

8.3 How *not* to motivate people

1

1 F – in 2000 (20-0 the most goals against)
2 T
3 T
4 F – archery is the national sport

2

1 Extrinsic motivation comes from something outside of the person being motivated, like money, and intrinsic from something within, like desire to do the task well.
2 Being relatively new to football, losing dramatically and being in position 209 of 209 in FIFA's ranking.
3 They didn't feel pressure being bottom as the only way was up!
4 Television and the Internet were allowed into the country in 1999, tourism is limited to package tours.
5 GNH is measured to help people strike a balance between material and spiritual concerns.
6 There were no new players to replace the ones retiring and funds were needed elsewhere for health and education.

3

1 extrinsic   2 giddy   3 coined   4 Archery
5 infamous

4

1 twelve   2 $300,000   3 training camp
4 humidity   5 free   6 ninetieth

5

1 b   2 h   3 e   4 f   5 a   6 c   7 d   8 g

6

1 be a team player
2 bond as a group
3 a sense of belonging
4 pull their weight
5 doing your fair share
6 Sharing the load
7 a part of things
8 go the extra mile

7

2 The enjoyment of the game itself provided the *motivation* for the team to play well.
3 The *awarding* of extra holiday as an incentive proved more effective than overtime payments.
4 He had extensive background *knowledge* of the match.
5 The crowd enjoyed the *excitement* of the game and festive atmosphere.
6 The *inconvenience* of travelling to Thimphu is because of the mountains.
7 The Thai team's *generosity* about training made competing possible.
8 The team's *commitment* to winning was high throughout the game.

8

1 off   2 in   3 around   4 at   5 on   6 towards

9

a 2   b 4   c 5   d 3   e 6   f 1

8.4 If you'll just let me finish …

1

1 Can I just say something here?   I
2 Could I just finish what I was saying?   S
3 If you'll let me finish …   S
4 I hate to interrupt ….   I
5 I know you're dying to jump in, but …   S
6 Sorry for interrupting, but …   I
7 Before you continue, can I just say …   I
8 If you'll allow me to finish …   S

2

2, 4, 5, 6, 8

3

1 I'd like to start the discussion by …
2 I'd also be interested in hearing your views on …

4

1 take   2 thoughts   3 continue
4 everything   5 finish

5

1 I'd like to <u>start</u> the discussion by asking if everyone's read the information sent around?
2 It'll probably make a difference to the <u>discussion</u>.
3 There will be a chance for <u>everyone</u> to have their say.
4 You mean with <u>hindsight</u> it was more useful than when you were actually doing it?
5 It could be a great <u>retention tool</u>, as well as promoting innovation.
6 I <u>would</u> like us all to suggest one or two employees to put forward and answer the questions.

6

a 3   b 5   c 1   d 2   e 4

7

1, 6, 7

8

1 also
2 Thanks to / As a result of
3 as a result of / thanks to
4 However
5 As a consequence / Because
6 As a consequence
7 Overall

9

(Example answers)

1

b I left at relatively short notice <u>because</u> the IT project was urgent.
c <u>As a result</u> I wasn't well prepared to fix the problem.

2

a <u>Because</u> the IT systems were identical we could 'speak' a common language.

b <u>As a result</u> we built good relationships.

3

a My counterparts didn't speak very good English and <u>also</u> I don't speak good German / <u>neither/nor</u> do I speak good German.

b My biggest challenge was not understanding German. <u>As a consequence</u> I had many confusing experiences.

c <u>However</u>, this experience improved my understanding of my European colleagues.

4

a <u>As a result of</u> learning to simplify my message I can avoid misunderstandings.

5

a <u>Overall</u>, I would recommend a basic language course before the programme.

WRITING 4

1

b, d, e, f, g

2

1 b **2** d **3** f **4** g **5** e

3

1 F **2** F **3** T **4** F **5** T

4

1 It was **a huge success** from start to finish.

2 We ended up being **pleasantly surprised**.

3 We couldn't wait to **do it all again**.

4 It turned out to be **the best way we could have spent our day**.

5 All in all, I'd say **it was worth every penny**.

5

a 2 **b** 3 **c** 1 **d** 5 **e** 1 **f** 3 **g** 5 **h** 5
i 2 **j** 4 **k** 3 **l** 2 **m** 4 **n** 4 **o** 1 & 5

6

1 It was great to get your message!

2 I've just had **the holiday of a lifetime** in Thailand.

3 **The first thing I want to tell you about is** the hotels we stayed in.

4 **It was a pleasant surprise when** we found out that all our food and drink was included in the price – great value for money!

5 **Then it was on to** Bangkok for a week.

6 I'd love to take you to Thailand one day. **Let me know what you think**.

7

1 breathtaking views P

2 welcoming people P

3 (the) ideal place P

4 (with) disastrous results N

5 dreadful weather N

6 (a) rewarding experience P

9 (Example answer)

Hi Sally,

Thanks for your message. How's everything with you?

I've just got back from the adventure of a lifetime! I left work on Friday and got the train from San Diego to Los Angeles, my first experience of the American railroad – their trains are so much bigger than the ones we have in Europe! In LA, I changed onto the train that travels across to Chicago. Can you believe it takes over two days to get there? Luckily, I was only on it for about 12 hours, getting off in Flagstaff.

I went for breakfast in a proper American diner, full of friendly people. At 9am, I was collected by a small tour bus which already had six other people on it, and the most enthusiastic guide I've ever met. Two hours later we arrived at what had been the goal all along: the Grand Canyon National Park. The guide made us get out of the van and walk along looking at his feet. He walked backwards and we weren't allowed to look up until he told us to. When we did, the view was truly breathtaking. The whole Grand Canyon was spread out in front of us, stretching away to the horizon. It was the perfect weather for taking photos, and through the day we stopped in loads of places to get different views of this true wonder of nature.

We've all seen photos, but that's nothing compared to the real thing. If you ever get a chance to go there, you definitely should! I hope you do!

Write soon,

Adam

UNIT 9

9.1 All it takes is 10 mindful minutes

1

1 He dropped out because he lost several friends in an accident and the stress led him to embrace full-time meditation.

2 He has a circus arts degree and is a mindfulness consultant, he has learned to meditate while being a monk and learned to teach it to others.

3 Andy Puddicombe contributes the meditation expertise and Rich Pierson the marketing and brand knowledge.

4 The question of how to present meditation in such a way that friends would give it a try.

5 To create a happier and healthier world by teaching the skills of meditation and mindfulness.

2

b Finding happiness through increasing mindfulness

3

1 living **2** valuable **3** Curing **4** happy

4

1 e **2** a **3** c **4** d **5** b

6

1 it really resonated with me

2 actually, rather the causes of happiness

3 or was likely to make us happy

7

1 Because she practises mindfulness activities most days and is interested in being present.

2 That although we live longer and are richer we aren't measurably happier.

3 Is it just as good to think about the past or the future when doing something, or is it better to stay focused on the present?

4 His finding that it's better to stay focused on the present.

8

1 T

2 F – He analyzed 650,000 real-time reports from 15,000 people.

3 F – When doing unpopular tasks, staying focused improved the happiness rating.

4 T

5 F – She is aware that the people she sees every day would be happier too.

9

1 a **2** b **3** c **4** b **5** a

9.2 Even holidays are stressful

1

1 exquisitely **2** beautifully **3** extremely
4 tastefully **5** importantly **6** completely
7 fully **8** completely **9** well **10** totally

2

(Suggested answers)

1 It's absolutely device free and completely peaceful.

2 Walking or riding in totally traffic free and beautifully quiet surroundings.

3 In the exquisitely modern spa and pool complex and the beautifully comfortable sofas and seats inside and outside.

4 Holidays should be totally relaxing and absolutely perfect.

3

1 extremely **2** completely **3** barely
4 freshly **5** locally **6** Amazingly
7 Expertly **8** completely

4

1 d **2** e **3** a **4** b **5** c

5

1 horribly busy **2** absolutely clear
3 naturally sociable **4** rapidly growing
5 blissfully happy

6

1 Although he was nervous, he delivered the presentation incredibly <u>calmly</u>.

2 After the sales team had used it for a year, it was <u>utterly</u> ruined.

3 He learned the skills <u>fantastically</u> quickly.

4 The spare parts are <u>readily</u> available in most electronics stores.

5 We discovered this place <u>accidentally</u> on the way back last year.

7

1 just   **2** while   **3** recently   **4** yesterday
5 tomorrow   **6** now   **7** When   **8** last
9 finally   **10** already

8

<u>I recently became acquainted with a couple</u> – both medical doctors – who travel every year to a different destination. <u>Unusually, they don't relax on the beach</u>, but take a busman's holiday where they offer their medical expertise in remote places to people in need. Before leaving <u>for somewhere completely different and utterly remote, they totally</u> remove any evidence of wealth and privilege. They travel with an organization and, <u>once thoroughly briefed, they work tirelessly to</u> <u>assist</u> the victims of natural disasters. <u>They are unreservedly enthusiastic about these trips</u> and arrive back eager to explain how much they have gained from the whole experience and the kindness of strangers.

9.3 Alert and alive

1

1 at   **2** about   **3** with   **4** out

2

1 Everyone who works.
2 Yes (well-documented; several studies).
3 The ridiculous in difficult situations, tense situations, yourself, jokes we come across on a break from work.

3

1 N   **2** D   **3** D   **4** D   **5** P   **6** P   **7** D   **8** N

4

2 joking aside   **3** you're missing an important trick   **4** well-documented   **5** break out of the cycle   **6** don't take it too seriously   **7** Take time out   **8** lighten up

5

1 d   **2** g   **3** a   **4** h   **5** b   **6** c   **7** e   **8** f

6

1 got cold feet   **2** makes my blood boil
3 up to my eyeballs   **4** keep my chin up
5 is a pain in the neck   **6** get it off my chest
7 let her hair down   **8** was a weight off my shoulders

7

1 f   **2** a   **3** d   **4** b   **5** g   **6** c   **7** e

8

1 quite   **2** very   **3** acutely   **4** extremely
5 deeply   **6** very   **7** totally   **8** absolutely

9

1 c   **2** d   **3** e   **4** f   **5** b   **6** a

10

1 lived through   **2** live down   **3** live up to
4 lives for   **5** live with   **6** live on

9.4 Have you got a minute?

1

1 you got a minute
2 I do for you
3 I wanted to talk to you about
4 the thing is
5 nuisance
6 couldn't
7 'm sorry

2

1 b   **2** e   **3** c   **4** f   **5** g   **6** d   **7** a

3

1 a Sorry, but if you have a moment …
2 a I have to apologize.
3 a Is there any way … ? b I have a favour to ask.
4 a That's a shame, but I understand. b Don't worry. It doesn't matter.

4

1 a P b A   **2** a A b P   **3** a A b P
4 a P b A   **5** a P b A   **6** a A b P

5

1 g   **2** c   **3** a   **4** h   **5** b   **6** d   **7** f   **8** e

6

1 claim<s>ed</s>   **2** alleged<s>ly</s>   **3** <u>making</u>   **4** admitted <u>by</u>
5 acknowledged <s>that</s>   **6** proposed   **7** agreed <s>of</s> <u>to</u>   **8** <u>are urged</u> / <u>are being urged</u>

7

1 acknowledged   **2** admitted   **3** accused
4 denied   **5** suggested   **6** insisted
7 agreed

8

(Suggested answers)

1 The team acknowledged that they don't always answer emails quickly enough.
2 They discussed briefly what was acceptable and agreed to reply to customers within twenty-four hours.
3 It was claimed that some emails need more time to reply to due to information gathering.
4 It was proposed that a short email be sent to update the contact concerned.
5 Two members alleged that they could see no system in who to copy into emails.
6 They urged us to look at today's emails as examples.
7 Several members admitted to copying in too many people.
8 All were asked to monitor things and reduce the number of recipients if possible.

PRESENTATION 5

1

1 b   **2** c   **3** a

3 (Example answers)

Organizational skills
managing groups of people, planning trips, making lists
Interpersonal skills
communicating with others, understanding others, organizing tasks
Financial management skills
managing a budget, making savings
Time management skills
maintaining a schedule, meeting deadlines

5

1 d, g   **2** a, h   **3** c, e   **4** b, f

6 (Example answers)

1 Today, we're going to look at an aspect of daily life and the skills that you can develop. I'm going to talk about how I've managed to gain some skills.
2 This relates to one of my hobbies – running. People don't realize how many different skills you can develop doing an activity like this.
3 I'm actually part of a running club, so I've been able to develop my communicative skills by interacting with the other members. Running is also a very demanding physical activity, especially when you're training for a race. I've proven to myself that I have been able to plan my time, been dedicated and committed to my training schedule, and taken care when planning my meals.
4 So, that's all about my skills. I hope you found my talk interesting. Have you got any questions for me?

UNIT 10

10.1 Protecting Twitter users (sometimes from themselves)

1

1 From the only member of the department to the Vice President of Trust and Safety in 2014.
2 To enable her to have a private as well as a public life.
3 Her work for PJFI, fighting child exploitation and bringing criminals to justice.
4 She has a tattoo on her wrist that symbolizes hope.

2

c Privacy and control in the modern world

3

1 Preferences   **2** others   **3** risks   **4** need

4

1 b   **2** e   **3** c   **4** a   **5** d

6

1 Michael (Cummings)
2 National Geographic Learning
3 friends and colleagues
4 teacher
5 classroom

7

1 Working abroad.
2 The diversity and the notion that they are fundamentally something good.
3 It made him think about what a relationship is, what social networking is and how he might be influencing the lives of people he doesn't even know.
4 That he has the ability to spread happiness or even obesity via his social networks.

8

1 T
2 F – It was his discoveries about widowhood.
3 T
4 F – The motto is to encourage people to make connections with people who share the same goals.
5 T

9

1 a **2** b **3** c **4** c **5** a

10.2 Not as risky as it sounds

1 were mostly considered
2 were reported
3 is widely believed
4 has generally been considered
5 is thought
6 have sometimes been known
7 is expected
8 is estimated

2

1 e **2** d **3** a **4** b **5** c

3

1 was said
2 was reported
3 is feared
4 has been agreed
5 was decided
6 is estimated / has been estimated
7 was alleged
8 isn't expected

4

2 Captain Edward John Smith is/was presumed to have drowned.
3 1,500 passengers and crew are known to have died.
4 A technical failure wasn't shown to be the cause in the surveyors' reports.
5 The Titanic is said to be the most famous shipwreck.
6 The Titanic was believed to be unsinkable when it was built.
7 The Titanic was considered to be a low marine risk by Lloyd's.

5

2 It is presumed that Captain Edward John Smith drowned.
3 It's known that 1,500 passengers and crew died.
4 It wasn't shown that a technical failure was the cause in the surveyors' reports.
5 It is said that the Titanic is the most famous shipwreck.
6 It was believed that the Titanic was unsinkable when it was built.
7 It was considered by Lloyd's that the Titanic was a low marine risk.

6

Lloyd's of London <u>is known to be the oldest insurance market in the world</u>. Technically, <u>it's not considered to be a company</u> but a corporate body of 94 syndicates or 'Names', as they are called. It was founded in a City coffee house in 1688 where merchants bought insurance for their ships. The Lutine Bell <u>was reported to have been rung when the Titanic sank in 1912,</u> as has been done for all other ships lost or missing since 1799. <u>In the eighties and nineties Lloyd's was shown to be at risk itself</u> and in fact incurred gigantic losses due to asbestos claims flooding the market. <u>It was announced recently that Lloyd's has opened offices in China and Dubai</u> where the insurance market is much less developed than Britain.

10.3 Follow your gut instinct

1 Students' own answers.

2 7 and 10

3

1 b **2** a **3** a **4** a **5** b **6** b

4

1 They don't always get honest answers as people tend to see themselves in an overly favourable way.
2 All the answers follow the same pattern so you can tell which kind of approach to risk each answer represents.
3 Some of the answers are not so obvious so people would be more likely to have to think about them. Also there's a good mix of situations.

5

1 run **2** poses **3** reduces **4** likelihood
5 odds **6** high **7** in

6

2 availability **3** generosity **4** clarity
5 anonymity **6** hospitality **7** authenticity
8 necessity **9** simplicity

7

1 facts **2** two-faced **3** on it **4** music
5 slap **6** long

8

a a slap in the face
b put a brave face on it
c face facts
d be two-faced
e face the music
f pull a long face

10.4 All things considered …

1

1 c **2** d **3** a **4** b

2

burglary

3

1 There are
2 Possibly
3 drawback
4 According to
5 wouldn't
6 downside
7 attractive
8 sure

4

1 the light of
2 third alternative
3 the best choice
4 All things considered

5

Presenting options
There are some pretty interesting options to choose from
Possibly the most obvious one is
Additionally X is another option to consider
A (third) alternative that might do the job is
Discussing pros and cons
A drawback of X is
On the plus side
The downside is
X makes it a very attractive possibility
Considering options
I'm not sure it's the best option
In the light of
Ultimately, the best choice does seem to be
All things considered

7

1 fairly **2** quite **3** pretty **4** a little, a bit, slightly **5** rather

8

1 T
2 T (rather and quite)
3 F – only one (rather)
4 T (slightly, a bit, a little and rather)

9

1 It was rather a waste of money.
2 They were slightly poorer quality than we'd expected.
3 The XJ7 model is a bit more complicated to install.
4 He was quite impatient and a little unfriendly when he explained it.
5 I found it rather uninspiring and pretty old-fashioned.
6 The company is fairly disorganized.

7 That's rather a worrying / a rather worrying state of affairs.

8 The model they chose was reasonably easy to use.

10

1 quite **2** fairly **3** rather **4** slightly **5** quite
6 a bit **7** rather

11 (Example answer)

The system's low price made it fairly attractive and it arrived pretty promptly. Unfortunately, it was a little faulty but we were given a slightly better maintenance service than I had expected. So overall the package was quite reasonable.

WRITING 5

1

a, c, e, f, g

2

1 a **2** e **3** g **4** c **5** f

3

1 F **2** T **3** F **4** T **5** T

4

1 d **2** g **3** f **4** a **5** h **6** b **7** c **8** e

5

1 knowledgeable **2** prompt **3** wealth
4 remarkably **5** professionally **6** dedication

6

1 regret **2** a time **3** Not only **4** fortunate
5 stood out **6** impressed **7** Once again

7

1 We will not hesitate to recommend you to our customers.
2 I will recommend your restaurant to all my friends.
3 I will certainly use your hotel again.
4 We look forward to doing business with you again soon.
5 We look forward to continuing our business relationship.
6 We have recommended your company to others ...
7 ... and will continue to do so

9 (Example answer)

Dear Sir or Madam,

I would like to express my gratitude for the wonderful experience we had at your hotel at the end of last month.

We landed at the airport late at night, very tired as our flight had been delayed. We were very relieved when we were met by one of your excellent members of staff, Maja – we had forgotten that the transfer was included. She came prepared with water and snacks to help us wake up for long enough to get to the hotel. It was the little touches like this which made our stay particularly memorable.

On arrival at the hotel, we were upgraded to a better room with a breathtaking view of the mountains as Maja had discovered it was our wedding anniversary during our trip and had passed this on to the reception staff without our knowledge. This was a pleasant surprise, and even better were the roses and champagne that appeared in our room on the day itself. Altogether, it was probably our most enjoyable anniversary since we got married eighteen years ago!

I would like to finish by complimenting you on your restaurant. However busy it was, the staff were always calm and professional. The service they provided was prompt and they were able to accommodate my wife's food allergies.

All in all, it was a very pleasant holiday and we will not hesitate to recommend your hotel to our friends. I hope that we can stay there again at some point in the future.

Thank you very much,

Yours faithfully

Len Holder

UNIT 11

11.1 How to build with clay and community

1

1 That he would learn to read and write.
2 He trained in carpentry, teaching and architecture.
3 He raised funds through the company he set up 'Bricks for Gando School'.
4 He'd won seven awards by 2015, he has been exhibited in Frankfurt and New York museums and is a fellow at both the British and American Institutes of Architects.

2

a Community matters matter

3

1 space **2** sustainable **3** surprising
4 design

4

1 e **2** c **3** b **4** a **5** d

6

1 a <u>extensive</u>   **b** ext<u>ensive</u>
2 a weird-<u>looking</u>   **b** <u>weird</u>-looking
3 a techno-<u>geek</u>   **b** <u>tech</u>no-geek

7

1 F – Baan showed homes in China, Nigeria and Egypt. Eftychis talked about his great grandfather in Greece.
2 T
3 F – Eftychis would like to learn more about it.

8

1 Funny, posh or extravagant houses some techno-geek or multi-millionaire has built.
2 They like to personalize their living environments and they are highly creative.

3 He feels his people also had to improvise and make homes in unusual situations, his grandfather for example.
4 He gave very interesting information and didn't make it seem as if this situation only happened in certain areas or to certain people.
5 Particularly to people who don't travel very much so they see what life looks like in other places (away from the tourist spots).

9

1 b **2** a **3** b **4** c **5** b

11.2 A vision for saving the world

1

1 when **2** Although **3** In spite of the fact
4 By the time **5** provided that **6** in case
7 once **8** whereas **9** Given that

2

2 The last time I ate banana bread was when I was living in Australia.
3 In case I'm late, save me a piece of cake.
4 As far as not wasting food is concerned, banana bread is an excellent idea.
5 It tastes very sweet, considering there's no sugar in it.
6 Whenever he smells the dish it reminds him of home.
7 In view of the fact that she didn't (or doesn't) like bananas, she chose carrot cake instead.

3

1 If **2** unless **3** As long as **4** Supposing
5 Provided that

4

1 as soon as **2** until **3** Once **4** After
5 By the time

5

1 As far as fruit and vegetables are concerned, buy them when they are in season.
2 If necessary, find new recipes to use up leftovers.
3 When in doubt, don't eat food that's past its sell-by date.
4 Unless told otherwise by your doctor, eat a variety of different foods.
5 Once you've learned to cook fresh food, you'll prefer it to processed meals.

6

The amount of food waste increases <u>as the world's economies develop.</u> Ninety million tons of food are thrown away each year by Europeans. Food sharing <u>started in the light of this to counteract the</u> colossal waste. Valentin Thurn's documentary film *Taste the waste* raised awareness and, <u>after crowdfunding 11,000 euros, a non-profit company was born.</u> The www.foodsharing.de website connects people who have food to give to people who need it and, <u>given not everyone is connected, there's a low-tech solution</u> at strategic points, too. Food sharing is happening in 240 cities in Germany <u>and, according to the website, it is growing rapidly</u>. It's not only individuals, but also businesses that benefit from this practice, <u>given that they can save waste collection fees by donating goods to the organization</u>. Finally, health and safety laws ensure that no one shares anything unfit for consumption.

11.3 A personal calling

1

1 b **2** d **3** a **4** c

2

An advertorial

3

1 F – Mainly small businesses.
2 F – The problem is communicating it to enough potential customers.
3 T
4 T
5 T
6 F – Sometimes it's a free gift or just an extra bit of fun.
7 F – The personal trainer's card is rubber.
8 F – It's the fact that people like them as objects and therefore they keep them and show them to other people.

4

1 non-existent **2** innovative
3 pricey **4** striking **5** cool

5

a 4 (striking)
b 5 (cool)
c 2 (innovative)
d 1 (almost non-existent)
e 3 (pricey)

6

1 d **2** a **3** e **4** c **5** f **6** b

7

1 see eye to eye on
2 overseeing
3 are on the lookout for
4 see about
5 looked up to
6 look into

8

Two other nouns.

9

1 deadline **2** workspace **3** shortlist
4 crossroads **5** notebook **6** self-esteem
7 shareholder **8** database

10

1 d **2** f **3** a **4** e **5** b **6** c

11

1 high **2** behind **3** pushed **4** make
5 kill **6** move **7** dead **8** hard

12

1 dead on time
2 make time
3 gave me a hard time
4 at an all-time high
5 killed time

11.4 A dream come true

1

1 d **2** a **3** b **4** c

2

1 c **2** a **3** e **4** b **5** f **6** d

3

a Wouldn't it be great to
b I can see myself
c If money were no object, we could
d I've always fancied
e I'd love to
f I can't envisage

4

1 f I can't envisage
2 a wouldn't it be great to
3 c If money were no object we could
4 e I'd love to
5 b I can see myself
6 d I've always fancied

5

1 a S b U **2** a S b U **3** a U b S
4 a S b U **5** a U b S

6

1 highly impressed, pleased
2 excelled at, was extremely good at
3 confident, natural
4 an admirable, a strong
5 completely, consistently
6 privilege, honour

7

1 consistently **2** an admirable **3** an extremely
4 confident **5** a pleasure **6** quick
7 consistently **8** best

8

1 e **2** h **3** g **4** b **5** c **6** d **7** a **8** f

9

(Example answers)

2 She was incredibly quick to solve problems proactively and creatively.
3 The coaching considerably improved our performance in decision making.
4 We were greatly inspired by the vision she helped us form.
5 The life coaching session helped us hugely to get the best from our new situation.

PRESENTATION 6

1

1 b **2** c **3** a

3

1 c **2** b **3** a **4** e **5** d

5

1 c **2** a **3** f **4** d **5** e **6** b

6 (Example answers)

1 Hello and welcome. Let's get started.
2 Where I live there aren't many things for people to do for fun. As a result, people don't seem very happy.
3 What we need is some kind of club to give people something to do. I would like to set up a film club so people can get together to watch films and discuss them.
4 We could do this by installing a big TV screen in a communal space. They're not all that expensive these days if you go for an older model. If we get a DVD player we can get people to donate their old films for everyone to watch.
5 I feel this is important because people need to spend time together. By making a space where people can relax and watch films, neighbours in the area would be able to get to know each other and friendships could develop.
6 Thanks so much for listening to me talk about this improvement that could be made. Does anyone have any questions?

UNIT 12

12.1 Image recognition that triggers augmented reality

1

1 He was Global Head of *Aurasma* and she was Head of Marketing.
2 She brought an advertising background.
3 She's now a founding Director of TRM&C.
4 He started working at Featurespace, working against fraud with high-tech solutions.

2

b Interfaces between technology, mind and matter

3

1 Redefining **2** Greater **3** eye **4** minds

4

1 e **2** a **3** c **4** b **5** d

6

Stressed content words **in bold**, grammatical chunks <u>underlined</u>.
1 One of my **favourite TED talks** <u>is the one</u> from Tan Le called 'A **headset** that reads your **brainwaves**'.
2 Tan Le <u>starts her talk</u> with her **vision** to expand **human** and **computer interaction**.
3 She <u>reminds us</u> that **interpersonal communication** is more **complex** than mere **commands**.

4 The **headset** will cost <u>only a few</u> **hundred** dollars, not **thousands**.

7

1 She's able to present it live on stage and the price isn't too high.
2 She thinks it's well explained, calm and seems effortless. Also she likes that Tan Le invited Evan Grant onto the stage to demonstrate the headset.
3 Opening and closing curtains, turning lights off and on and controlling a wheelchair through facial expressions.
4 To spread the message that technology can be used in our favour and for good causes, not only for fun and for entertainment.

8

1 background, demonstration, applications
2 comes, wears, carries
3 command, difficult
4 submitted
5 smiles

9

1 b   **2** a   **3** c   **4** c   **5** b

12.2 They saw it coming

1

1 were to
2 was about to
3 would
4 was bound to
5 wouldn't have been
6 was going to be
7 unlikely to be
8 would have been
9 was to be

2

1 going   **2** was   **3** bound   **4** were   **5** likely
6 would

3

1 d   **2** b   **3** e   **4** f   **5** a   **6** c

4

1 was to become
2 were going to be
3 unlikely to be
4 would not teach
5 would
6 were
7 to be passed

5

Thursday 13th at 10.30.

6

1 was wondering
2 did you have
3 was thinking
4 was
5 was hoping
6 did you want
7 hadn't been cancelled

No 7 isn't a tentative use of the past.

7

1 The project team was going to meet again <u>before</u> my holiday.
2 They were going to <u>cancel</u> the launch meeting.
3 I was thinking of <u>Thursday</u> morning.
4 I thought <u>Ricardo</u> was going to call.

8

In 1964, <u>were we more likely to have exciting predictions</u> of the future than we have today? Ryan Ritchey thinks so and explores the topic in his documentary, *After the Fair,* about the World's Fair in 1964 in New York. This fair <u>was going to enable people to encounter computers</u> and other technological and cultural trends face to face for the first time. It <u>was to have had 70 million visitors but in fact only 51 million</u> made it in the two six-month seasons it was open. It was a vision of the future, <u>so not everything would come to pass that was on show, for example</u> colonies on the moon and cities underwater. On the other hand, many visitors <u>were to have the experience of asking a computer a question</u> and getting an answer, something many of us do regularly now. There were also picture phones that <u>were unlikely to appeal to visitors then</u> because outward appearances were less important then than they are nowadays.

12.3 Half full or half empty?

1

1 d   **2** e   **3** b   **4** a   **5** c

2

a Generation Z   **b** Generation X   **c** Mature Silents   **d** Generation Y   **e** Baby Boomers

3

1 T
2 T
3 F – Generation X is probably most comfortable with change.
4 F – It's the Mature Silents.
5 T Baby Boomers are independent / able to find their own ways and Generation X.
6 F – The Baby Boomers were the first relatively fit generation but those following have been too.

4

1 more, more
2 some things, more
3 a great deal of, fewer
4 less, appreciate
5 return to, unlikely

5

1 bright side
2 hope
3 half empty
4 tunnel
5 bad things
6 half full
7 dark cloud
8 cloud

6

1 c   **2** e   **3** b   **4** a   **5** f   **6** d

7

1 sparsely populated   **2** strong-willed
3 open-minded   **4** well-educated
5 quick-witted   **6** poorly-skilled

8

1 d   **2** e   **3** f   **4** b   **5** a   **6** c

9

1 flash of inspiration
2 bundle of laughs
3 mine of information
4 glimmer of hope
5 drop of rain
6 stroke of luck

12.4 Is Friday good for you?

1

1 f   **2** d   **3** a   **4** e   **5** b   **6** c

2

It's about brainstorming ideas for the company's twenty-five year celebration.
1 I want to arrange to meet about
2 you could make the meeting
4 make something work
5 Let's pencil it in
6 can confirm with everyone else

3

1 I was wondering
2 How about
3 Would
4 That would
5 I can manage it
6 to be honest
7 out for me
8 afraid not
9 Let's
10 Sounds

4

1 supposed to
2 was meant
3 confirmed then
4 can reschedule
5 any good
6 postpone to

5

1 e (the kick off email)
2 a (mentions Bert and Liz so they haven't replied yet)
3 d
4 b (must come after d as she is due to be in the meeting that is rescheduled)
5 f (mentions the other replies)
6 c (confirms the meeting)

6

1 a Is <u>Thursday</u> afternoon any good for you?
   b Any time after <u>two</u> is fine.
2 a Would Friday at <u>nine</u> work for you?

b I'm supposed to be meeting Jake but I <u>may</u> be able to postpone it.
3 a It's not ideal, to be honest, but if we make it <u>ten</u> instead of nine I can manage it.
  b <u>Sure</u>, yeah, I'm around.
4 a How about Monday <u>morning</u>?
  b Monday's out for me but <u>Tuesday</u> would work.

7

1 Various suggestions
2 One proposal
3 was agreed
4 was suggested
5 Another suggestion
6 the objection
7 was discussed
8 been planned

8

1 two hundred: current and retired staff and families, catering staff and customers.
2 not agreed on
3 open
4 open
5 budget decided, local catering company to be used – which to be decided
6 speeches, announcements and a short film
7 open

9

2 (Overall theme) The suggestion was a Western theme – inspired by our latest product range.
3 (Highlight) Not everyone agreed on fireworks as the highlight.
4 (Activity 1) It was agreed a barn dance would match the theme and be fun.
5 (Activity 2) The suggestion was a rodeo bull-riding machine (as it's fun to do and watch).

10

1 We are pleased to present our ideas for the anniversary event, from our recent meeting.
2 For the overall theme the most appropriate suggestion was a Western theme – inspired by our latest product range.
3 One proposal for food and drinks was to use a local catering company with vintage BBQ carts, which fits well with this theme.
4 After some discussion, it was agreed a barn dance would match the theme and be fun.
5 The unusual suggestion for the second activity was a rodeo bull-riding machine that's fun to do and watch.
6 In the end not everyone agreed on fireworks as the highlight and it was decided that perhaps the activities are highlights enough.

WRITING 6

1

a, b, c, d

2

1 a 2 c 3 d 4 b

3

1 T 2 T 3 F 4 T 5 T

4

1 c 2 e 3 b 4 a 5 d 6 f

5

1 To begin **with**, by visiting a nature park people can experience the natural world first hand.
2 It would **therefore be** easier for them to watch programmes on their own television.
3 **Besides,** companies are much more likely to listen to the government than their customers.
4 It is **a** well-known fact that travelling on the underground is faster than using buses.
5 On the other **hand**, a rapid bus system would be much cheaper to develop than a new underground system.
6 Instead of **creating** a large area of solar panels, we could put them on individual buildings.

6

1 On <u>balance</u>, while both visits to nature parks and programmes about the natural world are important, I am in <u>favour</u> of the latter as the best way to teach people about the environment.
2 <u>Bearing</u> all that in mind, I believe that the government should focus on reducing the amount of plastic used in packaging <u>rather</u> than on trying to make us recycle it.
3 To <u>sum</u> up, while both types of public transport have their advantages and disadvantages, in my opinion, the benefits of a rapid bus system <u>outweigh</u> those of a new underground system.
4 In conclusion, if the advantages of solar power are <u>compared</u> to those of building new wind turbines, the <u>former</u> is clearly more useful to the community.

8 (Example answer)

Volunteering has many possible benefits for companies and their employees, but it is important that any scheme is set up in a way that allows both to make the most of it. In this essay, I will examine two possible structures for a volunteer scheme and say which I believe is the most effective.

The first structure to look at is where each person is given a certain number of hours to volunteer anywhere they would like to. This way they can find a project which appeals to them, increasing the positive feelings they get from it. If they are not forced to work on something which they have no interest in, employees are more likely to want to volunteer their time and will feel more motivated. The downside is that it may prove difficult for employees to choose where they would like to spend their time.

An alternative way of organizing such a scheme would be for each team to choose a project to contribute to. This will have all of the benefits of an individual scheme, as well as encouraging teamwork and collaboration. The skills each team develops will help the company as well, as they will be able to carry over their increased sense of team spirit to their day-to-day work. Fewer decisions would need to be made as one person can suggest a project and others can join in with it.

In conclusion, I believe that team projects are more effective since they promote collaboration within the company in addition to the other benefits of volunteering.

Audioscript

CD1

TRACK 2

My name's Karen Spiller, and I've put together the writing and editorial teams and worked with them to develop the *Keynote* course.

I really like this talk, and the way it's delivered. Dan Phillips is not the usual polished TED presenter – he's kind of like a cowboy. Listening to his lilting American accent and easy jokes, we feel as if we should have been sitting round the campfire with him. Dan shows and tells us – with a four-minute carousel slide show – why and how he does the things he does. He does it with a casualness that almost conceals his deep passion for the buildings he creates and the materials he uses. We want to see more of the quirky yet functional wooden homes he builds. We have to look again and listen to Dan's explanation to fully discover why they are so extraordinary.

His work is made up of almost entirely recycled material and other people's cast-offs and scrap – in fact between 70 and 80 per cent of his construction materials are pre-owned. He tells us he got hold of a complete wooden staircase for twenty dollars, including delivery. He shows us 'bumpy tiles' high on a wall that visually re-create tiled froth in a beer-themed bathroom. 'How do you get bumpy tiles?' he asks. 'You smash up toilets', he replies with a grin. Herein lies his secret and, for me, the main message of his talk: waste really is a matter of taste and what one person discards becomes another's treasure. It's upcycling on a large scale. It's about being as resourceful as our parents and grandparents were; my own mother used to collect among other things the twist ties from packaged loaves of bread – I've never really understood what for but I guess they came in handy for something!

I wish I was better at recycling things. My default position is to 'buy a new one' when something breaks down. I think that's partly because it takes time to see the potential in re-using or re-purposing something – and time is something I'm short of – but also I don't think I've got the right mindset or way of looking at things. I do see lots of examples of people who are good at this though – I've got an allotment, and quite a few plot holders have created sheds and compost bins out of objects that used to have a different function. I wonder whether there's a link between growing things in an allotment and giving old things a new life – a positive kind of renewal.

Dan is proud of making a feature of the blemished, of finding beauty in the irregular, the imperfect and the flawed. He inspires us to rethink our quest for perfection and embrace the diverse and the different. When we think outside the box in this way the previously rejected becomes interesting and the rubbish heap becomes a treasure trove.

It's a talk to get you questioning what is valuable and why. It challenges you in a very persuasive way to reconsider your attitude, choices and environment.

TRACK 5

I = Ian, B = Bob, C = Connie

I: I wonder if we could have a chat about my plans?

B: Sure.

C: No problem.

I: As you know, I'm trying to work out what to do next year. All I know is, I really want to study, but not immediately. I think doing a gap year could be just the thing for me. After all, I wouldn't want to waste money studying the wrong thing.

B: Absolutely not! We certainly wouldn't want that.

C: I'm guessing you'd be thinking of something abroad? Have you considered doing some voluntary work? Conservation work or something? It'd help you decide exactly what to study and be a chance to broaden your horizons – you know beyond here and school and before college.

B: To be honest, I'm not such a fan of gap years. Personally, I feel that you young people have too many choices and actually should just work like we had to do. Education is expensive and …

I: But the experience does help find out what to do and voluntary work abroad is seen very favourably by employers and universities nowadays, you know. It's great life experience.

C: It seems to me that it might not be a bad idea to find out more about it. Maybe we can ask around, look on the net …

I: Well, actually there's an information evening at school, lots of people are interested so the school got some organizations in to talk to us. And there are some reports from people who've done it already. I think a couple of them might even be there.

B: Uh huh, I see. When's that then?

C: Well, there's nothing to lose in finding out, is there?

B: I suppose not, but can I just suggest writing to your uncle Tony in New Zealand and running the idea past him? Maybe he has some contacts. You never know.

I: OK. I can do that.

TRACK 9

Hi. I'm Paula Mulanovic. I'm the writer of this Keynote workbook.

Pico Iyer's talk resonated deeply with me on a personal level. Like him, I find the questions 'Where are you from? Where is home?' challenging. I was born in the south of England, but I've lived abroad much longer than I've lived in Britain. For now, I call Cologne, Germany, home. Pico Iyer says home is a question of soul, not soil. This last statement seems to ring true for him, and it certainly does for me: the idea that home is something you carry with you, and the place where you become yourself.

Pico Iyer is such a crisp, clear and calm presenter. Although there are no slides or pictures, his story is extraordinarily animated. The animation comes from within Iyer, who quite visibly speaks from the heart and he makes the audience feel compelled to listen. His stories paint pictures I see in my mind's eye: 'the 1,200 feet of golden pampas grass running down to the sea' or 'tail lights of cars disappearing … seemed like my concerns of the previous day'.

Pico Iyer belongs to what he describes as the 'great floating tribe' of 220 million people worldwide. These are people living in a country that is not their own. He acknowledges that there are many in the tribe who didn't choose to leave their countries and have become refugees in others. But for these who can choose their homes and have transferable skills to make a living elsewhere, the world is an exciting place.

Iyer says 'home is the place where you become yourself' where you 'fashion your sense of self'. His idea of a home is not a place with four walls, as he learnt when his own home was burnt down in a fire. The story of the fire was key in the talk: without it he wouldn't have discovered two things: one, that home wasn't the building that burned to the ground and two, that he'd been hankering after stillness and silence. This second realization came to pass as he was looking for a new home and was presented with the chance to stay in a monastery. Iyer states that he isn't religious but the peace he felt on arriving at the institution (and imparts to us in the talk) is palpable. He found very quickly that the silence provided by no laptops, telephones, televisions and chatter allowed him to make decisions and do some of his most important work. He describes this more fully in the TED Talk he gave the following year, called 'The art of stillness'. He compares stillness with movement and home with travel as each gives the other meaning. Perhaps he discovered this in the stillness after the fire.

Finally, he quotes Marcel Proust, who said that the real voyage of discovery is not seeing new sights but looking with new eyes. With this statement we can check how we feel about our current home. Is it the place where we have become ourselves, or is it a place that is part of the work in progress?

TRACK 10

B = bank employee, C = customer

B: A great deal of unaccountable activity is evident in the account, you say. There are twice as many payments on your credit card statement this month as there were last month. Let's check the dates. Yes, 12, 14, 16 of March and 19 and 20 of March, all in the same week. If you didn't make those payments yourself, you may well have been a victim of a phishing scam.

C: Oh, no! Will they be caught? Will I get my money back?

B: Well, we'll cancel the card immediately. You'll need to be able to prove you didn't make the payments and weren't away. Unfortunately, only a very small minority of criminals are caught, but the credit card company does cover the losses in all but a handful of cases.

C: That's a relief at least. What did I do wrong? I haven't been aware of any crime or anything suspicious.

B: That's what's so worrying – the vast majority of victims don't notice until it's happened. We've had a fifty per cent rise in reports in this last year. It was probably an online transaction that triggered a phishing email or a lookalike site.

TRACK 13

N = Nancy, H = Henri, J = Jo

N: What do you think about the new dress code then? We can actually wear jeans!

H: But only smart ones, not scruffy ones – what was it? 'Dark and smart' I think.

J: Well, you'd actually look smart in anything you wear, Henri. It must be your French flair.

H: Oh, thank you, but actually I feel more comfortable in a suit and tie at work. I'd hate to come in gym clothes or tracksuit bottoms or old trainers.

J: Well, that's just as well as you're not allowed to – look at the poster! Don't wear sports clothes … I guess you can't wear your well-cut suits and tasteful ties any more either though.

H: Well, only for meetings, anyway. But I can wear jeans and a pullover and jacket, for example. So it's fine really. It'll save me money on dry cleaning.

N: What about the IT people? They won't be so happy, will they? They'll have to wear more appropriate clothes and less unconventional stuff – no more weird T-shirts.

J: Yes, it says here 'Don't wear hoodies and messy jeans'.

H: Or slogan T-shirts.

N: Yes, in the summer we can wear T-shirts. That's good.

J: I think Jan looks good, don't you? She's a little more casual but still really smart looking. I think it's a good idea. It brings us together a little more.

H: It is meant to, after all.

TRACK 14

C = coach, J = Jane, A = Anne, E = Erik

C: OK. Well, we've just watched the last of the interviews. Good job everyone! It's not easy doing an interview with an audience and a camera, and even more difficult to watch yourselves afterwards!

J: Oh, yes.

A: Too right.

E: Absolutely.

C: I'd like you all to think about what you'd recommend doing differently. I'd like to hear your contributions.

E: Oh, I'm embarrassed. I looked so shy.

C: Thank you, Erik. I agree but, to be honest, you weren't the only one. Most of you might want to sit up straight and try to use more positive body language. And Erik, one other thing to consider is making eye contact. Now, who noticed themselves smiling a lot?

E: Mmm.

J: Not really.

A: Well, I didn't.

C: Exactly. I didn't notice anyone smiling. You mustn't forget that people can't help receiving a more positive impression if you smile. It's the single most important thing to do in an interview.

A: I was so nervous I didn't answer the question properly.

C: Good point, Anne. How could you feel less nervous? Any ideas?

E: If you feel nervous, why not try breathing deeply? That helps. Practice probably will too.

C: Exactly. Thanks, Erik. Anne, it might be a good idea to remember that everyone feels nervous before an interview. It's not necessarily a bad thing; the extra adrenaline can help you perform better. OK, Jane. You were quite nervous too; your papers were visibly shaking, weren't they?

J: Yes, it was terrible.

C: I would seriously consider putting your papers on the table and not holding them.

TRACK 17

Hi. My name is Stephanie Parker and I'm one of the development editors on the Keynote series. I was very struck by this inspiring talk, which shows what individuals can do, and about the power of social media to connect them.

Ronny Edry is a graphic designer who started a peace movement. Using his art and social media, he made a simple and heart-felt gesture, which has had extraordinary repercussions.

Although his English is far from perfect, Edry is a natural communicator. He uses images as well as humour to tell his story warmly and directly with apparently ego-less delivery. The images make a big impact in the talk – they are so candid and show ordinary people from both sides, distinguishable only by their flags.

What's also appealing about this talk is that it has the feel-good optimism of a film. Actually, the only filmic element this talk lacks is the major setback you usually get two thirds of the way through, to heighten the drama. And, at the moment, it lacks a conclusively happy ending.

Edry knows how to tell and illustrate a good story; he launches directly into his tale of what happened one night when he put a poster of himself and his daughter onto Facebook with the caption 'Iranians we will never bomb you. We love [heart] you'. He was only asking for approval from his friends so he was totally bowled over by the extent and volume of the reactions he got. The story has a wonderful filmic arc, as he describes how the momentum built from that first night: first, all the unexpected responses to his poster, then the poster he made of his wife and of his friends. After that, the posters he made of the messages and photos that came back from Iran, the ones the Iranians made themselves, through to lots and lots of spin-off Facebook movements, online and face-to-face friendships across opposing sides and finally global news coverage. In between, he gives us snippets of information about the conflict between Israel and Iran but with a very light touch – without preaching or any political bias. I found this story very moving. At one point early on Edry says, 'Everybody's crying now' – and, to be honest, I was too, within the first few minutes of the talk!

All in all, he communicates a simple but dramatic story about the power of images: how positive images can spread peace and friendship while the negative images can create such false and damaging impressions. His aim is to counter bad with good; to change hate into love. It's a real message of hope but without any sentimentality.

This story touched me particularly because I have a brother who has been involved in the humanitarian peace process in the Middle East, which has made these conflicts feel closer to home. Alongside all the challenges he confronted, he also brought back pictures of beautiful places and stories of the intelligence and humanity of the people he met, which is rarely focused on in the media.

We should all watch this talk and take a leaf out of Ronny Edry's book. Next time I read about a nation in conflict, some very different pictures will pop into my head as a result of all these lovely posters of kind, committed people reaching out to others.

TRACK 23

A = Ant, J = Jenny, R = Richard, S = Stan, H = Helen

A: Do we have any views on which charity we're going to support? We've been discussing the proposals for a while now.

J: Well, it's important to choose something local, isn't it? So that we can see where the money goes. So, why don't we choose the special needs school?

R: I'll agree to the proposal so long as we choose something else next year. I thought we wanted something environmental.

S: Right. Absolutely. We did but we were also looking for something local if you remember.

A: What's your take, Helen? Are you for something local or something environmental?

H: I'd accept the local idea. I think that really makes sense on condition that we all agree. We all contributed to raising the money so I think we should find something we're all happy with.

J: What's your view, Ant? You've not really said yet.

A: I'd like to suggest that we go with the children's charity Childtrust. It supports children with special needs too, so that fits in with your idea.

J: Let's invite Childtrust to meet us and we'll take it from there.

TRACK 25

McGonigal talks about two studies and how they changed her own approach to stress – from something to be avoided to something that's a part of life that we can manage.

In the first study they measured 30,000 people's perceived stress load and their belief in how harmful stress was. People who experienced a lot of stress in the previous year had a 43 per cent increased risk of dying but only if they believed stress was bad for them. I thought it was interesting that the way we see things affects the way we approach stressful situations and then how we experience them. I've definitely seen how sometimes people can achieve better results, or really excel, when they face stressful situations but what I find fascinating is when McGonigal says that our beliefs about stress will affect whether we suffer when we're in a stressful situation and her question about whether we can actually change our body's response to stress, and thus stay healthier and feel less anxious.

The second study examined how stress can make people more social; it studied 1,000 adults over five years. Again, they first established the stress load and then asked how much time people had spent helping out friends or neighbours. What I found surprising was that they discovered that stressful life experiences increased the chance of dying by as much as 30 per cent but not for those who engaged in caring for others. The body's stress reaction can make us seek out social contact (thanks to oxytocin). And that for those who actually do, there are health benefits; the body actually becomes more resilient to stress thanks to this same chemical.

TRACK 26

I'm Sonia Jordana and I'm the ELT sales executive for NGL in Catalonia and the Balearic Islands, Spain. I particularly liked this talk because it can help us reconsider what we have traditionally heard about a feeling which is generally seen as something negative: stress. After listening to this talk, I believe I won't have such a negative reaction to stress from now on.

We learn from the TED speaker, Kelly McGonigal, that stress can be useful as long as you think positively about it. The difference between thinking positively about stress and getting stressed about stress, however, can be the difference between staying healthy or getting sick.

McGonigal talks about two studies and how they changed her own approach to stress – from something to be avoided to something that's a part of life that we can manage.

In the first study they measured 30,000 people's perceived stress load and their belief in how harmful stress was. People who experienced a lot of stress in the previous year had a 43 per cent increased risk of dying but only if they believed stress was bad for them. I thought it was interesting that the way we see things affects the way we approach stressful situations and then how we experience them. I've definitely seen how sometimes people can achieve better results, or really excel, when they face stressful

situations, but what I find fascinating is when McGonigal says that our beliefs about stress will affect whether we suffer when we're in a stressful situation and her question about whether we can actually change our body's response to stress, and thus stay healthier and feel less anxious.

The second study examined how stress can make people more social; it studied 1,000 adults over five years. Again, they first established the stress load and then asked how much time people had spent helping out friends or neighbours. What I found surprising was that they discovered that stressful life experiences increased the chance of dying by as much as 30 per cent but not for those who engaged in caring for others. The body's stress reaction can make us seek out social contact (thanks to oxytocin). And that for those who actually do, there are health benefits; the body actually becomes more resilient to stress thanks to this same chemical.

Although the talk is scientific in parts, it's never boring and she makes it accessible with pictures and examples. The speaker is clear and very good at presenting scientific concepts but at the same time she uses irony and humour to keep the audience's attention. The speaker's open and enthusiastic presentation style both engages the listeners and challenges them to think beyond their current assumptions.

The point she makes about developing resilience to stress by helping and caring about others is a good one to help us reconsider some of our actions. Nowadays our hectic lives make us focus too much on our present, our problems, ourselves ... but if instead we react to stress by seeking out support and connection with others, science suggests it will be beneficial to both parties.

I would recommend watching this talk to several friends, particularly those who, like me, have always considered stress as a risk, danger or threat. We all need help coping with stress.

TRACK 27

H = Henry, N = Nina, M = May

H: How long do you think it'll take before we get approval on the speed-reading project proposal?
N: I'd say at least a week, don't you think?
M: There must be dozens of project proposals – it seems as if everyone's working on one.
H: Don't forget that there are only about four or five proposals a year from the training department and they're usually IT related. Our research shows speed reading could roughly double our efficiency with all the information we deal with. That kind of project proposal gets approved fast.
N: Maybe the proposal approval team'll be the first to sign up.
M: We must have as many as fifty on the waiting list already – that's two workshops at least.
H: We've only asked for two days or so project time, after all. It's a pretty low budget project.

TRACK 31

D = Dana, G = Greg

D: So can you hear me now?
G: Yes, I can hear you fine now. Could you just go over that last bit again? I didn't quite catch what you said.
D: I was talking about sharing documents.
G: Yes. OK, good. What is it I click? Was it 'File' or 'View'?
D: Right, as I said, go to the top left menu and click either 'File' or 'Share' and you can share documents or the screen.
G: Can you explain why I would need to do both? You've lost me a bit, sorry.
D: You don't need to do both. It's two ways of doing the same thing – to share a document. Well, it's probably easier if I show you by you doing it. You see, you may want to share what's on your desktop or a document or something with other people.
G: Oh, I see. Are you saying that I can set things up beforehand? Or can I access things when it's running?
D: Good question. I can see you're getting it. Both and either are possible and very easy ...

TRACK 33

G: I'm not with you. Would you mind giving it to me one more time?
D: Sure. No problem. First go to the top left menu and choose 'Share' and in the drop down menu select 'Whiteboard'. See ... when you click it, it opens automatically.
G: OK. Yes, I see. That's great. Did you say we can all write things there? That'll be great for brainstorming.
D: That's right. You can also start a whiteboard session by clicking the plus sign in the middle of the screen above the whiteboard part.
G: Would you mind backing up for a second? I missed that last bit – I was trying out the whiteboard.
D: Sorry, I was speaking rather fast. Sound still OK?
G: There's a delay but it's clear. I'm probably just being a bit slow, but how can you check the sound when the meeting's in progress?
D: Well, up there in the top menu ... that's right ...

TRACK 36

My name's Laura – I'm an editor at National Geographic Learning. When I first watched Maysoon Zayid's TED Talk 'I got 99 problems ... palsy is just one', I was in complete awe over what an inspirational, vibrant and funny person she was. And I laughed all the way through!

Maysoon Zayid brims with confidence and charisma. She sits on a high bar stool, on stage, and her presence fascinates the auditorium. She begins by forthrightly saying that she isn't drunk but has cerebral palsy and that's the reason why she shakes. By answering the unasked question in everyone's minds, she clears the way for what she has to say.

The main content of her talk covers how she grew up in New Jersey with three older sisters and parents who treated her exactly like their other offspring and expected just as much from her. These loving expectations set by her family enabled her to live a 'normal' life and to succeed. She went to the same schools as her siblings and danced and wore high-heeled shoes and learned to drive like any teenager. There are lots of things that she has achieved at such a young age: things that I would love to do but would never have the courage to do, such as tap dancing on Broadway, walking the red carpet, setting up a charity and co-founding her own comedy festival. All in spite of the limitations people have tried to place on her because of her cerebral palsy, gender and Palestinian ethnicity.

Her quick wit is hilariously funny and often hard hitting – for example, she says she bets that we have at some point wished we were a little disabled if only to be able to park nearer shops. She found her niche in comedy after being refused roles in the acting profession because producers were only interested in casting 'perfect actresses'.

I found her mention of the negative remarks that people have made about her on social media so upsetting. She says that she never got hateful comments at school or at live gigs, only on the Internet. What a cowardly act to make comments like that with the distance and anonymity of the Internet. Hopefully, the more people who watch this brilliant woman's talk, the more the positive images of disability that she wishes to foster will spread.

The positive mantra, instilled in her by her father, that 'You can do it, yes, you can!' is something that everyone should take on board; it's about all of us being able to set ourselves challenges and having the confidence to try things. Her attitude is so infectious, it's inspired me to push myself to try the things that I've been too scared to do – maybe I'll start by taking up tap dancing!

TRACK 37

W: Oh, by the way, I bumped into Ivan last week at that party. He sends his regards. He wished he'd seen you too.
M: That's nice, thank you. How's he doing? If we hadn't had that setback with the project, I would've gone.
W: He seems really happy. He always said he'd rather work with people than computers. I wish I'd trained to be a teacher when I had the chance. If only we had six weeks' summer holiday like him!
M: Yes, of course. It would be great, but I'd rather not have all that marking. And anyway, I'm the opposite; I'd actually rather work with computers – they're much more logical.

TRACK 39

W1 = Woman 1, M = Man, W2 = Woman 2

W1: Sorry I missed the meeting. I couldn't rearrange an appointment. How was it?
M: Well, it was really interesting, wasn't it?

W2: Yes, it was! You missed something.
W1: How so?
W2: Well, we'd been really stuck coming up with ideas until Bob saw that we were at a dead end somehow. Then he produced some cards that he'd got at a seminar and it was like magic …
M: Yes, they were surprisingly useful, weren't they? I hadn't realized before that being structured could make things easier – I always thought having constraints was the enemy of new ideas.
W1: Me too, I've always thought that. Interesting.
W2: It was funny how, until we had the card 'eliminate', we were completely stuck. And then suddenly we got it! It seems obvious now but we were so busy trying to work out how to redesign it, or change the packaging, that we hadn't even considered the possibility of just not having any …

TRACK 40

N = Nathan, S = Sam, L = Lisa

S: OK. Let's try to put together a plan for the training event, shall we? We need to come up with a theme and a keynote speaker.
L: Yes, it's about time, you're right. But, sorry, I've no ideas at all except I really fancy the idea of holding part of it outdoors. It'll be summer after all.
N: Mmm, the weather isn't always good though. Anyone got any objections to "New technology" as a theme?
S: That would be a great idea. We all need to learn something about it. Or how about "Communication" as a theme or "Teamwork"?
L: Yes, I'd go along with all of those.
N: I'll add them to the list for later. Any thoughts on a speaker?
L: Sorry, the same goes for the speaker. I'm drawing a blank.
N: Well, I met that guy I told you about at a conference last month. He was really good and he's local. OK if I contact him? Anyone got a bright idea about format?
S: Sure, Nathan, go ahead.
N: Well, I was thinking of a day format and keeping it local to keep costs down.
L: That sounds practical. Right, which ideas can we reject?
N: Well, as we said, an outdoor event may not be practical.
L: I guess indoors is better.
S: That's also true of any event, really. The weather's just too unpredictable.
N: What about themes?
L: We should probably opt for technology rather than teamwork or communication. It's more interesting and more modern.
S: Mmm, it wouldn't be that easy to come up with something new for teamwork. OK. Let's go with the technology theme. We're agreed on that. Nathan, can you get in touch with the guy you mentioned and set up a meeting?
N: Sure. I'll get right on it.
S: Good. That sounds like a plan.

TRACK 41

1 Outdoor events aren't quite as <u>predictable</u> as indoor ones.
2 The speaker didn't get <u>such</u> good feedback, did he?
3 I heard the caterers weren't <u>especially</u> friendly.
4 The atmosphere wasn't <u>particularly</u> warm.
5 I thought the speaker wasn't <u>that</u> interesting, actually.
6 The room wasn't quite <u>warm</u> enough.

TRACK 43

I'm Nick Ventullo, Senior Content Project Manager, and I watched this TED Talk after reading the synopsis. It immediately caught my interest and did not disappoint. I feel like Amy Smith should be speaking to high schools all over the developed world recruiting future engineers!

I'd like to start by telling you about what particularly impressed me about this talk and why. The first thing is Amy Smith is an engaging speaker, inspiring and passionate about using her resources, the resources available in a developed country, to make the world a better place. She told us in detail the many issues faced by the people in Haiti and in other countries where she and her team have worked. Now that I've explained a little bit about her, I'll move on to describe what she said that was new for me. Although I was aware of the poverty in Haiti, I had no idea of the number of people dying due to respiratory illnesses from indoor cooking-fire fumes: over two million people worldwide die annually. Isn't that heart-breaking? I found it horrifying to think of, when I take it for granted that I can easily and safely cook a meal for my family each day.

I'd like to tell you what the solutions are a little later. OK, now for the work she tells us about in her talk. It really felt like people making a difference, a worthwhile investment. Ms Smith and her team of MIT students and Peace Corps volunteers are helping people help themselves; they're using recent technology to come up with simple solutions to improve quality of life. And that makes me hopeful for the future.

So, about the solutions. Although the goal of her team was to create a cleaner cooking fuel that would prevent the deaths of these mainly women and children, there were other benefits to creating the end product. What they did was use leftover sugar-cane fibre – called 'bagasse' – a by-product from sugar production. This material, unlike charcoal, does not cause deforestation like traditional wood cooking fires, and that's incredible. The fact that the team worked to create something useful and necessary out of waste is amazing. Although Ms Smith joked about the different things the team had tried, it was touching that they cared about the long-term social impact so much. Particularly her statement about not stopping farmers from becoming farmers, but helping them be successful farmers is striking. It's not even the case that one solution fits every country, as she herself found when she travelled to India to look there at the cooking-fuel fume problem. There they had to look for alternatives as in that region in India there wasn't any sugar cane – they had to find other waste biomass to use, which I'm happy to say they did.

Lastly, it's quite overwhelming to think of the problems people face every day just to get by. The statistics at the end were thought-provoking and just reinforced how fortunate we are. In my view, everyone is entitled to live with dignity and these solutions will allow people to do just that. This is about working with people to develop the tools they need to improve their day to day lives, health and economic situation. Having dedicated, innovative individuals working towards a better world, really made me feel hopeful for the future. I'm sure it will make you feel the same way too.

TRACK 45

G = George, L = Luke, S = Sally

G: What shall we do now? Any ideas?

L: If I knew, I'd be doing it. I'm completely lost! Maybe we should consider calling for help?

S: Well, what are our options?

L: Search me. I've never been here before. Why don't we keep calm and think of a plan?

S: What a crazy idea for teambuilding, and trust us to get lost. I don't believe it.

L: Oh, no! Where are we? Don't you know where we are either, George?

G: Sorry, no idea.

S: So what'll we do? We could go back till we recognize where we are.

G: You mean retrace our steps? Good idea. If we had phones we could ring someone.

L: But that's the point of this, isn't it? Not having the usual resources, we have to work together. Let's take stock. We've been walking twenty minutes …

S: Annoying, isn't it? I've had enough. Are you sure we'll find the last station?

G: No, we're not sure, but I'd rather keep looking. Come on. Let's give it a try anyway.

L: Yes, OK, let's try it. What have we got to lose, Sally? Nothing. You never know, the others may be worse.

G: Exactly. Let's retrace our steps to the tower, and then … maybe we should consider looking for the other teams.

S: Oh, I'm not too sure about that. Won't we just get more lost doing that?

L: Wait! Maybe we should try going the other way at the tower – the clue said something about a tower, I'm sure. I think we just took the wrong road.

G: I think you're right. It's worth a try. Look! I can see some people gathered around and some flags… looks like the rest of them.

S: Oh, at last, I thought we'd never find it!

G: Actually, I didn't think we would either!

CD2

TRACK 2

My name's Doruk Denkel and I'm the General Manager of the Abu Dhabi branch of National Geographic Learning.

This talk has personal relevance for me and not only me but for any professional. Everyone has some degree of motivation for choosing what they do for a living and in this talk James Cameron revealed some personal reasons why he made particular film choices.

James Cameron has an easy confident way of talking, without relying on emotional outbursts and high-pitched statements for his audience's attention. This confidence may come in part from Cameron's phenomenal business success, but I think it's also based on his belief in what he does. This belief is impersonal and fact based, in other words, he disconnects his ego from his work when he talks about it and he isn't the block-buster director but a man doing a job and living a life.

I found that Cameron's way of talking was especially compelling because of his lack of ego about his work.

In his talk, Cameron explains that, from an early age, he was driven by his insatiable curiosity and was always amazed by how boundless nature's imagination is. His narrative is so exciting that he doesn't need visuals to bring it to life – surprisingly for a film director, his presentation included no slides or film clips. He describes how he was always outside as a child, making discoveries by exploring the neighbourhood woods and looking at things under the microscope. He was also an avid reader of science fiction and read for at least two hours a day. Television, when he was growing up, was about going beyond the known world – man was exploring the oceans and space – two areas he was fascinated by. He would spend time drawing – as a creative outlet. He drew strange creatures and worlds. Being desperate to experience some of these worlds, he learned how to scuba dive but it wasn't until he moved to California that he was able to properly use this skill, and it wasn't until the film *Titanic* that he had a chance to make a personal dream come true. He wanted to see the Titanic wreck at the bottom of the ocean with his own eyes and making a film about it was the perfect vehicle to do this.

Cameron wanted to use computer-generated animation (CG) in the film *Titanic*. He'd already worked extensively on CG animation in a less successful film *The Abyss* and even founded a company to explore it further. He'd noticed that audiences were mesmerized by the magic of CG and he rightly saw this as a big opportunity.

This was the part that particularly grabbed me: how Cameron realized his dream in a way that also created value for others. He convinced the Hollywood studio it was necessary to film the ship's wreckage, the studio then funded the expedition, his movie became a success, delivering profit to the studio and entertainment to audiences. If he hadn't been driven by the passion of his own personal motivation, the film may not have been such a success.

I would recommend this talk to others and feel its message is important. Your ideal job will build from your personal interests and passions. Don't be afraid of exploring these for the benefit of both your work and personal life. In James Cameron's case, he'd imagined a reality where he could dive to the wreck of the Titanic and one day he found himself doing just that. As he said in the talk: 'Imagination is a force that can actually manifest a reality.' It has done that for me too.

TRACK 6

J = Jon, D = Danny, S = Simone

J: Has anyone seen or heard from Nicky this morning?

D: I expect she's on holiday. She was talking about a holiday last week.

J: Yes, but that's next month, not today. She was going to be doing a training course but it was cancelled at the last minute on Friday.

S: She's probably just stuck in traffic. I called her just now and got her voicemail.

D: Have you called her landline? She may've overslept.

S: That seems highly improbable with three children! I hope nothing's happened. It seems likely that she's stuck in traffic, but then she'd call in or something.

J: She might've forgotten her phone.

S: But she never forgets her phone. That doesn't seem likely at all. Perhaps she's gone to the doctor but normally she'd have mentioned it before.

D: Maybe there's been an accident that's delayed her. I don't mean she's been in one but that the road's maybe blocked.

J: That seems a likely explanation, something unavoidable for sure. But it's still strange she hasn't phoned.

TRACK 7

N = Nicky, J = Jon

N: Hi. Is that Jon?

J: Yes. Oh, hi, Nicky. Is everything all right?

N: Yes, we're all alright…

J: We've been wondering what happened and thought there's bound to be a sensible explanation.

N: … but there's been a fire in the building next to ours.

J: Oh, how awful! What happened?

N: We don't know exactly yet, but we've been out in the street most of the night and we're all suffering from shock so I'm afraid I won't be in today; we're really tired. But don't worry, there are no casualties and everyone's all right. It seems likely the firemen'll find the cause soon – I can't really talk, it's not my phone. I'll call again later.

J: OK, bye, take care. Thanks for letting us know.

TRACK 9

W: That can't be right that there's a light on across the road.

M: Oh, you mean because they're away? I think you're onto something there.

W: I'm not entirely convinced that everything is OK.

M: It certainly looks that way, or do you think they've come back early?

W: That doesn't seem at all likely to me. I didn't see their car on the street. Maybe they've got those automatic lights that go on and off even when you're away.

M: Yes! That seems a likely explanation but let's call them anyway. You never know.

TRACK 11

My name's Daniel Barber. I'm the writer of one of the Teacher's Books for the Keynote course. One of my favourite TED Talks is by a doctor, Atul Gawande, and it's called 'How do we heal medicine?'

I've heard Atul Gawande speak before about doctors, hospitals and the health system and he always impresses me as a speaker. He has a wonderfully calm voice, speaking slowly and thinking carefully about every word. I like to see the bigger picture on issues, and Gawande is able to take a step back from the detailed work of his job as a practising doctor to look at medicine as a whole. He sets out to provide clarity to problems that show bewildering complexity.

He explains this complexity by means of some facts and figures. Medical progress has meant that there are now 4,000 medical procedures and a doctor can prescribe any of the 6,000 drugs available. He says that's too much knowledge for anyone to 'know' and people need to be cared for by systems, not individuals any more. There was a study that compared the number of clinicians required now and in the past – in 1970 the average hospital visit required care from two full-time clinicians. By the end of the twentieth century the number had risen to fifteen. According to Gawande, another problem is the enormous cost of the technology and the human resources needed to make people better in the twenty-first century.

Despite our best efforts, these complex and expensive systems can fail: for example, 40 per cent of heart patient admissions don't get appropriate care, and 60 per cent of asthma or stroke patients don't either. Shockingly, there are two million people who pick up an infection, in the very hospital that should cure them, from staff not following basic hygiene practices.

Gawande's message is an important one: medicine is broken but there are answers to its problems so it can be fixed. He shows that there are surprisingly cheap and simple solutions.

In the next part of the talk, he outlines the methodology to find these solutions using three skills: find the failures, devise solutions and implement the ideas. His particular

interest was reducing the number of deaths in surgery and Gawande decided to look at other high-risk industries to see how they tackled complex systems. He looked at aviation and high-rise construction. He was startled by what he found: checklists. Something as straightforward as a checklist could actually help make experts better. He implemented the checklists in eight hospitals worldwide and complication rates fell in every single one. Death rates fell by a staggering 47 per cent. That point deserved the standing ovation it got.

My interest in medicine has grown ever since my daughter, who's eleven, was diagnosed with a rare genetic condition called cystic fibrosis. People with this disease used to live just a few years but, thanks to the sorts of technological advances in medicine that Gawande talks about, there is every chance my daughter will live a long and healthy life. I am reminded every day of the enormous cost to the local health authorities for her treatment and I am so very grateful that it is there for my family and the millions of people who benefit from the work of doctors and nurses.

We all operate in complex systems ourselves and we will all need the expertise of a doctor at some point in our lives, which is why I'd recommend this TED Talk to everyone.

TRACK 15

F: Did you read about Bhutan winning?

M: Yes, I saw some tweets coming in yesterday. It was quite exciting.

F: I didn't know they started at the bottom like that.

M: Yes, the bottom dozen play two matches against each other to qualify in the next World Cup.

F: I read that they nearly didn't take part at all because of the costs involved.

M: That's right, then FIFA made $300,000 available to support the teams and the Thai team let them have a training ground for a month to get used to the humidity.

F: That's right. They're used to playing at altitude but aren't used to humidity. That was pretty good of the Thais!

M: Their story is pretty amazing really – it's like going back in time. They've only had TV and Internet since 1999.

F: I read that when they played at home no-one had to pay to attend the match and civil servants had the day off work. It's quite a big deal, isn't it?

M: The coach reckons the players all play much better than he did thanks to television; they have access to games and interviews with other coaches. Even the captain said he wouldn't play like he does without television. He can't remember a time without it.

F: It's nice to hear something positive about TV.

M: They scored the winning goal in the ninetieth minute and said they heard the dragon roar. What a great story!

TRACK 16

B = Bela, K = Ken, A = Ali, J = Jordan

A: Can we start?

J: Yes. I'd like to start the discussion by asking if everyone's read the information sent around before the meeting …

J: OK. That sounds good. Anyone have any personal experience of a rotation programme before we continue?

A: Yes, actually I …

K: Sorry for interrupting, but could we just clarify what it is first?

A: … could I just finish what I was saying? I was going to say I've had experience. It was before I came here and I wanted to know the same thing as Ken – in case you understand something different here.

K: Sorry. I just didn't want to waste time.

J: Well, here we define it as a programme involving working in different departments that's good for gaining experience and good for professional development. Exactly Ken, we don't want to waste time. That's partly why I sent you the proposed concept so you'd have time to think about it. Currently, as you know, we use rotation on the trainee programme and with interns, but as we've been looking into better collaboration and …

B: I hate to interrupt, but …

J: I know you're dying to jump in, Bela and we'll come to you. If you'll allow me to finish …

B: Yes, you're right.

K: There'll be a chance for everyone to have their say.

J: Thank you. OK. As I was saying, we've noticed that innovation opportunities are in fact forged by making new connections and mixing teams up. OK. This is where Bela comes in as he was a trainee and he can tell us what he learned. In a couple of minutes, I'd also be interested in hearing your views on expanding the scope of the programme. But first, I'd like to return to the first question and …

TRACK 17

J: So Bela, what's your take on the benefits of changing departments?

B: Well, if you ask me, I can only praise any system that means you can learn about different parts of the organization, in a structured way. When I was on the trainee programme itself I didn't really see how valuable it was until I made use of the connections I made afterwards. Sorry, I didn't explain that very well.

J: Thanks. That's helpful – you mean with hindsight it was more useful than you realized when you were actually doing it?

B: Yeah, that's right.

J: OK. Any thoughts on the expanded programme? And before you continue – Ken, can I just say thank you for all your help with this?

K: Well, I think the crucial thing about talented employees is that if you don't help them find positions that they'll be effective in quickly, they'll end up leaving for somewhere else. The programme could be a great retention tool, as well as promoting innovation. It could be really exciting.

J: All right, I think that's nearly everything but I would like us all to suggest one or two employees to put forward and answer the questions I've prepared here. If you complete the information and get it back to me by Friday then I think we can finish there for today …

TRACK 20

I'm Helen Smedley and I'm the National Geographic Learning sales representative for the south of the UK and Malta. I watched Matt Killingsworth's TEDxCambridge talk 'Want to be happier? Stay in the moment'. This talk was of interest to – it really resonated with me because I try to practise mindfulness in my daily life.

Matt Killingsworth has a PhD in Psychology from Harvard University. His main subject is happiness, actually rather the causes of happiness.

His presentation style and way of talking emanated a distinct scientific feel although, as the topic is a universally relatable one, the talk was easily understandable. He conveys passion and enthusiasm for his topic that quickly builds rapport and interest with the audience. He begins by describing how we all seek happiness and that, despite being richer and living longer than we did 50 years ago, we don't necessarily lead happier lives. We aren't measurably happier. That is the paradox of happiness, what looked like it should bring – or was likely to make us happy – doesn't always.

What interested me particularly about the talk was what he said about staying in the moment and wandering minds. This was a main focus of the talk. His research with the tracking app 'Trackyourhappiness. org' has revealed that mind wandering is ubiquitous. Matt Killingsworth analyzed data from 650,000 real-time reports from 15,000 people hailing from 80 countries and from 86 occupational categories, and he discovered that on average our minds wander 47 per cent of the time. I attend yoga classes three times a week and meditate for 10 minutes a day to music, and try to stay mindful when doing household tasks, but I had a question at the back of my mind which was 'I sometimes think happy thoughts about pleasant past memories and have positive thoughts about future events – is this just as good for my mind as staying on the present?'

Matt Killingsworth addresses precisely this question in his talk and found in his research that mind wandering causes unhappiness because when we are not focused on the present, most of us inevitably think unhappy thoughts as well as happy ones. This made me realize that when I think happy thoughts about memories or future plans, I can sometimes drift and think about unhappier ones too, so it certainly isn't a good thing to focus too much on the past or the future! When research respondents stayed present

in a task, they reported a high happiness factor even when they were doing something that most people strongly disliked, like commuting. We are decidedly less happy when our minds wander. Killingsworth seemed surprised by these decisive results, as if he couldn't have predicted that it would have such an impact.

As a result of watching this talk, I'm going to take on board his advice and train myself to be more mindful in my daily activities – in fact I'm going to try this tomorrow when I have a three-hour drive. Driving is an activity where I am most distracted, so I'm going to be very conscious of staying present. If I'm happier, then the people I see every day will be happier too. In fact, the world could become a better place if everyone listened to this advice and appreciated the moment more and practised mindfulness every day!

TRACK 26

Hello, my name is Michael Cummings and I am the senior consultant for National Geographic Learning in the UK, Eire and Morocco. One of my favourite TED Talks is 'The hidden influence of social networks' by Nicholas Christakis. This talk struck a chord with me, having travelled and amassed many friends and colleagues across the globe as first an English language teacher and now a rep for NGL.

Indeed, as a teacher, I noticed that every classroom featured the beginning of a new social network and one that may eventually extend beyond the goal of language learning.

TRACK 27

Hello, my name is Michael Cummings and I am the senior consultant for National Geographic Learning in the UK, Eire and Morocco. One of my favourite TED Talks is 'The hidden influence of social networks' by Nicholas Christakis. This talk struck a chord with me, having travelled and amassed many friends and colleagues across the globe as first an English language teacher and now a rep for NGL.

Indeed, as a teacher, I noticed that every classroom featured the beginning of a new social network and one that may eventually extend beyond the goal of language learning. So my own social network grew beyond all recognition from when I was living in a small quaint town in the North of England to my various posts across the globe. Christakis made me realize that we are interconnected to hundreds or even thousands of people. I love the notion that social networks are fundamentally something related to goodness, as I value greatly the diversity within mine and I believe my social circle provides me with a huge amount of insight, perspective and opportunity. When my social network grew it fundamentally changed how I perceived the world.

This talk left me pondering a number of things: what is a relationship, what is social networking and how am I influencing the

lives of people I may not even know? His message was clear, concise and extremely relatable. After doing research into widowhood, he found that when someone is widowed its effects aren't limited to the spouses but extend to friends, neighbours and a wider community. He said that this knowledge changed the way he sees the world and it also changed the course of his research. He became obsessed with the influence of social networks themselves and studied obesity networks. He showed the results of a 30-year study about obesity with the use of coloured interconnected dots depicting their interconnectivity. Surprisingly, you have a 57 per cent higher risk of obesity if your friend is obese – the closer the relationship the higher the risk. He later studied other topics like happiness and altruism and how they relate to our social networks.

I had not previously considered the different ways in which my social network might affect those within it or those on the fringes of it. My ability to spread happiness or indeed obesity seems like quite a big responsibility!

It also made me want to examine how my own position in my personal network might impact my life in ways I don't even know.

Finally, this presentation reminded me of one other thing that I was told as a sports-mad young man: 'If you want to be a lion then you must train with lions!' It is important that those within your network share your goals and can help you reach your potential.

This talk made me more conscious of how I can positively influence those around me, in turn making the world a better place in my own miniscule way. I would recommend this talk to everyone in the hope that it goes some way to making them realize that our social network is a living thing that surrounds us, shapes us and binds us together.

TRACK 29

The problem with Attitude to Risk questionnaires – and in fact questionnaires that ask people to evaluate themselves in general – is that they don't always get honest answers. That's not because people are intentionally dishonest, but it's just human nature to see yourself in a favourable light. So in this case I think most people would like to see themselves as more adventurous risk-taking types. So they are more often going to answer B or C than A. And that's another problem with this. All the answers follow the same pattern: A for the least adventurous, B for the middle ground and C for the biggest risk takers. It would be much better if the answers were mixed up. Having said that, I like the fact that not all the answers are obvious – like in items 8 and 9. I think people would probably answer those honestly or at least have to think hard about the answer. There's also a good mix of situations – social, work, life in general.

TRACK 30

S = Sonya, B = Bert, L = Lewis

S: Well, as you've seen in the press there's been a spate of these recently and I think we should do something about it. We've invested a great deal and we don't want to put the business at undue risk.

B: There are some pretty interesting options to choose from, with different degrees of security and varying price tags, naturally.

S: Possibly the most obvious one is a camera.

L: A drawback of the camera is that the footage has to be monitored somehow, doesn't it?

S: Doesn't the security company do that?

B: According to the brochure, a combination lock is another option to consider. What about that?

S: Mmm … on the plus side we wouldn't need keys any more but the downside is we're only strengthening the door.

L: Oh, good point. Well then, is an alarm system worth thinking about? It protects doors and windows, which makes it a very attractive possibility.

B: Hmm, yes but considering the price, I'm not sure it's the best option.

TRACK 31

S: In the light of the increase in criminal activity in the area, I think we should invest in an alarm and a safe.

B: A third alternative that might do the job is a dog.

L: I thought you were allergic to dogs!

B: No, I'm just joking. Ultimately, the best choice does seem to be the alarm system.

S: Now you've got me thinking about a dog. Maybe we can have both.

B: No, come on, think how expensive and complicated that'd be. OK. All things considered, it makes sense to go with an alarm – now we just have to choose which one.

TRACK 34

My name's Eftychis Kantarakis and I'm the NGL Teacher Trainer and Sales team co-ordinator for Greece. One of my favourite TED Talks is Iwan Baan's 'Ingenious homes in unexpected places'.

My job involves extensive travelling, and this is one of the things I really enjoy about it. The topic of this talk really appealed to me as I've seen many 'weird-looking' homes around the world. Originally, the title made me think that it was going to be one more of those demonstrations of funny, posh or extravagant houses some techno-geek or multi-millionaire has built. You see pictures of those all the time in social media nowadays. The TED Talk had little if anything to do with all these, which turned out to be a very positive aspect of it, as it talks about everyday people and their lives.

What I liked the most about this talk was how it showcased the ingenious ways in which people, with nowhere else to live, found solutions to their problems! How they turned places like a slum tower awaiting the hammer into a living city for those who couldn't afford a 'real' home. He showed people living underground in China and on water in Nigeria, and the Zabaleen in Egypt, people who live in dwellings on and in the rubbish heaps. He has admiration and respect for the people because what they build is so ingenious and so varied. Generally people are unhappy with 'cookie-cutter' solutions; they like to personalize their environments. Even if they are disadvantaged, they are highly creative about shaping and designing the appearance and comfort of their homes.

It resonated with me because people in my country, too, have to find such solutions all the time. Albeit not always to such an extent. People in Greece have had to improvise solutions for their accommodation for many centuries.

My great grandfather had to live in similar settings when he brought his family to Greece as refugees in the 1920s along with thousands of others. I've heard stories about how they had to convert old wooden huts into brick ones, building the walls from the inside. Back then the first priorities were to build a kitchen, a bedroom and a place to pray.

I think Iwan Baan came across like a true TED speaker; he gave us very interesting information but also made us feel that this is not some isolated issue that happens only in certain parts of the world, and it is not necessarily something to be avoided or looked down upon. Diversity is key to human life as well as to the ecosystems we live in.

Nevertheless, I would really like to learn more about the reasons why people had to choose solutions like the ones shown here. Iwan Baan deals more with the results than the causes of the problem. Having watched this, I would recommend it to friends and colleagues, especially to ones who don't travel much. I think this talk would help them get a better idea of what cities can look like away from the tourist spots and off the beaten track.

TRACK 36

Our experience with B-Creative Cards was very positive. We have a small yoga studio which was only nine months old when we first contacted them. Our advertising budget was almost non-existent, so cost was a big consideration. The first idea they came up with was really innovative. It wasn't a card at all: it was a bendy drinking straw with a person doing a yoga pose on the part of the straw that bent. They were going to print our contact details on it too, but it was going to be too pricey. So instead they transferred the idea to a more standard business card. The design is very striking still and there's still a person in a yoga pose that flexes when you bend the card. Has it worked? Well, actually, loads of first-time visitors tell me they came along because they thought the card was so cool.

TRACK 37

C = Carolyn, D = Dan, M = Maja

C: So, the focus today is to clarify the direction you'd like your new business to go in.

D: Yes, that's right. We've always fancied setting up our own business but until now we haven't had the opportunity, but last year I was left some money by an aunt who passed away.

M: Until now we've worked in the service sector in hotels – helping people – but we're not sure if we'd like to carry on doing it as the hours can be tough for family life. On the other hand, I can envisage a quieter life, having a smaller B&B place somewhere nice.

C: Mmm. I see. You were on reception, weren't you, Maja?

M: Yes, and Dan was the manager. He's good at communicating with everyone.

C: Is that what you like doing, Dan?

D: Well, I always thought if money were no object, I'd buy my own hotel somewhere. But to be perfectly honest I'd like to do something different.

M: I know what you mean.

C: OK. So, apart from communicating, what else are you good at?

D: I like fixing things and making things work. I actually wanted to be a mechanic but I got a job in a hotel and I liked that too. I fiddle with cars and bikes in my free time.

C: OK. Thanks. How about you, Maja? Are you creative?

M: Yes, in some ways I am quite creative. I could see myself cooking in a restaurant or a café or doing events like weddings. I like doing things like that. But I can't see myself at the front desk any more. I need a bit more of a challenge. I'd love to work on special events and design the cakes and everything. I love doing that.

D: That's true, you always do the events really well. You're a good organizer – lots of people comment on it.

C: OK. Interesting. We've got quite a bit to work on …

TRACK 41

My name's Rosane Di Genova and I'm an English learning solutions manager in Brazil. One of my favourite TED Talks is the one from Tan Le called 'A headset that reads your brainwaves'.

Tan Le starts her talk with her vision to expand human and computer interaction to include facial expressions and emotions as well as verbal and mechanical commands. She reminds us that interpersonal communication is more complex than mere commands – taking non-verbal communication into account too. What follows is not the kind of new technology that you saw on a sci-fi movie that you watched ten years ago and thought: 'No way … it will never happen'. It is new technology so accessible that she demonstrates it live on stage – successfully. The headset will cost only a few hundred dollars, not thousands – making us think about how many people would benefit from that! More about that later on.

Although it's quite technical, it is well explained in three clear areas: background, demonstration and applications. Tan Le manages the whole presentation in such a calm, clear and collected fashion that it seems effortless. I liked the fact that she invited another TED fellow, Evan Grant, to come on the stage, wear the headset and help her demonstrate the system. He carried out two simple tasks that involved moving an image of a cube on a screen using just his thoughts – no verbal commands or use of his hands. First he tried a simple command – he chose 'pull' – and second he tried the much more difficult command "disappear". Mr Grant was a willing guinea pig and performed the first task perfectly. When the task to make the cube 'disappear' didn't quite work he submitted a second neural signal which then made the cube disappear perfectly too. Apparently, with repetition the signal becomes stronger.

It was an impressive demonstration, however, if Ms Tan had called someone randomly it could have given even more credibility to it, I feel. For example, she could have asked him to think about a task for the cube, without telling her what and then when the cube suddenly disappeared, the audience would've believed he was doing it completely unaided.

In addition, I think that she would've made more impact if she'd expanded the examples of how to use this technology in 'real life' in the applications part. For example, turning lights off and on, opening and closing curtains, which could be extremely useful for someone who has a physical disability. For me this is much more relevant than the tests with a person who can move a cube. She did show some footage of a wheelchair user using facial expressions to move left and right or straight on, using blinks and smiles – the potential of this clever technology is huge and very exciting.

It is inspiring to see that some people, like this young woman, are dedicating their time to developing systems that can help so many people. I would definitely recommend this talk to my friends to help to spread this message: that technology can be used in our favour and for good causes, not only for fun and for entertainment!

TRACK 42

I = Isabel, F = Frank

I: Hi, Frank. How's it going? Actually, I was wondering if we could squeeze in a meeting before I go away.

F: OK. Let's see. When did you have in mind?

I: Well, I was going to go to Frankfurt for two days, but that's been cancelled. So I was thinking of Wednesday the twelfth or Thursday the thirteenth.

F: Well, I was down to be in a teleconference on Wednesday afternoon …

I: It's just that I was hoping to hand over the project before I go away. How about Thursday morning?

F: OK. What time did you want to meet? Any time after ten is fine with me.

I: Let's say ten-thirty then. Thank you. That's great. It wouldn't have been possible if the Frankfurt trip hadn't been cancelled.

TRACK 45

The generation that you belong to is determined by the ten to twenty years in which you were born. Here are five terms to describe five demographics represented by the different generations alive today. The oldest generation, born in the late 20s until the mid-40s, are sometimes known as the Mature Silents or the Silent Generation; Baby Boomers are next and one of the largest populations in the USA and Europe – they were born between 1946 and 1964. Generation X follows and spans the second half of the 60s and the 70s. Generation Y, or the Millennials, are children of the 1980s and 1990s. Finally, Generation Z refers to those born after the year 2001.

TRACK 46

1 I reckon there will be more laziness as we use more automated things. But as the world gets more integrated and diversity grows we should understand each other better and find more productive ways of saving fuel and the planet.

2 I think in five years some situations will have improved and other issues will have worsened but I hope we help each other more locally and globally.

3 In five years, many things will seem the same but will have changed dramatically. Change is constant. In technology we'll connect to the Internet via our watches or glasses and make cashless payments. Smart phones are yesterday's news. Landline telephones will become more and more obsolete.

4 We're very lucky, we have longevity, we're healthy. In a way we should be less concerned with technological changes and more concerned with changes to quality of life. To live in peace and be satisfied with what we do have without always wanting more.

5 It's very hard to predict changes for the future. Everything changes so fast. I hope for something amazing that will ease the tension around the world. I know it won't happen but it would be nice to return to old family traditions and good social values and that we become less materialistic.

TRACK 47

S = Sam, F = Felix

S: Hey, Felix. Everything OK?

F: Yes, fine. How about you?

S: Pretty good, thanks. I'm glad I've bumped into you …

F: Sounds ominous.

S: (Laughing) No, no! Not at all. I promise you it's something good. I want to arrange to meet about the celebrations. I've been asking the others too. I was wondering if you could make the meeting next week, midweekish?

F: Oh. Sounds interesting. It's not ideal timewise, to be honest. Wednesday and Thursday are out for me, I'm afraid. But if we can do another day I'll certainly try and make it.

S: That would be good.

F: Are you planning the company's 25-year anniversary party?

S: Yes, and I'd like to organize a first meeting to brainstorm ideas and you're so good at that! Can we make something work? How about Tuesday morning?

F: Tuesday morning? I'm afraid not. I'm at a meeting. But Tuesday evening may just work. I'm supposed to be coming back by train from Amsterdam then. If I can participate by phone I can manage it. Would that work for you?

S: Sounds great.

F: Let's pencil it in, but I need to check train times to check I'm actually on the train then. About six should work.

S: Thank you. I hope Tuesday is good for the others. When you've checked, let me know and we can confirm with everyone else.

F: OK. Good. It sounds great. Really interesting.